Sketchbook 1966-1971

Max Frisch

Sketchbook 1966 - 1971

Translated by Geoffrey Skelton

A HELEN AND KURT WOLFF BOOK

HARCOURT BRACE JOVANOVICH, INC., NEW YORK

Parts of this book appeared originally in *Boston University Journal, Fiction,*
and *Partisan Review.* Pages 173-192 appeared originally in *The New Yorker.*

Printed in the United States of America

Library of Congress Cataloging in Publication Data

Frisch, Max, 1911-
Sketchbook 1966-1971.

Translation of Tagebuch 1966-1971.
"A Helen and Kurt Wolff book."
1. Frisch, Max, 1911-   I. Title.
PT2611.R814Z52413 838'.9'1203 [B] 73-19649
ISBN 0-15-182892-X

B C D E

The lines from "We Shall Not Be Moved," and from "Ballad for Bill Moore"
appear in *We Shall Overcome! Songs of the Southern Freedom Movement,*
compiled by Guy Carawan and published by Oak Publications.

"We Shall Overcome," new words and music arrangement by Zilphia Horton,
Frank Hamilton, Guy Carawan, and Pete Seeger, © copyright 1960 and 1963
by Ludlow Music, Inc., New York, and TRO Essex Music Limited, London, is
used by permission. Royalties derived from this composition are being con-
tributed to The Freedom Movement under the trusteeship of the writers.

The excerpt from an article in the New York *Times* by Judy Klemesrud on
euthanasia, copyright © 1971 by The New York Times Company, is reprinted
by permission.

The quotations from Tolstoi are from the following works: *I Cannot Be Silent*
and *Patriotism and Government,* translated by Aylmer Maude, and *The Law
of Violence and the Law of Love,* translated by Vladimir Tchertkoff.

For Marianne

1966

QUESTIONNAIRE

1.
Are you sure you are really interested in the preservation of the human race once you and all the people you know are no longer alive?

2.
State briefly why.

3.
How many of your children do not owe their existence to deliberate intention?

4.
Whom would you rather never have met?

5.
Are you conscious of being in the wrong in relation to some other person (who need not necessarily be aware of it)? If so, does this make you hate yourself—or the other person?

6.
Would you like to have perfect memory?

7.
Give the name of a politician whose death through illness, accident, etc., would fill you with hope. Or do you consider none of them indispensable?

8.
Which person or persons, now dead, would you like to see again?

9.
Which not?

10.
Would you rather have belonged to a different nation (or civilization)? If so, which?

11.
To what age do you wish to live?

12.
If you had the power to put into effect things you consider right, would you do so against the wishes of the majority? (Yes or no)

13.
Why not, if you think they are right?

14.
Which do you find it easier to hate, a group or an individual? And do you prefer to hate individually or as part of a group?

15.
When did you stop believing you could become wiser—or do you still believe it? Give your age.

16.
Are you convinced by your own self-criticism?

17.
What in your opinion do others dislike about you, and what do you dislike about yourself? If not the same thing, which do you find it easier to excuse?

18.
Do you find the thought that you might never have been born (if it ever occurs to you) disturbing?

19.
When you think of somebody now dead, would you like him to speak to you, or would you rather say something more to him?

20.
Do you love anybody?

21.
How do you know?

22.
Let us assume that you have never killed another human being. How do you account for it?

23.
What do you need in order to be happy?

24.
What are you grateful for?

25.
Which would you rather do: die or live on as a healthy animal? Which animal?

STATISTICS

The average life expectancy of a human being at the time of Christ's birth was 22.0 years; around 1600 it was 33.5 years; in 1900, still only 49.2 years; while today it is 68.7 years. The longer life expectancy affects the distribution of age groups. In 1900 young people up to the age of twenty comprised 46 percent of the population; in 1925, only 36 percent; and in 1950, 31 percent. According to calculations the proportion of young people in the year 1975 will be 28 percent of the whole. The proportion of old people (over sixty) increases correspondingly: in 1900 they comprised 7 percent of the population. In 1975 the figure will be 20 percent.

BODEGA GORGOT

His wife does not interrupt him, but everybody can see that she no longer listens to him, that she finds his conversation tedious. He is a goldsmith. His work is respected. He removes a prize certificate (National Exhibit 1939) from the wall. An apprentice and two other assistants are aware of—what? They don't know exactly, but they feel the old man is always trying to prove he is better than they. Even if he *can* prove it, they get him down. Now he sits most evenings in the Bodega. Bearded youngsters with their long-haired, trousered girls, etc.—it doesn't bother him that they are not working at five o'clock in the afternoon. The Bodega is gloomy even in the daytime. He worked when he was young, and the habit sticks. Afterward he goes back to his workshop. On one occasion she comes into the Bodega: he has been drinking and looks none too good. She is not surprised—that he knows. She puts her hand on his and takes the goldsmith home. His father was an elementary schoolteacher. In many matters, politics for instance, he knows more than his wife, in others less, and this is what matters: when she shows no interest in his political knowledge or opinions, he becomes unsure of himself. She declares that Trotsky was shot and he contradicts her, but she is not convinced; when he subsequently looks it up in a book, he is angry with her for being able to make him doubt himself. For weeks he stops going to the Bodega. Perhaps he has discovered another place she knows nothing about. A trained kindergarten teacher, she gave up her job to look after her own children; now she keeps the books for her husband's business, but there is not much to do; she is irreplaceable. Later he returns to his round table in the Bodega; he watches the bearded youngsters, drinks, but speaks to no

one. When he takes up a newspaper, he gets the feeling that he
has read it all before. Perhaps she has left him. What he is doing,
as he silently sits there, is justifying himself. After all, he has
built up a business on his own; after all, his work is respected in
the trade; and so on. His two children, now grown up and independent, feel he needs their admiration, but his self-conceit
makes it difficult for them. She has not left him; she knows that
the goldsmith needs her and she bears her cross with a good
grace. She is in her middle forties. Nothing will change now. He
has no real idea what her life is like. She comes into the Bodega
with her shopping bag and drinks a Clarete with him. Perhaps
she realized very early, even on the first evening, that he could be
made to doubt himself. He was generally considered a go-getter,
successful with women, etc. He persuaded her to go on the river
with him, to demonstrate his prowess as an oarsman and,
when it began to rain, took it as a personal failure. His present
failure makes no difference to her feelings for him. On the
contrary, it simply shows how right she was: the way he pays
for their wine in the Bodega, takes her shopping bag, and helps
her into her coat; the way he waits, not daring to say, "Oh,
come along!"; the way, when she nearly forgets her gloves, he
blames himself.

     BERZONA (Tessin)
     The village, only a few miles from the
     border, has eighty-two inhabitants, who
     speak Italian. There is no <u>ristorante</u>, not
     even a bar, for it lies off the main road
     passing through the valley. Town visitors
     immediately exclaim, "Oh, what air!" and
     then, rather nervously, "And how quiet!" The
     ground is steep, with the usual stone ter-
     races, chestnuts, a struggling fig tree, a
     jungle of brambles, two large walnuts,
     thistles, and so on. You have to watch out
     for snakes. When Alfred Andersch, who had
     been living there for some years, pointed the
     little property out, the building was in a
     dilapidated state--an old farmhouse with
     thick walls and a towerlike barn (now the

studio), all roofed in granite. The valley
(Val Onsernone) has no flat bottom: a deep
and wild gorge, into which we have never yet
descended, runs through the middle. The
slopes are wooded below and rocky above, and
will probably become boring in time. I
prefer it in the winter. The local people
used to make a living from basketwork, until
the market in Milan was flooded with straw
hats and baskets from Japan. Since then the
valley has become increasingly poor.

RESOLUTION

After five years abroad (in Rome) one sees many things more
clearly, though not to the extent of discovering any real significance in them. This being the case, I have resolved to make no
more statements concerning Switzerland—at any rate, not
publicly.

. . .

It does really seem that foreigners living in Switzerland have
a happier relationship to this country than we ourselves. Basically they do not criticize; our criticism they find rather embarrassing, and they prefer not to listen to it. What—apart from the
secrecy of the Swiss banks—attracts them here? Obviously
all sorts of things—scenic beauty, the central situation, the
cleanliness, the stable currency—less the people themselves
(there they occasionally lapse into negative commonplaces);
above all, however, a feeling of being let off the hook. All that is
asked of them is that their papers and their finances be in order
and that they have no desire for change. As long as the aliens
department refrains from annoying them, the foreign residents
have no complaints. What they are enjoying is the luxury of
freedom from historical associations.

. . .

My resolve to make no more statements about Switzerland
has already been broken ("A proud little nation sees itself in

danger: it has called for workers, and has been given human beings"). Perhaps I came home too soon.

Casa da Vendere

The things that can happen: a villa has been standing empty for a long time, no trace of its former occupants. It seems the people simply got up from the table and left without clearing up: moldy risotto in a bowl, an open bottle of wine, fragments of bread as dry as a bone. They did not even take their clothes, their shoes, their personal belongings. It was weeks before the lights went off because the electricity bill had not been paid: that was noticed. . . . Since then a number of things have been stolen; the front door was not locked. 'A porch with a naïve sgrafitto, above it a balcony, its railings rusted, the green shutters now closed, the stucco (the color of raspberry yogurt) flaking in patches. In the garden stands a notice: Casa da Vendere. I'm told it has been there for years.

THE GOLDSMITH

It will all come to a bad end. That he realizes when he is sitting in the Bodega. The Spanish waiter looks somewhere else as he plumps down the glass of Clarete on the table, is already speaking to the neighboring table. His father died of a heart attack, just like that, on a bus. Whenever some former acquaintance enters the Bodega the goldsmith gets ready to leave, putting his money on the table as soon as the other sits down. He cannot understand how an apprentice can get so far under his skin. As a young man, directly after leaving art school, he went abroad to work (to Strasbourg), returning home in 1939. He got rid of the apprentice and took on another, but this one also leaves the faucet dripping. It seems it is not only in his workshop (twenty-seven years spent working with a magnifying glass) that he is a fusspot: coming home from work he can't stand the sight of a dirty kitchen, for instance. He sometimes feels like setting fire to the house. She knows he can't stand a dirty kitchen, but finds it downright ridiculous that he should be bothered about such little things. The Spanish waiter in the Bodega is friendly enough, but serves him more negligently than all the other guests. He does not dare tell her to keep the kitchen tidy. She never has done anyway, from the very start; he has obviously become more touchy since his failure as a man. Even a simple request not to leave dishes standing around unwashed for days, because the sight of them revolts him, leads to scenes. After all, she is a trained kindergarten teacher and not his servant. The quarrels over the kitchen invariably end in him seeing that he is being ridiculous; when this happens, she washes the dishes without a word, but not a moment before. His shop and workshop are in an old part of the town, in which a fire would cause untold damage, particularly after midnight. Sometimes, when he is alone at home, the goldsmith washes and dries the dishes and even scrubs the kitchen floor, but he knows she has no reason to be grateful: it is a demonstration of protest. All the same he does it, because the unwashed dishes revolt him. Why doesn't she find herself another husband? If he does *not* do it, but leaves the dishes for her to wash, it is all he can do not to apologize: after all, she is not his servant. Not until he has had his first glass of wine in the Bodega does he feel reasonably good; he seldom drinks more. But a single glass doesn't last long. Afterward he goes back to his workshop, which is now empty, and turns off the dripping faucet. Once she made a bad mistake in the bookkeeping, but he did not point it out to her.

He gets no pleasure out of upsetting her. When she goes off to her parents for a week, he no longer finds the dirty dishes in the kitchen so irritating; he washes up only the evening before she returns. His income is not large, but it is enough. If not the dishes in the kitchen, there would be something else to show him that she feels no compulsion to do what he wants. That he knows. Of course it is not the dishes, really. He knows that as well. It is all too stupid. She is sorry for him. She no longer comes to the Bodega to fetch him; he finds it humiliating that she should come for him. He is difficult. It could be said in her favor that whenever he is ill, she nurses him with touching care. She still does that. He used once to have friends; now he hardly ever calls them up, feeling that the things with which he concerns himself are too petty. What people call marital squabbles do occur now and again, but not if he can help it, for at such times he says precisely the things he did not mean to say: that business of the unwashed dishes, for instance. Now and again she does take trouble. He has lost his interest in public affairs (the restoration of the old city), though he reads the newspaper when he is in the Bodega. Compared with what he reads in the newspaper, his own concerns are very petty. Beneath his dignity. If he should ever set fire to anything, that would be the reason.

In earlier days he never felt the need to take offense: a go-getter, successful with women, etc. Even until recently he did not always feel the need—possibly because he was not given the chance. For instance, his wife took the photograph of Strasbourg off the wall, got rid of it without a word. She is always frightened nowadays that he might be making a fool of himself. When somebody dials a wrong number and then simply hangs up without apologizing, he takes it personally and keeps repeating his name—"Huber"—although the other person is already off the line. In the mornings he sits at the back of his shop working by neon light, his glass screwed into his eye. His wife deals with the customers, he himself hardly ever now, or, if a customer insists on speaking with the goldsmith himself, he bends low over his table so the customer cannot see his face. There are still people who buy his brooches. Usually he says nothing, nothing at all, just wondering what has gone wrong to make him put up with everything now. Perhaps she thinks he doesn't even notice. And then she always says: "Are you sure you locked up at home?" Sometimes the goldsmith just looks at her, as if he felt like hanging himself. One of the waiters, the young Spanish boy, has noticed it, too, and has become more friendly since the goldsmith stopped removing his coat; with it he wears his beret. He unwraps meat loaf from rustling paper: it is obvious he is not going home for his supper. If the goldsmith gets involved in a dispute, he knows from the start that she is on the other's side; it is no use saying anything. She is always thinking of his own good and behaves as if he never makes anything but mistakes. At times he feels like ending it all. In the

Bodega it doesn't bother him in the least if the ashtrays are dirty. Once she let it slip out: "It's only you who makes the dirt." (Which is probably true.) It is always better if he says nothing. An hour after coming out of the toilet the goldsmith notices that his fly is undone; perhaps it has happened before and he has never even noticed. He feels safer with his coat on. In the Bodega he recalls a case he heard of as a boy: a mining worker who had cancer of the throat placed a detonator in his mouth; his brains were spattered all over the arcades in the Hechtplatz. A gruesome method such as the goldsmith himself would not care for. At about six o'clock the Bodega fills up, and then he makes way for others. Since he is already wearing his coat, he can withdraw unobtrusively, leaving his money on the table. Another case: when he was at art school, living in Wiedikon with his mother, he once, while cleaning his teeth in the bathroom, heard an unusual sound from the bathroom below, not very loud, rather like somebody breaking the mirror with a small hammer, only without the tinkle of glass. It was a shot; two hours later they carried the coffin out of the apartment block. The older you get, the simpler you want to make it. He knows places enough on the Albis where it could be done: no need to pick a Sunday, when a lot of people are out walking, families with children. Sometimes he thinks; I'll hang myself! for instance when she says to him; "Don't just talk—*think*." His visits to the Bodega become more and more regular. The first thing he does after sitting down is to look at the people around him, then he thinks—what exactly? A long-haired, bearded youngster at the round table wishes him a good appetite. Later, from a neighboring table, he hears somebody say the word "cock." The goldsmith must be careful not to fall into the trap of taking everything personally; in fact, he must always be very careful (and not only when he comes out of the toilet). All his life he has tried not to be distasteful to others: he has always opened the toilet window, always pulled his coat over his face when going to sleep in a railway carriage. Now in the Bodega he is known only with his coat on: an old man, happy with his meat loaf and his Clarete. Not an imbecile, as she seems to think at home, but all the same he must be careful. When laying out his money on the table in the Bodega, he always checks it twice, and after a while yet again. A way of making certain would be to jump off an observation tower, but that, when he comes to think of it, would be unpleasant for his relatives, and all his life he has tried not to be distasteful to others. The goldsmith knows it must occur before very long. Born near Zurich (Adliswil) and brought up in Zurich, he of course knows the Mühlebach-strasse and the Mühlegasse, yet just now on the street he gave somebody the wrong direction. Lucky she wasn't with him. When they watch television, she never agrees with his opinion: he is always on the side of the people she doesn't trust—Willy Brandt, for example. Once he thought of putting his head in the gas oven, but of course there is no gas in his home. She is always thinking of his own good: for instance, she wants him to go out and meet people. Then afterwards she tells him that as always he did all the talking, never listened to what others had to say, etc. All the goldsmith knows is that, if he ever does say anything, nobody takes it seriously. The only way that is both safe and not distasteful for the relatives is to take sleep-ing pills, which he thinks unmanly. All the same, he has begun during the past few months to collect sleeping pills, which he hides away in his workshop. But for this way, too, you must be in the right frame of mind: simply not to be frightened is hardly enough. You can't swallow thirty sleeping pills just like that, throwing three or four at a time from the palm of your hand into your mouth and having to wash each batch down with water or Chianti. When, in order to get into the right frame of mind, the goldsmith starts a quarrel over some trifle or other (she has again thrown away today's newspaper), she reacts reasonably, even maternally; afterwards she cooks his favorite dish, lets him turn on television. And later he begs her pardon. It's not her fault that things are going from bad to worse. "Childish"—that is just the sort of thing one says: she doesn't really mean it in the way he now takes it. There are many things she says exactly as she did ten or twenty years ago, and at that time the goldsmith thought nothing of it when she called him an imbe-cile. It wasn't meant literally, of course, otherwise she would never have spent a whole lifetime with him. They still sleep side by side in twin beds. It's not her fault if she has to tell him in front of other people: "You mean carbuncle—not carfuncle." Quite soberly and factually, and she had anyway already told him about it at home. It is terrible when one can no longer even speak properly. Once she said to him: "You're talking now like an old fool." But then she begged his pardon. She had really meant it—and she has never said it again since.

Actually, there is nothing more to decide as he sits on a bench at the edge of the woods: he is content with the view of the town, the Limmat, towers, the Schlieren gasometer, a pair of lovers going into the trees. The goldsmith now has his sleeping pills in his coat pocket. He is in his sixty-fourth year. What is he waiting for? He has to go to the toilet during the night anyway: ten times three tablets, each with a gulp of water, he can manage that. But it has got to be a certainty. He no longer goes to the Bodega (where he is not missed, though he leaves a gap: two or three old men are as much part of the inventory as the ancient iron stove, the flue along the walls, etc.), all of a sudden he no longer felt any reason for going there. If he orders more printed note paper or buys himself another new beret, this doesn't mean that he is now prepared to wait till he has his first stroke. That would be leaving it too late. His daughter-in-law in São Paolo has written that they will be coming to Zurich in September. The goldsmith will not be there to fall in with her plans, however nicely meant her proposal: family outing to the Vierwaldstätter-see for a meal of whitefish baked in *Bierteig*. She is of the opinion that the goldsmith works too hard. By the time he has to go to the toilet in the night it is already four o'clock, and if he isn't up by nine she will call for help and an ambulance will come with a stomach pump. It can only be done around evening time: not too late, or the ambulance will come too early; not too early, or he will fall asleep in front of the television. Snow flurries on the following day. In order that his decision to take the pills at about ten in the evening isn't noticed, he spends the day as usual: morning in his workshop, afternoon at the Bodega (for the last time). He drinks no more than usual, and reads the newspaper to pass the time. All she notices is that he has been in the Bodega again: "Still wasting your time in that Bodega." When you have a grip on yourself there is no need to take offense. The goldsmith does not even look at her, but simply turns the page of the newspaper as if he has not heard, and she repeats: "Wasting your time." But the goldsmith has a grip on himself as not for a long time; all he feels is that it is a pity she should have chosen today to say that. To discover the goldsmith dead on the very next morning, that would not be fair: she would blame herself for having said what she did. They are still sleeping side by side. At ten o'clock, when the news comes on, the goldsmith almost invariably thinks of it. He knows somebody who once had a stroke. Apparently it is only the eyelids that are affected, and you can get sunglasses to hide that. All of a sudden everyone will become very solicitous, not sure whether his mind is still functioning. Does such a person know he is babbling? He won't ever recover entirely, though he won't necessarily have a second stroke. The goldsmith still has a grip on himself, his mind is still functioning. There is another occasion when it can't be done: his wife tells him she must visit the doctor next day. The doctor tells her an operation may be necessary, though it is nothing to worry about, a matter of eight or ten days. . . . That long he must put it off.

The goldsmith is still living. The outing to the Vierwaldstättersee with their little grandson from São Paolo takes place in September. Okay, okay. Only Granny is not feeling her best; she talks about her operation the previous spring, while the goldsmith eats whitefish baked in *Bierteig*, thinking it doesn't taste as good as it used to. The son from São Paolo is a general manager for a Swiss-American firm, almost an American himself in the way he talks about Latin America while feeding Swiss swans. The goldsmith is told he has no need to worry about money at all, even if he lives to be ninety—no problem there. Okay, okay. It is not him saying it, but Granny, and she is saying it, not to him, but to her small grandson.

The way he now sits in the Bodega (the iron stove is still there, only the waiters are different), unwrapping meat loaf from rustling paper then chewing: his wife is dead, the shop sold, and he is living in a home for old people.

```
Berlin

All there is to see is what one already
knows.  I have often been in Berlin and have
always steered clear of visiting the Wall.
Uwe Johnson conducts us round like an of-
ficial, though without commentary.  Since he
```

is very tall, he stoops politely whenever
some technical information is asked for,
removing his pipe from his mouth; he is
dressed as always in a black leather jacket,
his head shaved bare. He doesn't call him—
self a refugee, but he is not allowed on the
other side. A sunny day with a cold wind,
wide expanse of bright northern sky above the
barbed wire. Seeing the Wall, there is
nothing one can say, but, equally, one
cannot speak about other things, either.
Only later in a bar (lying practically in
no—man's—land) does the conversation become
personal, though even then he does not take
off his black leather jacket, which he also
wore during that summer in Rome. A uniform?
The tobacco pouch I take from my pocket is a
gift from him, ostensibly because I was sup—
posed to have said——not in Rome, no, but in
Spoleto, and not in the bar but at the news—
stand . . . What a Homeric memory this man
has! Mecklenburg (the province of his
youth, which he can no longer visit, but
about which he is writing a novel trilogy)
may depend on it.

REMINISCENCES OF BRECHT

My first sight of Brecht: November 1947, a few days after his
arrival in Europe. It was in the small book-burdened apartment
of Kurt Hirschfeld, literary adviser to the Zurich Schauspielhaus, which had staged the first performances in German of
three of Brecht's plays. There he sat on a bench in the corner of
the room, looking like the rare photos I knew of him: gray,
silent, thin, rather shy, a stranger in a country that happened
to speak his language. He seemed grateful for the walls each
side of his shoulders. My arrival interrupted his account of the
hearings of the Un-American Activities Committee, which he
had just undergone. I was thirty-six then, an architect. Since
he did not know Zurich, I showed him the way to the Stadel-
hofen. He showed no curiosity about the city in which he was

now planning to settle down for an indefinite period. I talked to him about Germany, what little I knew of it from my travels, and the war damage in Berlin. He asked me to visit him in Herrliberg to continue my account. "Maybe you, too, will one day find yourself in the interesting situation," Brecht remarked at the railway station, "of hearing someone tell you about your native country and listening as if you were being told about some place in Africa."

The apartment had been lent to Brecht rent free by young Mertens and his wife. Brecht's financial situation while living in Zurich was wretched: the journey to Europe had been paid for by the sale of his house and furniture in America; his earnings at that time would hardly have kept a young student alive. True, he was negotiating with the publisher Peter Suhrkamp, but Suhrkamp at that time had no capital either. Possibly I was misled by the only luxury he allowed himself—expensive cigars—and his hospitality. Brecht, who never talked about his financial situation, did not appear any worse off than later, just as later he did not seem better off than in former days.

Did we see Brecht as a German? A Bavarian? A citizen of the world? This last he would, as a Marxist, have objected to. There was one respect, in comparison with other emigrants, in which he seemed very un-German: he never put things into national pigeonholes—not even Hitler's war. (On a later occasion, in Weissensee, he did once say grudgingly, when asked his opinion of certain Communist officials: "Don't forget, Frisch, they are Germans"—but this was a rare exception.)

What Brecht brought back from emigration was an immunity to ideas of "foreignness": he was neither impressed by the fact that different countries have different customs, nor did he feel impelled by this knowledge to insist on his own German origin. His disapproval was directed toward one social system, his respect toward another; the affectations of world citizenship— the usual refuge for national inhibitions—were unnecessary to him. He was a native of Augsburg who worked in Berlin, with his roots in his own language. His origin was not a distinguishing mark, but an inescapable fact of life. Accepting this fact without question, he was able to regard negative national characteristics like self-hatred as relics of the past, not worth bothering about.

23 April 1948: Bertolt Brecht's first—and only—public appearance in Zurich. In a small basement, the secondhand department of the Volkshaus bookshop, a hundred or so people sit jammed between book-lined walls for one of the reading sessions the librarian now and again arranges. Brecht listens docilely to my short speech of welcome, thanks me with a polite little nod, and seats himself at the small table, tentative rather than expansive, not looking at his audience, Brecht with spectacles and a sheet of paper in his hand. It is doubtful whether the people in the back rows can hear him as he quickly announces the title. Oppressed by the nearness of the audience—those in the front could have rested their arms on the little table (though of course they don't, but sit back with folded arms)—he reads his poem *An die Nachgeborenen* ("To Posterity") in a low voice, rises swiftly, the sheet of paper (no, three sheets of paper) in his hand, and moves to the side, where it is dark. That's enough from him: now the great experts, the actress Therese Giehse and Helene Weigel, take over, and Brecht's presence is forgotten. Afterwards, upstairs in the bookshop, there is little of Brecht's work to be seen; much of it is still unpublished. Some of the guests, putting on their overcoats, eye Brecht from a distance: the gray little man is not waylaid. Later we gather in a little group over beer: Brecht, Weigel, Giehse, the grateful librarian, who cannot pay much for the reading—just the usual hundred francs. Brecht seems quite satisfied.

Once when I visited Herrliberg I found two Brechts sitting in the living room, both with the same haircut and dressed in similar gray linen jackets. One was rather leaner and awkward, friendly in a cramped sort of way; the other was Paul Dessau, the composer of the incidental music for Brecht's later plays. Caspar Neher, his scenic designer, was also often there. Then Brecht would be more relaxed, almost jovial, a different person: Brecht enjoying himself.

When Brecht was in the company of people he did not know well—usually younger people—and they met in a private apartment, rarely in a restaurant where strangers could overhear, he preferred to be comparatively silent. He was there mainly to find out: the center of gravity in the little circle, but not the center of attention, which was a topic, not a person. I can hardly remember Brecht ever holding forth. He did not like to give raw material away. He was never expansive, but restricted himself whenever possible to short anecdotes that, even if he were perhaps telling them for the first time, always sounded in some way cut and dried. Only rarely did he feel the need to describe. I never heard him fantasizing, inventing, throwing off ideas for the sheer fun of it. But he could do what fantasists can never do: listen, whenever anything was being described, in an encouraging, unselfish way. He did not have much to say, if anything at all: his critical attitudes toward the events described imparted themselves to the teller of their own accord. It was to Brecht the listener rather than the debater that one succumbed.

Once we went on a tour of workers' houses, hospitals, schools, etc. The assistant from the district surveyor's office, which had arranged everything at my request, took us all over the place in an official car. He did not understand his guest's questions as, in one development after another, he pointed out the same things, while Brecht, impressed at first by so much comfort for the workers, began to feel more and more oppressed by this very comfort, which seemed to ignore all the basic problems. In a nice new building he suddenly decided that all the rooms were too small, much too small, unfit for human beings; and in a kitchen, fully equipped and gleaming, he impatiently broke the tour off, anxious to get back to work by the very next train, angry that workers should be hoodwinked by this fraud, and still hoping that such attempts to stamp out socialism with comfort for everyone would stay confined to Switzerland.

Brecht must have been a passionate taker of notes, yet he never gave one this impression. I never had the feeling, when I visited him, that I was interrupting: he cleared a chair of books and papers, transforming himself at once from a writer to a listener, to an inquirer, switching his whole field of interest at the same time. Never a word about his own work: that was pushed right aside. When one left him after two or three hours, he seemed as alert as ever: evenings were never talked to a standstill. Whether he went back to work afterwards I cannot of course know. I think of him as a sort of Galileo: never preoccupied but always alert, open to new discoveries. He would, I feel, have been happiest at a standing desk. I cannot visualize him, whether working on his *Little Organon* or his *Antigone* verses, lying in wait like a cat before a mouse hole. I see him rather plucking, pinpointing, noting, defining, experimenting, keeping supple through a constant change of position. Otherwise it would be hard to explain the sheer bulk of his work, of which he himself, it seems, was hardly aware. Peter Suhrkamp told me once that Brecht, when discussing with him the format for his collected plays, pleaded for larger type, feeling that his work needed stretching out a bit: it ought to be made to fill at least five volumes.

"Legend on the Origin of the Book Tao-Te Ching During Lao Tzu's Journey into Exile": I read the poem during the war, standing in the street, as one reads daily bulletins; the carbon copy was almost indecipherable. With the copy came the request to make further copies and pass the poem on. In my studio (I had two draftsmen but no secretary) I typed, with eight copies:
Denn man muss dem Weisen
seine Weisheit erst entreissen,
Drum sei der Zöllner auch bedankt:
Er hat sie ihm abverlangt.
("For first a wise man's wisdom must be extracted. Thanks, then, to the customs man admit: He was the one demanded it.")

It belongs to the memories about myself which I should prefer to forget: there was I, sitting at least once a week in the Herrliberg apartment, but never did it occur to me to ask Brecht for anything, even when Helene Weigel once mentioned in passing what that trunk in the corner contained. Brecht was then fifty-one, an acknowledged master however unassuming his behavior, and the disciple never realized that it might perhaps have pleased him to be asked for something from the luggage that now, as a collected edition, fills a whole bookshelf. He was working then, among other things, on the *Little Organon for the Theater*. The disciple would not have asked to see even that if Brecht had not one day offered it of his own accord—as a piece of homework. He wanted to know, he said, whether it was comprehensible. Of course I read it that same night, but did nothing with it for days afterwards. When eventually I returned the manuscript, I still did not really believe that Brecht was waiting for my opinion, and simply put it on the table with a word of thanks and went on, shamelessly enough, to talk of other things; I left it to Brecht to bring the subject up. That happened up on the sanded roof: Helen Weigel cooking down below, Brecht questioning me as we walked up and down the terrace, Brecht very attentive, very persistent, interested in my misunderstandings, prepared to consider whether the fault lay in me or in the text. It was the only time I read a manuscript for him. Yet I, the beginner, thought nothing of it when the master asked to see my things, and felt it quite normal that he should not wait until the next meeting but sit down at once to his typewriter to give me his views.

At one time Brecht kept pressing me to write a drama about William Tell: it should demonstrate that the peasants' revolt, though successful, was really reactionary in relation to the Habsburg Utopia, a conspiracy of cranks. But it would have, he felt, to be done by a Swiss writer. The theory, which he made attractive enough in theatrical terms, is at least nearer to historical truth than the panegyric for which we rewarded Schiller with the Rütli monument, but it seemed to me all too readily adaptable as an excuse for present-day colonial governors. I never knew whether Brecht, when he was being crafty, imagined that one could not see through him. Another suggestion: Henri Dunant, the founder of the Red Cross: that would be a good patriotic subject for me—a powerful denunciator, a benefactor who beat down attacks from all sides and won, yet lived to see his work misused. Then a third and last suggestion: to adapt DeRojas' Celestina for Therese Giehse, Brecht himself offering to supply the songs I should need here and there. I sat in a public park with the borrowed book, which he had already marked with titles for his songs. It was very tempting. I began to feel frightened. Brecht, if he was allowed to, transformed everybody.

Something in Brecht's manner of thinking, as expressed in conversation as well as in the theoretical writings, gives one the impression: this is not the man himself, this is his method of treatment. That is the danger for Brechtians: they refine the treatment, but lack the genius to make it work.

What he obviously could not stand was somebody who felt obliged to flatter him. An actor who once tried it at table was ignored for the rest of the evening. Too stupid a person. Brecht never demanded proof from people that they were familiar with his works; praise irritated him, praise as a substitute for understanding.

Once, when we were on the lake with a thunderstorm approaching, he betrayed signs of fear. I played the local weather expert and assured him we should be home before it broke. He shrugged his shoulders: "I shouldn't want to be struck by lightning," he said. "I grudge the Pope that favor." He was really on edge.

Brecht's first stage-directing job (together with Caspar Neher) took place at Chur in February 1948, more or less in private. In Zurich we saw Helene Weigel in *Antigone*, but only in a single matinee performance, and the theater was not full; the main thing was that Brecht had been given a chance to try something out. He was in no hurry for a comeback. Whether in Chur or Zurich, Brecht was rehearsing for Berlin. The play he allowed the Zurich Schauspielhaus to bring out was the comparatively innocuous Puntila, written a long time previously in Finland, and he did not mind being obliged, as a foreigner, to omit his name from the program as director. These were all limbering-up exercises, and the less noticeable the better. During rehearsals he stayed in the background. Now and again he dropped a hint: a talented young actress from a well-to-do family had to play a little servant girl with a washtub. When Brecht sniggered, she did not know what she had done wrong. She was carrying a stage prop that was too light. He simply demanded—politely and not forgetting to add a general word of praise for the talented young lady—that in all future rehearsals a pile of wet washing should be placed in the tub: that was all. Three weeks later he remarked: "You see? Her hips got the idea." . . . Brecht on stage: always rather awkward, as if he didn't belong; all the same, one recognized the special gesture he wanted but could not demonstrate properly—it always looked more like a parody.

He could be indecisive. What doesn't work today will perhaps work tomorrow or the next day if one doesn't try to settle it today, if one is prepared to wait and not to make up one's mind at once whether it will ever work. He did not rely on theory, but observed and reacted; the effect was the important thing, though of course Brecht knew what he wanted and never gave in to effect for its own sake. At rehearsals (at any rate in Zurich, where he was working mainly with "nonpolitical" actors) he never used political words to make his point. When Matti, the servant, has to inspect the countryside under the enthusiastic prompting of Puntila, the big landowner, his indifference, conveyed in mime, invoked simple comments like "better," "funnier," "more natural," just as it was immediately "much better" when the maid, for all her youthful uprightness, did not walk around like a tennis player when carrying a washtub. All just questions of taste. One scene I thought rather vulgar. Brecht: "What's that?" He brushed my praise of other things aside: "What do you find vulgar about it?" I couldn't say exactly. "We'll meet afterwards," he said. "Think about it in the meantime." It turned out, after thorough discussion, that my taste betrayed unconscious political overtones. Brecht laughed. "You want Puntila to behave like a gentleman, but when he becomes vulgar that's exactly what he is doing." During rehearsals the actors were often surprised by sudden loud laughter from the back of the orchestra seats: it was Brecht.

All of a sudden, at a meeting soon after, he was wearing his convict's face again: little beady bird's eyes sticking out from a flat face above a too-bare neck. A frightening face, perhaps even off-putting if you didn't know him already. The cap, the linen jacket—borrowed, you might suspect, from plump Paul Dessau —only the jutting cigar looked authentic. A prisoner with a cigar. One felt like giving him a muffler for his neck. Hardly any lips. He was washed, but unshaven. No *clochard*, no Villon. Simply gray. His haircut at such times looked like a treatment for lice or an attempt to humiliate him. His walk lacked shoulders. His head seemed small. Obviously he was no cardinal—but not a workingman, either. In fact Brecht never looked like a working-man—that would be to misunderstand his outward uniform— but rather like a Caspar Neher stylization of an artisan: a carpenter, say, with a head that, with the required props, would

have provided the Roman Catholic Church with a very present-
able cardinal. At the moment, however, as I said, the cardinal
was not in evidence: the Brecht one walked along with was as
embarrassing a companion as a cripple. He was not in a complaining mood: on the contrary, he was busy praising Therese
Giehse. We sat down in the Café Ost, which no longer exists,
opposite an empty *Stammtisch* decorated with students' em-
blems. What are the essential qualities of an actor? We pondered
over it as if Brecht had never written a line about the subject.
He had both time and inclination for talk, his conversation was
alert and lively, inventive: nothing of the cripple about him now.
But back on the street he again seemed to become a pitiable
object, a down-and-out, his gray cap pulled low over his eyes.
And above all that neck—so bare. He walked fast, but his arms
didn't join in. That gray farmer's jacket—as if he had been
dressed at random from the shelves of some institution. Only
the cluster of pencils that he always carried in his top pocket
was personal, plus the inevitable cigar. He did not know what to
do with his hands and thrust them flat into his coat pockets,
as if to hide their nakedness.

5 June 1948, Puntila première in Zurich: the public not very
enthusiastic, Brecht himself, however, satisfied. "One must put
on plays like this over and over again, until people get accustomed to them," he said, "as they've grown accustomed to Schiller. That will take some years." And so he talked of it as if it
had just been a rehearsal.

Only once did I see Brecht together with a member of the
bourgeoisie: the city surveyor insisted on inviting us to lunch
in a place with a view over Zurich. Brecht, instead of admiring
Zurich as expected, asked me whether I had been in New York.
I must see it, it was worth it, but I mustn't wait too long: who
knows how much longer it would be there? . . . The city surveyor
was silent after that.

Ideological discussions, unavoidable in the early days, became
less and less frequent: not because of my objections, but because
I was not expert enough for him, and Brecht had better things
to do than to teach me. He preferred being shown around my
building site and hearing about construction methods, archi-

tectural problems, even more modest matters such as the organization of a largish building site. Technical know-how, especially when seen in practice, filled him with respect. While Ruth Berlau, who was with us, soon became bored, Brecht conscientiously (if rather nervously) climbed among the scaffolding and even up on a ten-meter observation platform, from which one could survey the whole site. Up there, however, he displayed little interest in explanations, though full of respect ("Admirable, Frisch, I take off my hat to you!"), and when Ruth Berlau, camera poised, asked him to step further out along the platform, he refused. Only when we were once again on firm ground was he ready to listen to statistics. "You have a good honest profession." His farewell greeting was often perfunctory: not supercilious, but light and casual. Now, after looking around my building site, he was very demonstrative—in fact, collegial.

When in August 1948 we crossed the border between Kreuzlingen and Konstanz, Brecht was setting foot in Germany for the first time in fifteen years. It was only a short evening visit. The main reason—providing Brecht with a welcome excuse— was to attend a performance at the Deutsches Theater in Konstanz, where Heinz Hilpert—who, during the Hitler era, had been manager of the Berlin *Deutsches Theater*—had produced my first play, which I should have preferred not to see again. (In November of that same year—that is to say, later— Brecht traveled to Berlin via Prague and then returned to Zurich for several months, before finally settling in East Berlin in 1949.) One of the Zurich stage technicians, owner of an ancient Lancia, drove us to the customs barrier. Brecht: "Let's walk across." Passport control, still at that time regarded as a minor adventure, went smoothly, Brecht demonstratively unmoved. Then we walked into the town, a very German town left untouched by the war, with shop signs still in Gothic lettering. After we had gone about a hundred yards, Brecht suddenly stopped, breaking off a conversation about something or other, to relight his cigar, which had apparently gone out. With a glance upwards: "The sky is no different here!" at the same time making that involuntary movement which was frequent with him: moving his lean neck from side to side within the wide collar, a sort of loosening twitch. Then the meeting with Heinz Hilpert and his disciples. Effusiveness always made Brecht awkward: he retired into his beer while a young actor (who had heard of the *Three Penny Opera*) held forth endlessly on the merits of the theater in Konstanz. Brecht listened in amazement: the spate of words left him speechless. After the performance Brecht expatiated on German beer, still the best in the world, then, almost at once: "Let's go." He said nothing until we were back in Kreuzlingen, when a word from an actor, Wilfried Seifert, who was with us, led to a sudden outburst. It began with a cold snigger, and then he screamed, white with rage. Seifert did not understand what was the matter. The way these survivors—however uncompromised—spoke, their behavior on stage, their complacent unfeelingness, the shameless way in which they simply went on as if nothing had happened, as if it were only their houses that had been destroyed, their art for art's sake attitudes, their haste to make their peace with their own country: all this was much worse than he had expected. Brecht was shattered, his outburst one long denunciation. I had never seen him so clear, so direct as here, when, in that quiet midnight café, he hurled out his challenge after his first re-encounter with his native soil. Suddenly he was eager to return: "Here we must start all over again from the beginning."

"Take this photo with you to Poland," he said, "You'll probably see some people from the government: ask them if it's true." He handed me an illustrated periodical, which, though it did not actually say so, showed pictures suggestive of outrages in Silesia, concentration-camp conditions. "Ask everywhere whether it's true," Brecht demanded. I could not imagine that people from the government would be willing to comment on such matters at an official banquet, for instance, but: "There's no harm in asking," said Brecht. He was completely in earnest. "If these things are happening in Poland," he said, "something must be done about it." When I returned from Poland, he was eager to hear from me, rang me up as soon as he heard I was back. I cycled over to Herrliberg with a lot of things to talk about: Breslau (now Wroclaw), Congrès International des Intellectuels pour la Paix, Warsaw. I expected the conversation to be difficult. Everything I had to report was double-edged, Brecht expectant. Greetings from Anna Seghers. Alone with Brecht, who had not yet seen the eastern European countries with his own eyes, I simply spoke as things came, doubtful, pleasing, depressing, or unclear. Everything in concrete terms: impressions of a journey through Silesia; conversation with a Polish farmer who spoke faultless German—a former farmhand in East Prussia, where he gained experience and saved enough to buy a farm of his own in East Poland. Then war, eviction from his home by the Russians and now he was settled on Silesian soil—a whole life story. Brecht was an attentive listener, which made the telling easier, showing pleasure or dismay as the occasion demanded, but on the whole more concerned than otherwise. The manipulations of Fadeev and the brilliant Ehrenburg angered him: "If you're going to have a conference at all, such things shouldn't be allowed to happen." Now and again he called down to Helene Weigel, but we remained alone, Brecht edgy, often speechless, openly concerned, but showing no tendency to deny the unpleasant aspects. Just once a reproach to me for not having openly asked certain questions at an official reception where hundreds of intellectuals were gathered around a buffet. What I had seen of the recovery plans in Warsaw (scrapped after the downfall of Gomulka) or what I had learned in basement bars beneath the ruins—out of reach of official optimism—about real living and happy people: all this I enjoyed telling him; Brecht took it as proof that I was not merely engaging in polemics and showed all the more concern for the negative aspects (those which seemed negative to him, that is). "That's not right," he said frequently, "that must be changed." Later Helene Weigel came to join us: I had to continue my report, even repeat some of it; but it no longer worked. It wasn't only that she was always ready with the pat official explanation to put me, the eyewitness, right; Brecht, too, was now a different person, no longer indignant about Fadeev, but about me. I felt I was taking an examination that the examiners had already determined I should fail. Now put right about what was really happening in Poland, I rode off on my bicycle.

Certainly warmheartedness was by no means the prime characteristic of this man who did not like giving raw material away, and feelings are raw material. Nor in his presence could one display warmth: his habit of using more or less the same vocabulary to express toleration or respect or affection in his personal relations gave him an almost judgelike air. His gestures (I am always coming back to his gestures, though they were never flamboyant, but at times almost automatic and stereotyped) conveyed above all a sense of parody—and how many things there were to be parodied! Brecht must have been conscious of a sentimental streak in his nature, and anything that showed the slightest tendency in this direction he clamped down on. His courtesy was not expressed in flourishes, but in the manner of his greeting or behavior at table: a gracious sort of courtesy was all he would permit in the way of showing affection. Familiarity he shot down at once, when necessary with considerable harshness. It clearly made him uncomfortable. Feelings—normally held at bay by gesture and wit— Brecht admitted only in his poems, where they were under artistic control. He was bashful. Unlike most men, he did not change when women were present, felt no urge to show off; women on social occasions were either comrades (and consequently neutralized) or silly geese who, once identified and handled accordingly, did not disturb the conversation for long. At such times he showed more than his usual cordiality— to an extent indeed that made one wonder—toward men.

Berlin, spring 1950: *The Private Tutor*, a tragicomedy by Lenz adapted by the Berliner Ensemble, for the first time the curtain with the white Picasso dove, and afterward Brecht (without aura) on the sidewalk outside the Deutsches Theater. He was clearly pleased that people were coming to Berlin to see the Ensemble's work. No famous actors, a few friends from Zurich: Hans Gaugler, Regina Lutz, Benno Besson. It was like an electric shock: for the first time I see what theater can be. A vindication of his theories? One forgot them, since their promise had been met—probably very inadequately, compared with the Berliner Ensemble's later productions or those of the Piccolo Teatro in Milan, now in danger of atrophy. . . . Brecht seemed younger than usual. He invited me to stay the night at Weissensee; he wanted to talk. First, however, there was a May Day ceremony in the theater to be attended. Not a demonstration— that had taken place in the streets during the day. Now there was dancing, good fellowship, provocative almost in its absence of neckties, everybody determinedly good-humored, making the party go with vouchers exchangeable at the buffet. The question "How do you like it here?" made me feel rather embarrassed. Wolfgang Langhoff, another old acquaintance from Zurich, greeted me guardedly. I saw myself, whether I wanted it or not, in the role of a westerner, sniffing around the East Zone in a surreptitious search for evidence of restricted freedom, of misery and poverty. I was ill at ease. Brecht was there, doing his duty but otherwise unobtrusive. Uplifted as I had been by the performance I had just seen, I began to feel dreary and depressed, Even the buffet (hungry as I was) seemed to be trying to give me lessons in how to live here: all this chumminess—what spirit of comradeship! But it all had a faint air of compulsion, and if one tried to resist it one immediately felt the hostility, which the obligation to see everything positively only heightened: even silence was likely to be misunderstood. Helene Weigel, festively effusive, led me, the outsider, out to dance, but I was now past saving: everything seemed so demonstrative—and therefore suspect. Outside, a firework display began above the dark ruins. Brecht, like everyone else, went to the window. Smoking, he stayed for the final set-piece explosion, then came up to me: "We can go now, Frisch, or do you want to stay on?" Out in the dark street after slipping off unseen, Brecht talked about theatrical affairs. The ruins were not topical, nothing less important than ruins. Brecht was at his best—springy, light.

The rumor that Brecht, installed in a palace by the Russians, was living like a prince amid the poverty of East Berlin and that Helene Weigel had been buying up priceless antiques in the penurious East Zone, proved (as I had expected) to be false. A villa like a thousand others in Berlin: standing rather dilapidated, but unbombed, in an untended garden, roomy but, as far as I can remember, almost uncarpeted. A fine old cupboard, a few bits of furniture in pleasant style—little enough on the whole and, as always with Brecht, temporary looking. I slept in an attic, formerly a maid's bedroom, the walls covered with Marxist classics. Next morning: Brecht already at work, but with time to spare; five minutes with his guest, who had never seen the Weissensee, down at the lakeside, then back to the workroom in preference to a seat beneath a budding willow. The tutor's self-castration in Lenz's play as a technical stage problem. My feeling that conversation in Weissensee was different from that in Herrliberg could hardly be supported by evidence, yet I had the feeling then. "Plays must now be written by people who know the problems of this state from their own experience," Brecht said. "That can't be done from over there." Though the Berlin Wall was not yet built, there was already a "here" and an "over there." All the same he was very concerned that there should be no boycotting; he asked me to speak to Barlog, the manager of the West Berlin *Schiller Theater*, about an actor who was having difficulties in West Berlin because he had played in Brecht's Ensemble. Apart from that I remember nothing of our long conversation, but I do remember how Brecht managed so effortlessly to adapt that typically bourgeois villa to his own uses without rebuilding or anything of that sort. He felt not the slightest need to resist the architecture: he was the stronger. It was not like a requisitioning or a transfer of ownership: the question of whom the villa belonged to did not even arise. Brecht simply used the house as the living always use dead men's buildings, as part of the historical process. Later we drove to the theater, Brecht with cap and cigar at the wheel of an old open car, the banners of yesterday's May Day celebrations in trafficless streets, ruins all around beneath the thin Berlin sky, Brecht asking cheerfully: "When are you coming to join us here?"

Another time in Weissensee: "You have been accused of formalism. What do these people mean by formalism?" Brecht tries to shrug it off: "Nothing." He is irritated when I persist, leans back in his chair, puffs out smoke, puts on an amused air of unconcern: "Formalism means that certain people don't like me." What is actually irritating him comes out when he adds, rather angrily: "In the West they would probably have another word for it." We talk about other things, and it is only later, when I had ceased expecting it, that the real answer comes out in a completely different context: "As refugees, you see, we learned to work for our bottom drawer. Perhaps a time will come when people will dig out our work and be able to make use of it."

I have met only a few people who could be recognized as great and, asked what it was about Brecht that showed his greatness, I should be lost for an answer. In fact, it was always the same thing: only after leaving him did one feel the real impact of his presence. His greatness worked retrospectively, always lagging a bit behind, like an echo. In order to bear it one had to see him again, for then he helped one out by his unpretentious manner.

About Brecht's behavior during the workers' rising in Berlin on 17 June 1953 I later spoke to two members of the Berliner Ensemble, the stage managers Egon Monk and Benno Besson. Had Brecht, I asked, made a speech to his company when the first news from the Stalin-Allee came through? We know that rehearsals (*Der Zerbrochene Krug* and *Don Juan*) were broken off. Where did Brecht go in the course of that day? How had he assessed the events or as much as he knew of them: as a demonstration by workers with whose complaints he was in sympathy, or as mutiny? How much did he really know about it? Was he concerned that the West might take advantage of the leaderless rising, and that it might lead to war? Did he have a chance to intervene? What was it? Were his feelings divided? Was he indifferent? panicky? inactive? Did he ask members of his company for advice on how they should behave? Was Brecht (as people were saying at the time) a coward, a traitor to the workers? Or was he worried that the workers were placing themselves in jeopardy through romantic acts? Was Brecht shocked by the intervention of Russian tanks, or did he consider it necessary, in order to keep the West from attacking? Even the two Ensemble people I questioned gave me interpretations rather than answers, and their interpretations were conflicting. Peter Suhrkamp sent out copies of Brecht's letter to Ulbricht—the complete version.

My last encounter with Brecht before his death, was a short, somewhat stiff visit in the Chaussee Strasse in September 1955. An apartment with view over a cemetery. I felt ill at ease: Benno Besson, a Swiss whom I knew better than the other Ensemble people, happened to be there, and political blinkers had soured our relationship. After an unremitting series of quarrels Besson and I were still completely at odds, and as I entered Brecht's room we greeted one another with restrained coldness. Was Brecht aware of it? I came in the middle of a working discussion, and we stood for several minutes until politeness constrained Brecht to dismiss Besson with a gesture, though there were urgent decisions still to be made. Alone with Brecht, whom I had not seen for some time, I found the formal atmosphere persisting. He told me the Ensemble was firmly established and he could now leave the running of it to others. He felt the urge to get on with his writing. He looked gray and ill, and was sparing in his movements. I had come from rehearsals in West Berlin: Hanne Hiob, his daughter, was playing one of the main roles and Caspar Neher was designing the scenery. At lunch he wanted to know what people in the West felt about the danger of war. Now, if one came from the West, one was coming from a distant land. The habitual question: "What are you working on now?" was not asked. Helene Weigel was also present: she asked me what I thought about the persecution of Konrad Farner in Switzerland. Our meal was punctuated with periods of silence. No jokes. I remained ill at ease. An inhibited conversation—hardly a conversation at all. The feeling that I was to blame for the lack of frankness was lacerating, and could not be dispelled with accounts of how Suhrkamp was getting on—which was badly. The problem of reunification? Brecht: "Reunification would mean another spell of emigration."

Why Brecht ordered a steel coffin for himself remains a mystery. What was it supposed to protect him from? The people in power? Resurrection? From joining, like the drowned girl of his poem, the rest of the world's carrion on the riverbed (*Aas mit vielem Aas*)?

There is a saying that fits Brecht, though it was not written about him: "In spite of the one-sidedness of his teaching, this legendary being had an infinite variety of aspects" (Maxim Gorki speaking of Leo Tolstoi).

```
ZURICH
Mother dying.  At times she imagines we are
in Russia together.  She is ninety.  Has
Odessa changed much since 1901?
```

POSTSCRIPT TO A JOURNEY

In a room late at night somebody produces a piece of paper, an official form in Russian script, gray and crumbling, the reverse side filled from margin to margin with tiny handwriting, hardly legible without a magnifying glass. A comrade had been deported, though she never found out why. After a year in camp she asked for a single cell, where conditions are much worse (rats, etc.). Her second request was for paper. Both were granted: she was given these official forms by the prison administration and spent three years in solitary confinement. There she translated Byron's *Don Juan*—from memory. When she had completed it, she asked to be released from her solitary cell. Back in the general block and working on the land, she kept the manuscript hidden against her body. After eight years in all (if I remember rightly), she was declared innocent and released. Now, in 1966, her Byron translation is to be published, and may be read in public in a large theater.

. . . .

I have some rubles—900 rubles—payment for a novel printed in the periodical *Inostranya Litteratura*. It takes a worker half a year to earn that. There is nothing I can do with them: hotel and air fares have to be paid in dollars, and I am not allowed to take them out of Russia. Nothing for it but to drink Champansky and eat caviar. There is none in Odessa. An air flight to the Crimea is not possible, firstly because I cannot use my rubles; secondly, because I have no dollars left; and thirdly, because we should need another visa from Moscow. So we spent our time (having already inspected the fine Potemkin Steps and being unable to visit the Liebknecht collective, held up as a model in a gleaming prospectus: it was reachable only by dollar-taxi, but, though we had just enough dollars, it was closed to us on account of foot-and-mouth disease—"a disease you also have in the West")—so we spent our time at a football match, tickets (numbered) through Intourist. The young man sitting beside us happens to speak German and is interested in literature: he knows Heinrich Böll, Erich Maria Remarque. Then from his briefcase he pulls out the familiar periodical with the German novel he is at the moment reading—how extraordinary that I should be the author, yes, indeed, what a coincidence. Our young friend knows less about football. Evening with Champansky. Talk about God and the astronauts. Boris is a lecturer earning 80 rubles per month, and he lives in a single room with his wife, who is studying for a doctorate or a diploma —not sure which. Anyway, Boris is at our disposal if there is anything we want to know. Another evening with Champansky, but I still have 630 rubles left on the evening of our departure. What shall I do? Next morning, three hours before plane time, Boris turns up, saying in an odd voice that he must speak to me. At once. Not in the hotel lobby (where I have the impression he is known to the staff, though I am not supposed to notice). Outside on the terrace above the harbor: he cannot possibly accept the money I stowed away in his periodical. I explain my position to him. Should I leave my rubles lying here on the wall? No Soviet person, he says, would touch it. Money as a reward for work, yes, but not like this. So should I let myself be arrested at the customs barrier for these rubles I earned in Moscow? I say: Boris, listen, please—glancing at my watch and holding this bundle of notes in my hand. It had been the most expensive journey I ever made: one ruble to one dollar. Since I won't put it in the State Bank (which disappoints Boris), I can always buy something with it. Two fur caps, already bought in Moscow, are as many as I need; phonograph records are too cheap. What, I ask, cost 630 rubles? A motorcycle. Or—easier to transport—a camera. But I don't take photographs, nor does my wife, and my children already have a camera. But this is the best camera in the Soviet Union. So what else can I do? Boris takes me there. Why on the way did I have to ask yet again which was Isaac Babel's house? In the store to which he led me I should have been lost without Boris; he has a pass that obliges the girl to serve us at last, though her manner remains sullen. What the gentleman from the West is buying attracts several onlookers. I know little about cameras, the girl even less, but Boris assures me it works. I don't doubt that, but somebody should tell me how. Boris tells me something quite different: the girl serving us is very pleased—she has now achieved her sales target for the day, exceeded it, in fact. I readily believe him, though the girl has no smile for me. Boris takes the rubles to the cash desk. All settled now. We drink up the few remaining rubles at the airport. . . . In Warsaw I don't get very far with my story of the encounter at the football match in Odessa; they all laugh. Boris is what they are most of them called. Maybe so. But we liked our Boris.

WARSAW

Little to be had, if one were to want it, yet all the same one gets the impression that they live better than the Russians. They can smile at themselves. What they display in the shop window: taste without goods, imagination, gracefulness. It looks almost like bravado.

Where in 1948 there was nothing but rubble to be seen—I think of Viska, who was our guide at that time and our argument whether there was any sense in rebuilding houses just as they had been before—now I admit she was right: even the sham acquires a patina. I sit on the public square in a Biedermeier armchair: it just happened that furniture was standing on the pavement awaiting transport, and the photographer girl sat me down in this old chair. Quite right: it is twenty years since my last visit, and I feel quite historic myself.

He, this heir to a royal name, is not an unquestioning party comrade of the usual sort. Born as a large landowner, he was once reviled as the Red Prince and spent years in Hitler's concentration camps. At lunch with the Writers' Association (he is a translator from the German, now working on Musil) he tells me he often visits the peasants on his former estate. They are not living well, no, but better than ever before. He is a Catholic. Some people are worse off than in earlier days, but he is glad that 90 percent of the people are doing better.

A Chinese delegation at the airport, all in Mao jackets. Do they find us as impenetrable as we find them? An acquaintance from Switzerland, a professor who has been to a scientific conference, speaks to me: he finds Warsaw poor, dirty, drab, etc.

```
ZURICH
In a little restaurant (Wolfbächli) I grad-
ually get the youngish man opposite talking
as he eats his fried eggs.  Painter and
decorator with six employees, plenty of work,
he will be busy all through the night.  By
all sorts of byways (night work rates,
```

sport, architects' habits, spray techniques,
foreign workers, etc.) I finally get to the
point: Which work do you like best? I
would rather paint a wall than window frames,
bright colors rather than dull matching
tones. Why is that? He doesn't understand
the question. Which does he prefer dealing
with, redecorated or new buildings? One just
does both—tonight redecorating. Does he
dislike night work? One just has to put up
with it. Since he is the boss and can therefore select, I ask: Which part of the work do
you keep for yourself? Undercoating must be
boring enough, but removing old paint even
worse. Which gives you more pleasure using a
brush or spraying? His specialty, he says,
is hard finishing: that's where the profit
lies. So back to current rates: bit by bit I
find out what his annual turnover is, even
his own average income, once I have sworn
that I am not a spy from the tax office. His
income isn't huge, but respectable; he has
his regular customers; but it's hard nowadays
to find workers who can do a good job, and
then they are always leaving or taking days
off, it's not an easy job, with its dead-
lines, the price of materials, botched work,
etc. Back to my question: What in your work
do you occasionally enjoy doing? His answers: Spraying is more profitable, redecora-
tions bring in very little, the rates for
windows are much too low, on the other hand
he does well from hard finishing, and after
all he has a family to support, night work is
profitable. My further question: Doesn't
it annoy you when people choose colors that
you personally find wrong? I know, of
course, that, he is simply working for a
living, but all the same I ask my question:
Wouldn't you sometimes like to select a
different color? One tries out patterns in

the hall and then can be amazed with the
finished result: doesn't he look forward to
seeing how it will turn out? He doesn't
really understand what I am trying to get at;
he has told me his income. Don't you some—
times feel like taking up another profession?
Well, of course: when a job doesn't pay
because of the low rates (with the exception
of hard finishing, which is his specialty),
then his income goes down. So he enjoys
hard finishing? He wouldn't exactly say
that: hard finishing is a job that not
everybody can do and consequently the rates
are rather better. Finally (he really
ought to go, or his employees will get slack,
but I have just ordered two more beers), I
ask whether he believes his workers would be
less slack if it were their own business, I
mean, if they had a share in the profits and
in his understandable worries; in other
words, did he believe that a business run
on socialist principles could succeed—and if
not, why not? What, he asked was that—a
business run on socialist principles? Short
explanation from me, proving that I know
nothing about the decorating line: somebody
must go out after orders, somebody must
keep the books, and the workers know nothing
at all about that and don't care a hoot about
it, somebody must keep an eye on the dead—
lines in order not to lose customers yet take
care that nothing is botched, as it certainly
will be if the boss doesn't watch it. That's
how it is. And that's why he must go now,
which he does, not offering his hand, un—
smiling. . . .

SKETCH

There is nothing to be said ... But he doesn't even say that.
His wife does all she can to make him speak, in recent times

even by picking a quarrel—which ends in tears, because he won't argue. He stands at the window, hands in pockets, as if considering a reply. Silent. Then, when he at last turns around, he asks if the dog has been fed.

. . .

As the years go on, things get worse.

. . .

All the guests keep on talking and don't notice that he, busy with his duties as a host, is not talking. Their usual conclusion: a nice time. Only his wife is unhappy. Afterward she says, "You used to have ideas of your own." He doesn't deny it. "Haven't you anything at all to say?" Of course, if he makes the effort, he can say something; it's just that he has the feeling he has already said it all before. Who could be interested, except at most the other people?

. . .

He is in his middle forties, thus not old.

. . .

His wife at first puts it down to their marriage. There are couples who no longer have anything to say to each other. She goes on trips, etc., in order to revitalize their marriage. When she returns after two or three weeks, there he is at the station or the airport, waving. He takes her bags, kisses her—but there is nothing to be said.

. . .

There are words he never utters: he knows what they mean when others say them; if he says them himself they mean nothing, the same words.

. . .

He is a lawyer, head of a trust company, president of the House-owners' Association. He has a lot to do, much of it boring, but he never complains, even about that. He meets plenty of people every day, all sorts of things happen. "Why do you never tell me anything?" Then he turns on the television. "You and your football!"

. . .

Taken to the zoo in his childhood, he thought that fish couldn't speak because they were under water; otherwise they surely would. . . .

. . .

People like him. His quiet ways. There are always enough people around with something to say; it's usually sufficient just to listen. As a guest he comes in the category of those who stay seated, who never realize it is time to go, but just silently remain seated. Nothing occurs to him even when he is alone.

. . .

When she says to him, "You must be thinking something!" he gets up as if a conversation has just ended, goes out and feeds the dog, which simply wags its tail and eats and has no desire to make him talk.

. . .

His clients respect his habit of not saying what he thinks; all they want him to do is look after their interests.

. . .

His hobby: chess. No opponent would ever dream of asking: What are you thinking about now? All he needs to do is in his own good time make a move, silent as the chessmen themselves. His patience as his opponent now reflects, his air of relaxation, etc., he does not feel bothered when his opponent suddenly calls, "Check." What is there to say to that? He is grateful for every game, even when he loses after two hours—hours free from conversation.

. . .

He turns on the radio the moment he gets into his car.

. . .

Views on Nasser and Israel, on heart transplants, Ulbricht, Franz Josef Strauss, on the Common Market, *Der Spiegel*, on women's rights in Switzerland, on the statute of limitation for war crimes—everybody has views of some kind, naturally. Which is why his wife says, "That's what Heiner thinks, too," as he is uncorking a bottle.

. . .

The dog becomes more and more important. He spends hours walking with the dog. His wife can't stand walking for hours beside, in front of, or behind a man who has to exert himself even to say, "There's a hare!" If she starts talking, he listens until an answer is called for; then he suddenly stops and looks at something: Nature as an excuse for not talking. . . . When he goes out alone with the dog, he doesn't notice that for hours he hasn't spoken his thoughts, and, if he has none, the dog doesn't notice.

. . .

What he likes: films. But he always avoids films that excite controversy. He prefers Westerns.

. . .

Only people who don't know him ask the usual question: What is your opinion? Then he says something or other, but he could just as well have said the opposite; he is confused, as he used to be in school when the teacher said, "Quite right!"

. . .

When he has drunk too much he does talk, without asking himself whether he has anything to say. Next morning he can't remember, and that bothers him: what could he have found to talk about from nine in the evening till four in the morning?

. . .

His daughter has also noticed now that he never speaks. He is just fatherly. He can usually tell her what she wants to know, but he doesn't elaborate: he just knows what "idiosyncrasy" means (according to the dictionary), and then he pretends to be busy. Mowing the lawn. If his daughter shows signs of being bored at home, he wonders what the trouble is; he asks her. He permits her almost everything. He reads Mao in order to understand her—then plays ping-pong with her.

. . .

The doctor has forbidden him to smoke. But he can't stop—not with people around waiting for him to say something.

. . .

He has to go to the hospital for an operation. An enjoyable three weeks: all he needs say is that he has hardly any pain, then leave it to the visitor to talk about the weather outside, the heat in the city, a divorce among their acquaintances, etc.

. . .

Eventually he loses contact even with the dog. The dog stops running after the fir cones he throws. The dog stops coming when he calls. The dog finds its own amusement.

. . .

Once, at some public ceremony, he has to speak on behalf of the management. He acquits himself excellently, not without humor, in front of two cameras. When he sees himself on TV he admits he did it well. No difficulty there—as long as he doesn't have to say what he thinks.

. . .

When he has the house to himself he may suddenly start frying a couple of eggs, though he is not hungry. The minute one has nothing to do there is a danger that one might think something.

. . .

It's true that he used to have opinions. He can remember that. For example, he (more than Doris) was of the opinion they should get married. Now he has no opinion even about that.

. . .

Sometimes in his dreams he has something to say, but then the fact that he wanted to say it wakes him.

. . .

It has nothing to do with Doris.

. . .

How odd it is that people can hardly be in a room together before they know what to talk about—the same on the telephone or in the street! They greet one another and then at once know what to talk about.

. . .

He now avoids any situation in which he can hear his own silence. He stops at building sites: the noise of drills, etc. But every noise ends some time.

. . .

For a time, earlier on, he possibly used to speak to himself when silent: he still knew—in words—what he was keeping to himself.

. . .

From the outside he seems quite normal.

. . .

A suicide plan goes astray because in the letter he feels he would owe his wife he has nothing to say. . . .

. . .

Funerals never upset him, even when he was fond of the dead person. Everyone in black, some grieving, all admitting they don't know what to say, a consoling hand: there is simply nothing to be said.

. . .

Later he does it without a letter.

> BERZONA, June
>
> Phone call from Moscow: <u>Literaturnaya</u> <u>Gazeta</u> wants a statement on the bombing in North Vietnam. At once. They will call again at the same time (noon) tomorrow. "You ask what Western writers have to say about the American air attacks in North Vietnam. Your request is based on the assumption that we shall be able to state our opinions freely. That is very largely true. If you can promise Western writers that you will publish their protests even when these are not directed against the United States but (for example) against the sentences imposed on Soviet writers, then I should be pleased for you to publish the following statement concerning the American bombings in North Vietnam." Phone call as arranged at 12:10 P.M. The person writing it down on the other end speaks German without difficulty, sounds,

```
however, sour at the mention of Soviet
writers. I ask for confirmation: all or
nothing. Ten days later another call from
Moscow: my contribution has been rejected.
Voice very friendly. The reason: I did not
stick to the question.
```

QUESTIONNAIRE

1.
Do you still find marriage a problem?

2.
When are you more in favor of marriage as an institution, when you consider your own marriage or when you consider other people's?

3.
Have you more frequently advised others:
a. to separate? or
b. not to separate?

4.
Do you know of reconciliations that have *not* left a scar on one or both of the partners?

5.
What problems are solved by a happy marriage?

6.
How long on average can you live with your partner without losing your self-integrity (meaning that you no longer venture even in secret to hold views that could shock your partner)?

7.
How do you explain to yourself the urge, when contemplating a separation, to look for blame—either in yourself or your partner?

8.
Would you of your own accord ever have invented marriage?

9.
Do you feel in harmony with the mutual habits of your present marriage? If not, do you believe your partner is happy with them, and on what do you base your assumption?

10.
When do you find marriage most of a strain:
a. in everyday matters?
b. on journeys?
c. when you are alone?
d. in company with others?
e. when just the two of you are together?
f. in the evenings?
g. in the mornings?

11.
Does marriage produce common tastes (as the furnishing of the marital home seems to suggest), or does the purchase of a lamp, a carpet, a vase, etc., always mean a silent capitulation on your part?

12.
If you have any children, do you feel a sense of guilt toward them when a separation occurs? That is to say, do you believe that children have a right to unhappy parents? If so, up to what age?

13.
What induced you to marry:
a. a desire for security?
b. a child?
c. the social disadvantages of an irregular union, for example, difficulties in hotels, gossip, the tactlessness of others, complications with officials or neighbors?
d. custom?
e. simplification of household arrangements?
f. consideration for your families?
g. the experience that irregular unions can equally lead to habit, boredom, disenchantment, etc?
h. the prospect of an inheritance?
i. a trust in miracles?

j. the feeling that it is only a formality anyway?

14.
Would you like to add anything to the marriage oath as used in church or registry office ceremonies:
a. as a woman?
b. as a man?
(Please give precise wording)

15.
If you have been married more than once, at what point did your marriages most closely resemble one another, at the beginning or at the end?

16.
If you find after separation that your former partner does not cease blaming you, do you conclude from this that you were more loved than you had realized, or do you feel relieved?

17.
What do you usually say when one of your friends gets a divorce, and why didn't you say it to the person concerned before?

18.
Can you be equally frank with both partners in a marriage when they themselves are not frank with each other?

19.
If your present marriage can be called happy, state briefly to what you attribute this.

20.
If you had to choose between leading a happy marriage and following a call that might endanger your marital happiness, which would you consider more important:
a. as a man?
b. as a woman?

21.
Why?

22.
Do you think you know how your present partner would answer
this questionnaire? If not:

23.
Would you like to see your partner's answers?

24.
Conversely, would you want your partner to know how you have
answered this questionnaire?

25.
Do you consider that having no secrets from each other is a
necessary part of marriage, or do you feel that it is precisely
the secret between two human beings that binds them?

ZURICH, December

Ceremony in the Schauspielhaus: the man who
is being celebrated makes a declaration that
is listened to reverently and finally greeted
with applause. At last it can be said again:
that there is such a thing as decadent literature. Which writers are meant is not
stated. The Professor of German literature
from Zurich, dignified in the knowledge of
his own courage and speaking not without
thought but rather with a noble determination
to speak here and now the simple truth, asks
the question: Among what sort of people do
they live?--meaning, of course, the writers.
We have long been on Christian name terms, I
owe him much friendly encouragement for apprentice work, we have picked mushrooms and
smoked cigars together; he will find it hard
to understand why I today stand up in public
against him.

"Take a look at the subject matter with which recent novels and
plays are filled. They teem with psychopaths, with antisocial charac-

ters, with utter abominations, deliberate acts of perfidy. They are set in murky places, and show great powers of invention in everything that is despicable. Yet when people try to persuade us that such things are evidence of profound disgust, of mental anguish, of some sort of serious concern for developments as a whole, we sometimes—though not always—feel constrained to express our doubts.

"And today? We are met with the slogan 'Committed literature.' But this is no comfort for those who truly love literature as literature. Literature is losing its freedom, it is losing its true, convincing language, its capacity to outlast the changing times when it turns itself so eagerly and directly into an advocate of supposed humanitarian, social, and political ideas. Thus we see in committed literature only the degeneration of that urge for communion which inspired the writers of the past."

". . . This legion of writers, scattered throughout the Western world, who have made it their life's work to root among all that is mean and beastly in this world . . ."

"When such writers claim that the sewer is a symbol of the real world, that pimps, prostitutes and drunkards are representative of the real, unadorned world, then I am bound to ask among what sort of people these writers live."

"Let us relay the plain and solid foundations on which that great cultural edifice was built."

"Let us return to Mozart!"

—Emil Staiger on being presented with the Literature Prize of the City of Zurich on 17 December 1966.

MARRIAGE AFTER DEATH

A youngish widow, three years after the death of her husband, feels suddenly appalled: his public image, still generally respected, has no reality for her. His professional achievements are still known in the city and beyond; that—his professional achievement—had been real: nobody is seriously trying to question that. The obituaries were too flattering—that she had felt in spite of her grief—but they would have pleased him. Of course she never tells anyone. Whenever the talk is of Marcel (less and less as time goes on) she appears a model widow: one can discuss things with her and she is always reasonable, never claiming for her dead husband the right to dictate to his successors in office, she demands no more than the respect he enjoyed up to his death. She has read his early letters: the trouble does not lie there. They are good letters, often amusing. Nor has anything come to light since his death that could have appalled her, no piece of evidence that might suddenly make him seem a different person. A fleeting love affair, to which she would not perhaps have been as indifferent once as she is now, is quite in keeping with the lively personality he had revealed outwardly. She is still living in the same apartment; his collection of crystals, still kept shining with a feather duster, the overlarge collection of photographs of yachting regattas (he had enjoyed sailing in his spare time), the Indian souvenirs (reminders of a journey they made together)—all that is still there, as well as the maidservant, who still refers to the dead man as Herr Doktor. Suddenly, the less she thinks of Marcel, some ordinary remark of his returns from nowhere to surprise her. He had in fact always tended to deceive himself—not flagrantly but still to a certain degree—without being conscious of it. His friends, it seems still believe in him implicitly, and that, they imagine, binds them to his widow. Once or twice, as she suddenly breaks out in tears, they console her with words that could have come from Marcel himself. That frightens her. Eight years of marriage, a happy one on the whole; he fell to his death on a climbing expedition; the children are now of school age. He would certainly not have objected to her marrying again: she knows exactly what words he would have used to persuade her. It is only that, the longer he is dead, the less she believes him. The marriage still remains. In fact, the only thing about him she still believes in is his death. . . .

1967

INSCRIPTION FOR A FOUNTAIN

A sculptor, commissioned by the city of Zurich to provide a fountain for Rosenhof, a quiet square, shows me his stone and asks for a text to carve around it; the authorities made no stipulations, but naturally want to see the text beforehand. My text is approved—not without some shoulder shrugging—but approved.

Here lies
no great
Zurich
philosopher
statesman
or rebel
farseeing
planner
of freedom
etc.

1967 nobody
contemporary
patriot
reformer
of Switzerland
of the 20th century
founder
of the future
which yet will come

1967

No famous refugee lived here
or died hereabouts for the
honor of our native city.
Here no heretic was burnt.
Here no victory was won.
Here no fable glorifying us
calls for a memorial in stone.
Recall here our deeds today.
This memorial is free.

Here lies no cold warrior.
This stone, which is dumb,
was erected at the time of
the war in Vietnam.

1967

PRAGUE, February

Public ownership still apparently does not induce people to look after things. I ask why the road leading to a development of something like five hundred houses is still, after two years, not properly surfaced. A few bulldozers are scratching around. When it rains, the residents have to wade through a morass. I am told that two official departments cannot agree. Don't the residents complain? Not they—there are too many people waiting for houses like this. Many things remain unsaid. We

view a large hospital. Here, too, the approaches are such that
the ambulances are jolted. The medical staff has been complaining for years—in vain. The surgeon conducting us around—
friendly, factual without wasting words—is a loyal citizen. A
new major hospital is being built. The old one, built by the
Germans, reminds one of a military hospital: an emergency
structure still in use twenty years after the war, out of date and
in many ways inadequate. We must do our best for the patients,
the surgeon says, with the means available. Medicaments?
They get all they need—from the West as well. He would like
to visit the West some time for a medical congress, but is not
allowed. Medical books? They are available—not in the hospital,
but in the city library; the authorities are tight with foreign
currency and cannot be persuaded how important it is for the
doctors, who are overworked anyway, to have medical journals
on hand for their few spare moments. They can always go down-
town if they want to keep up with scientific advances. Why can't
the authorities, in spite of repeated petitions from the doctors,
be made to see sense? Because they are functionaries, and their
first duty is to the Party; it is to the Party they owe their positions,
not to their own aptitudes. The room in which the surgeon gets
ready for work, and also sleeps, is by my reckoning no more
than three yards by two or two and a half. I visit wards. A sad
sight . . . Yes, says the surgeon, we all hope things will get
better in time!

My female guide feels it her duty to provide only information
that will in her view make a good impression, and she is therefore always terrified that one might land among the wrong
people. She is most surprised that I, a guest of the Czechoslovak
Writers' Association, should wish to see an ice-hockey match.
Was it for that I was invited to Prague? But all right, if that's
what I want—the guest must feel free, completely free. I do
not know whether the hotel to which I have been assigned is
bugged. It doesn't worry me anyway: I don't think aloud. A
well-known but undesirable man, whom my guide does not
recommend, tries for two days to reach me, but is informed by
the hotel that I have already left. He argues with the receptionist, assures him he has an appointment with me. The receptionist sticks to his "Already left," while I am upstairs in
my room, waiting. When we at last meet by chance in the lobby

and express our delight, the receptionist feels no need to apologize: the mistake is part of his duty. I make a trip into the country, together with other artists, and meet a young writer of great promise. An ordinary day among friends: no subversive remarks, the state is simply not there—all the more so, in consequence, the countryside, the people in it, and their work. We talk about poetry. Poetry as protest? One evening I visit another man in his home and stay late: people are glad to meet visitors from abroad. The man goes out in the street to get me a taxi, a deserted suburb in the midnight hours, no people, no traffic, but as my taxi moves off I notice another car that, parked within seeing distance, turns on its lights and takes the same route into town as ourselves, keeping the same speed. Not until we are in sight of the hotel does he turn off: it could, of course, have been a coincidence . . .

Ilya Ehrenburg is staying at the hotel. My guide, already rather put out after having to spend a week with a guest who makes new acquaintances or renews old ones on his own (among them people who were not allowed to meet me at the airport, but also Party comrades who make the unavoidable encounter with her as short as possible—I feel rather sorry for her), my guide is suddenly a new woman since handing me a card from Ilya Ehrenburg; suddenly her mistrust has all but vanished. Her friendliness becomes less diplomatic, she is more relaxed, charming—as if I had been rehabilitated. I rather dread this meeting with Ehrenburg. (An old friend, once one of Gottwald's young supporters, said with a little smile, "Just listen to what he has to say." And also: "He's now writing his memoirs—but others have memories too . . .") I remember Ehrenburg from a conference in Breslau twenty-one years ago: I was as disgusted with him as I was with Fadeev, a Stalinist who later committed suicide. Ehrenburg is now an old man. We sit in the hotel lobby, on show, now and again a camera flashing in his direction. He knows one of my novels in Russian translation, a play production, he knows Enzensberger and Böll. You were in Moscow a year ago? That's right, I met theater people there, no well-known writers: they were all at the Black Sea. Ehrenburg: Whom did you meet in Moscow? My memory of the conversation, lasting two hours, falls into three phases.

First phase: Admiration for Isaac Babel; Ehrenburg talks of

his friendship with his contemporary, whom he describes as the greatest of Soviet writers, though he is not recognized as such (says Ehrenburg) because he was a Jew. Is that so? say I. Ehrenburg reminisces, and Isaac Babel becomes more alive than anyone in the hotel lobby.

Second phase: Since we were speaking of Isaac Babel, now dead, it follows naturally that Ehrenburg talks of the Stalin victims who survived. He describes the fate of a certain man: I had already heard it—from the man himself. I listen. Ehrenburg: Didn't you meet him in Moscow? Moscow is a huge place and I was only there a week; I am surprised that he should single out this one particular man. But Ehrenburg mentions another whom I did meet in Moscow and whom he describes as a good friend. What a small place the world is! This man, as I know, spent ten years in jail under Stalin, is now back in the Party, rehabilitated, though recently in difficulties again for signing a protest (disguised as a petition). Ehrenburg is right: he is a fine man. How do we come to be talking about him? Since Ehrenburg obviously knows that I met this man at gatherings of the Soviet Writers' Union and the Gorky Institute, but also alone, I ask Ehrenburg to give the man my greetings. (Three months later he writes to thank me for the greetings, which Ehrenburg had passed on to him.) I ask Ehrenburg what is going to happen to Daniel and Sinyavsky. He is hoping for an amnesty on the anniversary of the October Revolution. So we are agreed: a real man, a wonderful man, helpful and true, and so a courageous man . . .

Third phase: Asked what I think of Prague at the moment, I speak of the theater, the housing development we were shown, the hospital, the negligent Party bureaucrats. Ehrenburg: You don't have to tell me. Surely the Party, which calls itself the people's government, should be interested, I observe, and am not given time to finish. Ehrenburg: You don't have to tell me. I assume there's no microphone near; Ehrenburg is talking as no Czech would dare to. What do I think of the young people in this country? Having been here only a week I can give no true opinion, but the patriarch wants my impressions. One of them: Political apathy. Ehrenburg: It's no different with us. Why is that? (he finds it regrettable). The young people, says Ehrenburg, did not experience conditions before the revolution, nor the revolution itself, nor the war. But then he admits this explanation is too simple: the real reason is more complicated. And since Ehrenburg now orders tea (as far as I can remember it was tea), and is obviously in no hurry to leave, I question him further. Ehrenburg: That's how it is. But why? Ehrenburg doesn't blame the young people, the fault, he thinks, is not theirs. I do not know how frank the conversation really is: what seems like frankness can also be just a tactical ruse. Perhaps I am wrong—I don't know—but the thought is behind the cautiousness that everyone, here as in Moscow, learns in the same way as he learns to spell. Ehrenburg asks whom I have met in Prague. I mention Professor Goldstücker, who successfully got the ban on Kafka lifted, and turn the conversation to Kafka's grave, which I visited today. Ehrenburg is again paged in the lobby. He stays seated. We must try to understand the young people, he says when the waiter has gone. His exact words: "Naturally the young people ask us how the Stalin era could have been possible: were we all criminals or lunatics at that time? And it's difficult to answer . . ."

DIAVOLEZZA

My companions are already at the starting
point, since they want to do the descent
three times: we arrange to meet later on the
Bernina Pass. A curious feeling even as I
strap on my skis: not anxiety, for the
descent is not difficult, the snow just as it
should be. And everything goes all right, no
tumbles—yet still that curious feeling.
What is different from before? Maybe it's
the spectacles: so I stop along the track
and polish them. The curious feeling remains
until I reach my goal and unstrap the skis,
when I realize I had done the whole stretch
with my pipe in my mouth. That was a year
ago. To start writing about approaching age
it was enough for Michel de Montaigne to have
lost a tooth. He wrote: C'est ainsi que je
fons et eschape à moi ("Thus do I dissolve
and take leave of myself").

INTERROGATION I

A. Do you approve of using force to achieve political ends? People like yourself who wear spectacles usually take care not to become personally involved in scuffles, yet they advocate the use of force for political ends.
B. Theoretically.
A. Do you think it is possible to change society without the use of force, or do you condemn all forceful methods on principle —like Tolstoi, whom you are just reading?
B. I am a democrat.
A. I see you have marked some passages while reading. This, for instance: "The most dangerous people, according to the governing classes, have been hanged, or are in penal servitude, in fortresses and in prisons . . . One would think nothing more could be wanted! And yet it is just now, and just in Russia, that the collapse of the present organization of life draws nearer and nearer."
B. Written in 1908.
A. Since you call yourself a democrat, I take it that you find the power exercised by the governing classes in czarist Russia repugnant?
B. Yes.
A. Would you think it justifiable to use violence against such practices, that is to say, counterviolence?
B. Tolstoi was against it.
A. I am asking you.
B. The conditions are different here. Can we even talk of the governing classes, as Tolstoi did, and thus of people who are considered by the governing classes to be dangerous and who must therefore be dealt with by force, which in turn produces counterviolence? We in this country nowadays have an easy time compared with czarist Russia, compared with Spain or Portugal or Greece—even with the Soviet Union. The people considered dangerous by the majority are never hanged here just for their opinions; they are hardly even sent to prison unless they happen to have broken the law. The most people have to suffer for their opinions is occasional discomfort, nothing more: promotion difficulties at work, perhaps, but no banishment to Siberia or Jaros, no loss of rights. A teacher may lose his job, but he is not expelled from his profession. He may be

abused by the state-supporting press and consequently subjected to malignant gossip, but the state itself does not punish him. Freedom of speech, as laid down in the constitution, is upheld. The same with strikes: the workers can put forward their demands and there will be negotiations, for they are not slaves. Those who don't want to work at all can loaf around: there is no forced labor here. If you still want something changed, you can say so publicly; you won't be given a post at a university or invited to speak on television, and perhaps your telephone will be tapped, but you can still say whatever you like. You won't even have your passport taken away. As I say, there is no loss of rights. Of course, you won't be given any form of state aid, but that is simply your bad luck, it is not violence: nothing will happen to you when you cross the street. People whom the ruling classes consider dangerous even retain the right to vote; the majority decides. And before the law all men are equal, the weak as well as the strong. If any of these people hope to become judges themselves, they will soon find out their mistake, but they will not be arrested or punished. In other words, reprisals are kept within the bounds of the constitutional state.

A. Are you in favor of the constitutional state?

B. I am in favor of the constitutional state.

A. What do you understand by it?

B. That nobody is exposed to the arbitrary power of those who are temporarily on top, that the rights of the individual are respected, that social conflicts are resolved without the use of violence.

A. But you spoke of reprisals . . .

B. There is, of course, such a thing as force without violence— something that looks very like a constitutional state. It is in a certain sense a peaceful process, by which I mean that to prevent an outbreak of violence conflicts are denied and arguments stifled. But the ruling classes do not use force of the kind Tolstoi was attacking in his pamphlets. The constitutional state guarantees protection from violence. That is why I am in favor of the constitutional state.

A. You have already said that.

B. One cannot say it often enough.

A. Then what do you mean by reprisals?

B. These have nothing to do with the law, but affect the persons concerned, so not the constitutional state as such. Violence, on the other hand, offends against the law, through assaults, damage to the property of others, etc. The police, who are the protectors of the constitutional state, can intervene against violence, but not against reprisals—which may give the impression that they are protecting only the ruling classes. That is not so, however: they are protecting everybody from violence. The false impression stems from the fact that the ruling classes do not themselves indulge in violence. They do not need to, since their right to rule is guaranteed.

A. Why do you pick on Tolstoi to read?

B. Because Tolstoi interests me.

A. Here you have marked: "I cannot and will not. First, because an exposure of these people who do not see the full criminality of their actions is necessary. . . . And secondly because (I frankly confess it) I hope my exposure of those men will in one way or other evoke the expulsion I desire from the set in which I am now living, and in which I cannot but feel myself a participant in the crimes committed around me."

B. He meant the executions—

A. Of which there are none here.

B. And wars.

A. "Strange as it seems that all this is done for me, and that I am a participator in these terrible deeds, I cannot but feel that there is an indubitable interdependence between my spacious room, my dinner, my clothing, my leisure, and the terrible crimes committed to get rid of those who would like to take from me what I have."

B. That is the count speaking.

A. "That is why I write this and will circulate it by all means in my power both in Russia and abroad—that one of two things may happen: either that these inhuman deeds may be stopped, or that my connection with them may be snapped and I put in prison, where I may be clearly conscious that these horrors are not committed on my behalf; or, still better (so good that I dare not even dream of such happiness), that they may put on me, as on those twelve or twenty peasants, a shroud and a cap and may push me also off a bench, so that by my own weight I may tighten the well-soaped noose around my old throat." Why did you mark that?

B. I thought it very striking.

A. Now, as you yourself have said, there are no crimes of this sort in our own country. A sentence such as this: "There is an indubitable interdependence between my spacious room, my dinner, my clothing, my leisure and the terrible crimes"—that could nowadays be applied only to certain events in the Third World?

B. Yes.

A. Did you think of that?

B. Perhaps Tolstoi would have thought of it.

A. Here is another passage: "Violent revolution has had its day. Whatever it has to give men it has already given them . . ."

B. I did not understand that. Written in 1905, in the conditions Tolstoi had just described—a statement that I did not understand.

A. Looking at what you have marked, I see, firstly, that what concerns you most is obviously the problem of violence.

B. And counterviolence.

A. Tolstoi condemns both.

B. And what else do you see?

A. "Every revolution begins at a time when society has outgrown the philosophic basis on which the existing pattern of social life rests and when the difference between life as it is and life as it could and should be becomes so clear to the majority of men that they find it impossible to go on living under the former conditions."

B. That is well said.

A. Do you believe in revolution?

B. Where?

A. Here is another marked passage: "The aim of the revolution which is now beginning in Russia and which will spread throughout the whole world, lies not in the separation of church and state or in state ownership of the social product, not in the organization of elections or the apparent participation of the people in government, not in the foundation of the most democratic, or even socialistic, republic with votes for all, but—in true freedom."

B. What is that?

A. "Genuine as opposed to apparent freedom will not be won by barricades, not by murder, nor by any sort of order introduced by force, but only by people ceasing to condone any form of human coercion, whatever name they care to call it by.

B. I do not believe in anarchy.

A. Then you would not agree with this passage, which you have also marked: "To deliver men from the terrible evils of armaments and wars, which are always increasing and increasing, what is wanted is neither congresses nor conferences, nor treaties, nor courts of arbitration, but the destruction of those instruments of violence which are called governments, and from which humanity's greatest evils result."

B. Sentences like that—and there are a lot of them in Tolstoi—I marked because they make me realize how well-behaved, what a good citizen I am.

A. All the same, you are interested in change.

B. The constitutional state, in my review, does not exclude changes being made in the laws when historical developments demand them. For example, existing laws protect property. Anyone who possesses more property than anyone else does not have more rights, but the law gives him power. That is why it is always the strong who love the constitutional state. The need to change laws is always primarily the need of the weaker people, not of those who are enabled by the law to rule without apparent force, since their power is a legal one, acquired through property.

A. You say: without apparent force.

B. It is true that conditions here and now are peaceful. Power that can rely on our obedience is never or almost never violent, and as long as the law that gives one person power over the others is not challenged, the weaker brethren will be allowed to live completely unmolested.

A. What do you understand by power?

B. Money.

A. You call yourself a democrat. That means that you recognize the right of the majority. Elections show, however, that the majority does not want change.

B. Since it is precisely the weaker people who form the majority, that does not surprise me: the weak wish to remain unmolested. After all, they are left in no doubt that they are the weaker whenever those in power feel themselves challenged or even threatened and consequently become violent. The people in power possess an army. When the weaker, though being in the majority, confirm the power of a minority, it means that the majority is dependent on this minority.

A. That is what you understand by democracy?

B. No.

A. Here is another passage from Tolstoi: "The error at the root of all the political doctrines (the most conservative, as well as the most advanced), which has brought men to their present wretched condition, is always one and the same. It is that people considered, and still consider it possible so to unite men by force that they should all unresistingly submit to one and the same scheme of life and to the guidance for conduct flowing therefrom." It goes on: "It is intelligible that men, yielding to passion, may by force oblige others who do not agree with them to do what they wish. . . ."

B. What are you trying to ask me?

A. Do you approve of counterviolence?

B. Counterviolence in what situation? An attempt on Hitler's life, if it had succeeded, I should not, for example, have condemned as ordinary murder.

A. I mean counterviolence inside a democracy.

B. One must distinguish between violence and power. Martin Luther King preached nonviolence, but not nonpower, when fighting for civil rights for the colored population; what petitions were unable to achieve in decades was achieved by a single bus strike in Alabama—not violence, but a demonstration of potential power.

A. And this you approve?

B. Certainly.

A. And acts of violence?

B. Even in photographs or in newsreels I am horrified by any act of violence. That is why I support the argument that violence alters nothing. He who lives by the sword, and so on.

A. Here you have marked the following passage: "However much they may assure themselves and others that the violation of all laws human and divine which they continually commit is necessary for some higher consideration, they cannot hide either from themselves or from men of good will the guilt, immorality, and meanness of their conduct. . . . All the czars and ministers and generals know it, however they may hide behind the pretense of higher considerations."

New paragraph: "It is the same with the revolutionaries of whatever party, if they allow murder for the attainment of their aims."

B. Tolstoi was a Christian.

A. If you consider social changes absolutely necessary, and clearly see that certain persons are relying on their constitutional power to prevent those changes by constitutional means, would you be in favor of using force?

B. What would be the alternative?

A. Doing without the changes.

B. That is not the alternative. Experience has taught us that history never stands still. Or not for long. One can say that, I believe, even when telephones are tapped. I am afraid of violence, and so prefer the argument that change can be brought about by reason.

A. Your motto is, therefore, reform.

B. There I find myself in curious company: the argument that nothing can be changed by force is also used by the people in power, who block all reforms. Their annoyance when risings occur is understandable. These can be successfully put down, of course, but nonviolent suppression, reprisals in a framework of law and order, are less dangerous—for the people in power, too. There is always something provocative about the official use of force: it demonstrates all too clearly that the doctrine of nonviolence is always being preached to the victims of oppression.

A. You find this a justification for counterviolence?

B. I am no less opposed to violence because I am obliged at times to understand the use of it. Take, for instance, the growing violence among the colored people: they are presumably in the same situation now as the peasants, soldiers, and workers were in Tolstoi's time. Tolstoi wanted to help them, but he could not persuade the czar so they had to help themselves.

A. You expect another revolution, then?

B. Before every revolution that has ever occurred I should probably have said the same thing: namely, that I see no real chance of success. I suppose this means I am not a revolutionary at heart.

A. Don't you think that a general improvement of living standards does away with the need for revolutions?

B. It makes them less likely.

A. Does that worry you?

B. When I read Tolstoi I find myself asking, for example, what would have happened if the czar of that time had done away with the need for revolution by improving the general standards of living. We should still have czarism.

A. But a different kind.

B. Czarism, nonetheless.

A. Do you not feel that the threat of counterviolence can also create obstacles, since it hardens the attitude of the people who happen to be in power?

B. If Fidel Castro, instead of conquering Cuban villages and dispossessing foreign owners, had gone lobbying in the United States, Washington's attitude would certainly have been less hard (which might possibly have led to the failure of the experiment), and the American exploiters would still be sitting in Cuba.

A. Let's keep to our own part of the world.

B. The questions are the same.

A. So you are in favor of change . . .

B. Yes.

A. But you feel that the people in power will resist all attempts to change the law—with force, if necessary—in the name of the constitution.

B. Naturally.

A. You are careful not to say: It can be achieved only by counterviolence. Is this because you are, as you say, afraid of all acts of violence, or because you are still hoping that social changes can be made without the threat of counterviolence?

    End of April

    Military coup in Greece to prevent democratic elections. Young King Constantine, hauled out of bed to approve the rebellion with his signature, is reported to have hesitated until the (German-born) Queen Mother talked him into it. Papandreou and other politicians arrested, deportations, suspension of the constitution on grounds of a Communist threat. It has all happened before: military junta to preserve law and order, democrat-

ically elected parties banned in the name of
the fatherland. The people rush to Piraeus,
their hopes on the American Sixth Fleet in
the Mediterranean, anchored within sight:
but no military intervention in the internal
affairs of a country with American investments. (Our Neue Zürcher Zeitung, also not
intervening in the internal affairs of a
country with Swiss investments, points out
that the impending elections might really
have resulted in a majority for the Socialist parties: one must try to understand the
army officers, too.) Result: A Fascist dictatorship inside NATO. Photographs of Greeks
standing helpless before NATO tanks flying
the Greek flag.

CONCERNING THE PLAY

The plot that seeks to give the impression that it could only
have happened in this particular way may always seem very
satisfying, but it is untrue: all it really satisfies is a dramatic
form, inherited from classical times—a form based on Providence and climax. This great heritage affects not only one's
literary judgment but life itself: basically, one is always waiting for the classical situation to occur in which a decision
delivers one inexorably into the hands of Fate, and the situation
does not arise. There will be great scenes, no doubt, but no cli-
maxes. Real life offers something far more exciting: it consists
of a series of actions that remain fortuitous—things could always have happened differently, there is no action and no omission that does not provide future alternatives. The only event
that provides no alternative is death. Does a story become ex-
emplary simply because one ignores its fortuitous nature?
Something happens: it may lead to various consequences or
even to none, and something that would have been equally
possible does not happen. There is a pattern to which most
things can be seen to adhere, but this has no more than an approximate value, and what happens does not mean that with
the same characters things could not have developed differently, producing another result than that which has now become

biography or world history. It would be absurd to believe that the attempt on Hitler's life on 20 July 1944 could not have succeeded. No modern playwright could put over as *necessity* the fact that the bomb, correctly placed and then fortuitously pushed aside, failed in its object. That is just the way it happened. And the same is true of any story. Any attempt to present its development as the only possible one and thus to make it appear convincing is purely literary—unless, that is, one believes in Providence and consequently also (among other things) in Hitler. But I do not. So all I can do, in order to make a story convincing in spite of its fortuitous character, is to seek a dramatic form that deliberately accentuates its fortuitousness. . . .

5 June 1967

Neighbors returning from shopping in Locarno
bring the news: war in Israel. Confirmed by
the radio. Anxiety for friends, work seems
senseless, feeling of helplessness. Reports
vague all morning, but one thing remains:
War. Incapable of judgments. Nasser's familiar threats, then the closing of the Gulf
of Aqaba, then the march on Sinai. Who is
the aggressor? In the papers: the relative
strength of both armies.

10 June

Waiting for a cease-fire. The danger of
world powers intervening, particularly the
Soviet Union, which has invested on the Arab
side: the lands of the oil sheikhs as Socialist countries. It none of it fits. Reports
from the front line, maps, pictures: so hor-
rifyingly matter of fact. Figures lying on
the sand are dead: figures with hands above
their heads are prisoners. Their guards with
rifles on their backs are not maniacs, but
young people in steel helmets. The sight of
smashed tanks always gratifies me. Israel is
pushing on toward Jordan and Syria. A pre-

carious frontier. Memories of the mountains
there . . .

16 June

Discussions. Is Israel now out for terri-
torial expansion? Jubilation in the Federal
Republic from right of center: blitzkrieg is
a solution. There are people here, too, who
think everything is now settled.

25 June

Letter from the Hazorea kibbutz. How many,
one wonders, speak in this tone? But at
least there are some: We are alive, and so is
our son, who is in Sinai, but please don't
think we are celebrating.

26 June

Metamorphosis of anti—Semitism? In the overwhelming support for Israel? To make up for
it, the Arabs are assigned to the category of
subhumans.

CONCERNING THE PLAY

The only reality on the stage lies in the fact that one is playing
on a stage. A play permits what life does not. Life does not
permit us, for example, to ignore the continuity of time; to be
in several places at once; to interrupt the action (with songs,
choruses, commentaries, etc.) and to proceed only after we have
grasped the cause of it and the possible consequences; to elimi-
nate what is simply repetition, etc. In real life we can perhaps,
through a later action, make good some mistake that has occurred, but we cannot wipe it out, cannot cause it not to have
happened; we cannot select some other behavior for a time that
is past. Life is historical, definitive moment by moment, it allows
no variations. A play allows these things. Flight from reality?
The theater reflects it, but does not copy it. Nothing is more
nonsensical than an imitation of reality, nothing more super-

fluous: there is reality enough already. The theater of imitation (Martin Walser's phrase, I believe) is a misunderstanding of the theater's function. There are producers who are very good at it, turning audiences into voyeurs and then deceiving them. In order to be a voyeur I must set aside my own consciousness and forget that it is only a play I am watching, and, when I don't succeed, it is doubly embarrassing. The original theater (with cothurnus, masks, verse, etc.) was, of course, never a theater of imitation: the audiences of those days were always aware that the ensemble contained no real gods. . . . Brecht's answer to the theater of imitation was for the actor to disassociate himself from his role by his gestures (the so-called alienation effect), to interpolate songs, written slogans, etc. Friedrich Dürrenmatt answers it with grotesqueness, Samuel Beckett with a reduction to the bare essentials, while Martin Walser urges the theater of consciousness, that is, a portrayal not of the world but of our consciousness of the world. Whatever the label, the aim is to seek (and sometimes in various ways to find) a form of theater that does not claim to portray reality (only one particular school of acting does that; the playwright's job is so to construct his play that the possibility of imitation is eliminated). . . .

VULPERA–TARASP

Everyone with numbered drinking glass in
hand. Saint Boniface, help us not to grow
old; Saint Lucius, forgive us our years.
Half an hour later, after a walk back to the
Kurhaus, everyone to the toilet, then breakfast according to individual diet. In the
course of the day, massage, weight check,
afternoon walk on tidy paths through the
woods, ozone, until it is again time for the
pump room. Saint Boniface, observe our
ascetic habits; Saint Lucius, save us from
calcifying. Evenings in the great hall:
shipowners from Hamburg, diplomats on holiday, directors, manufacturers, professors,
all still active in their jobs. Dance band

> playing, waiters taking short cuts across the
> empty dance floor. Elderly gentlemen enter,
> book in hand: the memoirs of Konrad Adenauer.
> The only young faces are those of the Italian
> waiters. Nobody looks at all ill; health,
> it seems, can be bought. Everyone sun-
> tanned. There is nobody else in the bridge
> room. All the men in dark suits, ladies with
> jewels. Waiting for the elevator, they study
> the diet sheets for tomorrow.

In the Kurhaus they don't, of course, know the nature of the club that has booked a hundred beds for the weekend. The management, obliging as always and particularly obliging toward the end of the season (it is already snowing in the mountains), apologizes yet again for having only one masseur. . . .

Meeting place: the bridge room.

This morning in the pump room I tried to recruit new members. One has, of course, to be careful, or they will take fright. An association, I tell them, for the rejuvenation of Western civilization. This makes them prick up their ears. Rejuvenation: everyone thinks it means his own rejuvenation. A former cabinet member. Alt-Regierungsrat Huber, taking the cure here for the eleventh time, will attend the conference; though no longer in office, he is always good for conferences, known as a tough negotiator. Another man, a famous pianist, whom I approached in the pump room, has been ordered to bed by his doctor and will not be there. I am under no illusions: I know that not everybody coming to the conference will want to join when it is disclosed this afternoon what the rejuvenation of Western civilization means. At the moment only the chairman and myself know that.

By lunchtime only six have put in an appearance. They are none of them markedly different from the other patients: four rather corpulent, three bald-headed, five with no apparent artificial aids—nobody would call or even think of calling them old men. Only one holds on to the banisters as he comes down the stairs.

Thinking of the manuscript in my pocket, I feel less confident that my opening remark ("Gentlemen, we can all recognize in ourselves the symptoms of growing old") is the right one. When I look at these men in the hall—sedate, perhaps a little tired from the journey, calm, one looking rather gloomy but not unsprightly, none of them youngsters any more, sitting with legs spread wide and no doubt wearing braces beneath their waistcoats, men with memories ("at the time the border was occupied") and experience ("I've been smoking a pipe for forty years"), but all in touch with events ("did you read in the paper today?")—it will be difficult to say to them: "Gentlemen, the world will go on without us."

M——, once a respected painter, comes accompanied by his newest fiancée, and I have to tell him this is not allowed. (Why not will still have to be settled; at the moment all I know is that women are not going to be admitted to the society, or even to know about it.) The hotel porter comes to our rescue, shows her the most comfortable excursions in a map, cable railway to Naluns; fortunately she has never seen a marmot in her whole life and finds the prospect alluring.

Constrained atmosphere among the still very small group gathered in the bridge room, everybody reluctant to sit down, hoping the others may have got lost in this vast Kurhaus. Porter asked whether there is another bridge room (people had been asked in writing to be punctual). Porter's reply: This is the only bridge room. I voice another hope: maybe they have confused the Kurhaus with the Waldhaus: could they telephone the Waldhaus? I mean, the Kurhaus? Now I am becoming confused, too. . . . Perhaps our invitation was unhappily phrased. Maybe too vague to arouse interest, or too explicit—though it wasn't exactly an open invitation to kill oneself. It is a pity more of the absentees didn't let us know they would not be coming: it gives our little group the feeling of not being taken quite seriously. Perhaps it would be best to start now? I am in favor. The chairman, who happens to be my dentist and who was originally responsible for the whole idea ("When I realize one day that I'm becoming senile, etc."), wants in any event to await the arrival of the next bus. Meanwhile, from the Kurhaus (or Waldhaus): Nobody in the bridge room there. I suggest we at least sit down.

4:00: the Kurhaus band begins to play outside.

Little to hope for from the next bus, which runs between the railway station and the various hotels: there is no train due around this time. I don't understand my dentist: does he expect a special train? Alt-Regierungsrat Huber repeats his panegyric (which we already heard in the pump room this morning) about underwater massage: you feel reborn, every time reborn. A vigorous seventy-year-old.

The small bridge tables covered in green felt have been pushed together to form one long table with seats for a hundred people: eleven sit down. We hadn't expected an Easter parade, but a certain air of disappointment cannot be concealed, even when we remind ourselves that historical revolutions have often stemmed from small beginnings. . . . Gentlemen, says our chairman, I will now open the proceedings—I am sorry to see— all the same something must be done: the aging of our existing society—

A waiter interrupts.

One after the other orders mineral water, as if we were some dieting sect, so I order Veltliner. Three order coffee—two of them Sanka. Only Alt-Regierungsrat Huber, not always on the best of terms with me, orders Veltliner, too.

Well, then . . .

But the chairman waits until the young waiter closes the door behind him. There is nothing we can do about the band playing outside. Opposite there is a tennis game in progress. I light up a cigar (Monte Cristo) in order to be at ease when it's my turn to speak.

The idea:

But first I read out the statistics, expecting objections to statistics on principle: infant mortality at the time of Christ's birth . . . After a lot of palaver, which the chairman unfortunately permits, agreement is reached that a certain (I had said a catastrophic) degree of aging is discernable in our civilization, though it can't be expressed only in figures. I say: Look out through that window. (It was not without a purpose in mind that we chose this place for our conference.) Look out through that window, gentlemen, and you will understand—

Interruption:

The young waiter comes in with our orders, silence all round the table, but since he can't carry it all at once, he has to go out and come in again, more palaver about the unreliability of statistics in general, until the young waiter—an Italian, thus causing communication difficulties on top of all else—at last gets the drinks (three coffees, including two Sankas, and the mineral waters, four Henniez and two Passugger) to the right people. Once again the chairman has to ask him to close the door.

The idea:

In view of the fact that the number of people living too long has risen catastrophically and still continues to rise . . . Question: must we live as long as modern medicine enables us to? . . . Death, cutting short a life in its prime, is becoming a rarity; fear of death has been transformed into a fear of becoming old, that is to say, of becoming stupid. . . . We control our entry into life, it is time we began to control our exit. . . . Gentlemen . . . without going now into the theological aspects, the sacredness of life and so on, which anyway, as you all know, is generally taken to refer primarily to the white races and not necessarily to life in Africa or Asia, and in particular to the life of a certain social class, not necessarily to life in the slums . . . what I am saying is that since, as statistics show, we are now able to prolong the average life expectancy of a human being, so that today, in contrast to previous generations, the majority of people have to reckon with living on into old age, aging has become a social problem as never before. It is not a question of building homes for old people, which can at best make the treatment of our aging society more humane, but contributes nothing toward the rejuvenation of that society . . . it is also an individual problem: a problem of people who cannot simply leave everything to surgery and pharmaceutics but must in future, as I see it, determine their own demise. Gentlemen . . . If the association that we have decided to set up has the aim of making voluntary death a moral prerequisite of our civilization, we are nevertheless aware, firstly: . . .

Etc.

The chairman thanks me for these introductory remarks and invites discussion, though the gentlemen are asked to confine themselves at the moment to observations of a general nature: the rules and statutes of the association are not yet open to discussion.

Silence.

They drink.

The band plays outside.

Since everyone is silent—only old Hanselmann, head of the well-known importing firm of Hanselmann & Sons, wants to know what the association is to be called: I suggest Voluntary Death Association (the counterproposal of the painter, who has considered himself a wit ever since people stopped taking him seriously, finds no support: Harakiri Club—it sounds too much like Rotary Club)—since nobody has anything to say about the idea in itself, the chairman explains how the proposal must be understood: the association will contribute to the rejuvenation of Western civilization by translating the new idea of ending one's life as a social duty not only into words but deeds. This means that members must pledge themselves to carry out what will be required of them when the time for it comes.

Silence.

Whom, asks the chairman, can I now invite to speak—or would the gentlemen prefer to have a short intermission here?

Addendum by me:

The association would be international, open to everyone over the age of fifty without regard to religion or politics; the members would meet once or twice yearly to draw each other's attention to signs of aging; members guilty of staying alive beyond their time would be expelled; for that purpose there would be an annual general meeting, which would carry out a series of examinations, memory tests, etc.; the annual general meeting would pay tribute to those members who in the course of the previous year had carried out their resolve to dispense with a prolongation of the aging processes, etc.

AWAY FROM HOME

If there were no newsstands from which one could daily purchase the overall view, I really don't know how people like ourselves would know what is going on in the world. Ordinarily beings can scarcely see around the next corner or hear past the next two or three without immediately feeling threatened, confused, or upset; perhaps only indifferent—but above all uninformed. I always

feel easier when I am reading the top-grade
newspapers, simply because they know much
more than we do. However dreadful the news
the teleprinters keep transmitting, I feel
easier when I read what the editors have to
say about it, with their expert knack of
putting every significant detail into the
grand perspective. How näive I then find
myself to have been with my sympathy, my
trust or my concern, my anger, my perplexity!
As a rule I overestimate the seriousness
of things. These men think further than
people like ourselves: the fresher the paper,
the more one can feel that. Who reads old
newspapers anyway? Some items are boring,
and one skips them, but at least these prove
that top-grade newspapers are not simply out
for sensations: they give us things, as they
are, boring or not. They have a sense of
responsibility. It's disgraceful how casual
people like ourselves tend to be about what
is going on in the world. Above all, we
always regard things so personally. For
example, with that military coup in Athens I
immediately jumped to the conclusion that the
Americans were mixed up in it, though I had
no proof. The top-grade newspapers on the
other hand (or at any rate those which
deserve the name) remain objective. Not
only do the teleprinters keep them better
informed, but they can sustain a level of
thinking that goes above mere opinion. We
feel the touch of something impersonal,
whether the item is signed or not, some hint
of the <u>Weltgeist</u> being confirmed by daily
events, insofar as the facts are correct.
When (perhaps in the Trans-European Express)
one happens to meet the man who has just
written some part of it, one is not disappointed: he knows more than he has written--
sometimes a great deal more. Usually, too,

he personally believes that he has written,
that is, he says in private more or less the
same thing. But now he has acquired a face,
perhaps even a pleasant one; it is not his
fault that I, a reader of top—grade news—
papers, almost fell into the silly error of
assuming that newspaper views, in contrast to
our own, are always untinged by personal
feelings. I admit I do not see or think as
independently as they do. If that were the
case, people like ourselves would not always
be running to the newsstands. They can de—
pend on our curiosity, our lively forgetful—
ness, our concern according to their view.

VOLUNTARY DEATH ASSOCIATION

A member cannot, of course, be ordered to terminate his life.
All the annual general meeting can do is establish which members, were they to remain alive, would be contravening the
rules. Two-thirds majority in a secret ballot. Members who despite that decide to go on living will be expelled, with an expression of sympathy from the association. Should a member
consider himself unjustly condemned by the two-thirds majority, he can appeal; he would then have to undergo an additional
test, for example, make a speech on a theme of his own choice;
the accent would not be on fluency (in which old people in particular are seldom lacking), but on the ability or inability to
see a problem in a different way from yesterday, to question
his own answers of the day before. A Marxist, for example,
might know all there is to know about classical Marxism-
Leninism; if, however, his speech contains not a single thought,
even in passing, that he has previously considered unthink-
able, then he has shown himself to be an old man.
Annual general meeting:
To include hikes and also drinking sessions, whereby the
main thing to be watched is the condition on the morning
after, which will include shorter hikes, to be followed by discussions, reaction tests, etc., and in addition a written examination to establish whether members are still able to express
themselves in the vocabulary of the day. (A list of words and

phrases that are considered out of date will have to be drawn up every year. Expressions such as escalation, consensus, meaningful, hopefully, as of now, eyeball-to-eyeball, etc., might one day have to be added to the list.) In the evening parties, which will be recorded on tape; anyone recalling the same youthful experience more than three times will be booked.

Proposed:

That beside full members (people over fifty) associate members will be accepted: people under fifty, who will not have to undergo any tests but will take part in discussions and have the right to vote. This will help to ensure that full members will not involuntarily, as they grow older, tend to relax their standards from year to year.

Proposal adopted.

False teeth and dyed hair are permissible, as well as wigs. Outward appearances ("How wonderful you are looking!") will not be taken into account in the assessments. Members suddenly appearing on crutches will not be booked on that account. Slipped discs are admissible, since they are as irrelevant to a member's mental and spiritual vitality as a bald head. A red nose will also not affect the ratings. On the other hand, the annual general meeting will not allow itself to be deceived by a robust appearance, which can be achieved through health treatments or work in the garden; relatively slim and tanned members in ski suits or tennis dress will still have to undergo the tests. Factors to be noted: presence or disappearance of the combinatory faculties, approachability, capacity for new experience, readiness to discuss matters without reference to past achievements, but above all spontaneity, to be tested by means of appropriate happenings.

Proposed:

That every member should give an account at the annual general meeting of his professional progress during the past year, to include such things as widening of business interests, conversion to automation, establishment of branches and (in intellectual and artistic professions) new appointments (vice-chancellor, manager of a theater, etc.)

Proposal rejected.

(It was felt there was a danger of encouraging members in the wrong direction: assiduity disguised as youthful ambition. It cannot be the aim of the association to increase the assiduity

of elderly gentlemen, since it is precisely this that leads to the
aging of our civilization. One has only to think of the economic
field, universities, parliaments, the Vatican, as well as general
staffs.)

P.S.

Since among the seven full members I am the only professional writer, I have been instructed to draw up a list of symptoms of old age for the benefit of the first annual general meeting. It will be a list, not of physical infirmities that can be treated
by doctors, but of intellectual and emotional signs of senility.
A sort of handbook, not available in bookshops, for members
only.

> 25 October
>
> Road accident on the stretch between Cadenaz-
> zo and Giubiasco. Though the two cars lie
> beside the road and both drivers are still
> alive: Luck, but so public . . .

VOLUNTARY DEATH ASSOCIATION

According to statistics, more rich people than poor outlive
their usefulness. The reasons are obvious. Conclusion: senility
occurs primarily in positions of power. The objection against
our association—that it consists mainly of well-to-do people—
is therefore invalid. An old handyman, now dependent on his
old-age pension, has no power to force his calcified thinking
on his fellow creatures; a calcified managing director or judge
is more dangerous. I am glad that our members (now risen to
eight) belong among the well-to-do: this social class is more
vulnerable than the working class to the temptation of un-
naturally preserving its life, not only because it has the economic means to make the physical troubles of old age bearable
(vacations as they please, service as needed, treatments by
specialists, free choice of work, comfortable housing, underwater massage, diets regardless of expense), but above all
because its members consider the power their wealth gives
them as a proof that society needs them. An old waiter, dismissed because his hands tremble as he is serving, can hardly
make this mistake.

Observations made at the first annual general meeting:
1.
The examination procedure must be altered. Unforeseen factor: an old man's quickness of uptake. Men over sixty have learned to reply to questions by providing apt answers to questions which have not been asked, thus giving an impression of mental alertness.

2.
The members become friends. How can that be prevented? The export chief, the collector of crystals and my dentist, the only one of his kind in our circle, have no reason not to like each other. In addition, it turns out that all our members (excepting myself) are ex-officers, differing only in rank and arm of service, which is not enough to cause controversy: on the contrary, it encourages buddy relationships. Once we come to respect one another, we tend, owing to absence of any real conflicts of interest, to lie in support of one another.

3.
Members who do not bring their wives are at an advantage. (Women are not allowed to attend meetings, but join in meals and walks.) Bachelors or widowers are not under constant supervision ("Have you got your scarf?") and, when ash falls on their waistcoats, no one brushes it off; so they appear independent, self-possessed. Those with wives always feel caught out when they pretend to be younger than they are. On the other hand, one sees how much the female custodians naturally need their men. One feels pity for the wives—or one feels tempted to protect their husbands from them. In either case, objective judgment becomes difficult. It would be better without wives.

4.
Meals slacken discipline.

5.
Regarding my handbook of senile behavior: I appeal again for written contributions, but all react as if they had nothing to report from first-hand experience.

ZURICH
Brecht's death mask hanging in Konrad Farner's big library. Nose too crooked, recognizable only from a single angle. Looking at
the profile one might, for a moment, think it
was Friedrich Schiller. That irritating
smile on the dead face—not a grin, but sharp
mockery directed at no one in particular.
The eyes, closed in their deep sockets; even
when they were open they were set far back
under the brow as if in a lair. . . . Our
conversation in overcoats (the library can't
be heated) would bore the police.

Revival of interest in the theater: so long
as they are rehearsing in some public room or
other—this time in a police building. On
the floor below people busy with residence
permits, marriage banns, voting lists, etc;
the entrance plastered with Wanted notices.
The actors in their own personal pullovers,
with their own personal hairdos as they feel
their way into the fictitious situation,
script still in hand. Illusionless theater—
yet the fictitious situation involuntarily
establishing dominance over its office-fur-
niture surroundings. Question to the author:
What does Antoinette mean when she says that?
That is the director; the actress uses the
first person: Do I love him on this particular morning or not? Hard to say until
Antoinette exists: she begins to exist at
the moment when voice and gesture make us
believe that she loves Kürmann or that she
doesn't love him. Later, after the performance, the actress asks: Is that how you visu-
alized Antoinette? That would be untrue: I
never even knew her. I write dialogue as a
sort of Wanted notice, and one day there she
is word for word as described, and so I get
to know her—on one stage after another,
different every time.

1968

1933

Public appeals over a list of signatures as
prominent as possible, Nobel prizewinners
preferred, which means the same names appear
again and again, each time losing in value.
The public already knows: he is against the
American invasion in Vietnam, the military
putsch in Athens, torture everywhere, in
favor of amnesties in Portugal and in Spain;
no wonder he has now got it in for Dow
Chemical in Zurich for manufacturing napalm
for Vietnam and salving its conscience with
awards for artists. After all, one knows
these public protesters: We, the undersigned
scientists, artists and authors, condemn this
and that, we demand . . . What does one hope to
achieve with such earnestness? And always
the näive assumption that ethics are a factor
in politics. Results? Might reacts only to
might, which is exactly what the signatories
have not got: their appeal demonstrates it.
One is left with a nasty feeling of inflating
one's own importance. I resolve (not for the
first time) not to sign any more public appeals.

VOLUNTARY DEATH ASSOCIATION

Ten years after foundation: all seven founder members are
still living. There has been only a single occasion on which the
annual general meeting notified a founder member (not Hanselmann, to whom we owe our house halfway between Vulpera
and Tarasp), by a two-thirds majority, that his time had come.
(I voted in favor, though I must confess in my opinion old Hanselmann should in that case have been condemned, too.) After
the result of our secret ballot was announced, there was dead
silence in the room. It was, as I said, the first time the prescribed
formula had been spoken: After careful consideration the association has come to the conclusion, etc., in accordance with
our statutes, etc., it is left to the discretion of the member concerned, etc., the association reminds all members of their writ-

ten undertaking, etc., and thanks the member concerned in anticipation. Of course, nobody at first looked at the member concerned; some sat with folded arms, gazing up at the fine carved ceiling (Swiss stone pine) or somewhere else, others fingered the pages of the annual report. After the formal question: Does our member accept this majority decision? the silence continued. The member concerned—I was sitting beside him—was cutting a cigar: he hadn't heard his name spoken. When I—at the same time offering him a light for his cigar—drew his attention to the fact that the chairman was awaiting his answer, he showed no signs of being upset, but with a watery-eyed grin on his still ruddy face said: You watch out for yourselves! and sat back to smoke his cigar, which was as wet as a baby's comforter. The decision was given him in writing. When it came to the appeal and so to the extended examination on the following day, it turned out to be predominantly the younger full members, in their early fifties, who displayed the greatest tolerance. Why they in particular? I don't know. The appeal was granted. Perhaps because it concerned a founder member. One thing is clear: at the first vote, of which nobody can know the outcome, members vote more objectively; at the appeal, humane considerations win. As an associate member, helping me into my coat, remarked: After all, he's still a human being. That, incidentally, was our first annual general meeting in the new house, and so quite a number of years ago.

Yesterday, then, our tenth anniversary.

When one of the founder members says: If Picasso, when he was eighty, and Theodore Fontane, too, as we're told—and when Baltensperger adds: Let's not forget Titan!—then I say: Gentlemen! and, rising to my feet: Our association stands in great danger, gentlemen, of becoming an old boys' reunion. (The younger members, early fifties, laughingly protest.) I am now sixty-seven, I admit it, but I believe I can say (Interjection: Keep to the point) and if not an old boys' reunion, gentlemen, then in all events a Methuselah Club. (No contradictions, causing me to lose the thread and become aggressive): Export and import are all very well, Hanselmann, but if you, Hanselmann, try to get out of it with Theodor Fontane and you, Baltensperger, try to get out of it with Titan, then I must say (Interjection: Bertrand Russell!) . . . You say that (I call out to the back of the hall), but have you seen Bertrand Russell recently? (Interjection from the front: Where would France be without General de Gaulle?) Gentlemen (I say calmly, but again an interjection: And Albert Einstein? A whole chorus: Einstein, Albert Einstein! I say even more calmly): You are in your early fifties, among us older men you see no Einstein and not even a Bertrand Russell, I find it nauseating that we should begin to console ourselves with famous exceptions. Is that the point of our association? (Silence.) You all know the rules. Not a single one has followed them, gentlemen, not a single one of you. (Interjection: What about you?) I meant to say: not a single one of us. If things go on in this way, gentlemen, we shall still be sitting here together as ninety-year-olds promising a rejuvenation of Western civilization. (Sniggers from the early fifties.) Gentlemen, it is nothing to snigger about—nor for head shaking, Herr Alt-Regierungsrat Huber, though you may today still look like a sixty-year-old. (Sounds of agreement.) But that is not the point. (Interjection from Alt-Regierungsrat Huber: Then what is?) I know, gentlemen, we have got to the stage, and not only in this small gathering, we have in general got to the stage of thinking it something when a seventy-five-year-old looks like a sixty-year-old, and if a ninety-year-old looks like a seventy-five-year-old we behave as if all problems had been solved. Let me say by the way, gentlemen, that I consider yesterday's slide lecture to have been a mistake: If the Georgians live to be one hundred ten or even one hundred twenty, that is their affair. It is not enough (I say, recovering my composure) that our membership is constantly increasing. Incidentally, I can now tell you that the figure is no longer forty-three, as in the annual report, but forty-five, since this morning in the pump room two further full members were enrolled: Sir Ralph Emerson, former consul in Bombay, whom I welcome as the first foreign member of our association, which was always intended to be international. (The Englishman rises.) And Herr Peider Caflisch, former tennis instructor, now serving, as you know, in the pump room. (No one rises.) Herr Caflisch sends his excuses, since just now he is busy in the pump room, but I also extend a welcome to Herr Caflisch on behalf of the Voluntary Death Association. (Nods of approval.) But what I wanted to say: it is not enough, gentlemen, for us to sit here smoking Churchill cigars to show each other what we're still capable of, or for others to take great care of themselves. Every year you are getting older. The aim of our association is what it always has been: the rejuvenation of Western civilization. . . .

Etc.

Etc.

Etc.

HAPPINESS

Somebody might pass on the happy news that his trouble is definitely not cancer, but casually: it concerns only himself. On the other hand, the news that somebody has died or will soon die of cancer seems to affect us all, even when at the moment we are feeling happy. This may often be due to no more than the condition of the weather, the climate of a particular city (Berlin, for instance) or a feeling of physical well-being, a consciousness of one's own presence, an article of food, a meeting in the street, a letter, etc.—there are countless causes for private happiness. Why do I not note them? The paeans of happiness that have been handed down to us have all dealt with occasions of a nonpersonal nature—something we now seem to lack. Landings on the moon or on Mars will not supply them. Our revolutionaries promise us justice, not happiness. Only believers in drugs speak of happiness, by which they mean the ecstasy of escape from a world that offers no prospect of delight.

FEBRUARY

Depriving those few people whose freedom has
been achieved at the expense of the working
population of their property and power
cannot be the aim unless freedom for the
working population is the result of it. The
new men in Prague speak soberly, but what
they are attempting is bold: to develop
socialism in the direction of its own promise. Will they succeed? It would be wrong
to assume that this attempt means nothing
more than a rueful return to capitalism, and
any approval in this sense would do harm, be-

cause it would provide the enemies of demo-
cratization with the very excuse they need to
suppress it. Any more of this false applause
for Dubcek (both here and in Federal Germany)
is betrayal—and not without an ulterior
motive. "Socialism with a human face": that
is something our rulers do not wish to see.

TO COME BACK TO CHAPLIN

"Every reviewer imagines nowadays he'll fall panting by the
wayside if he isn't kept on his feet with constant shots of social
relevance."

"To come back to Chaplin—

"Millions and millions have seen his films—clowning based
on class consciousness—and what in your opinion has Chaplin
achieved?"

"You consider yourself a political person because you ask
questions about the political effects of literature."

"Politics as a literary fashion?"

"To come back to Chaplin—"

"Or to Brecht—"

"If literature ever feels the need to justify itself by its social
relevance, it will be lost. Its contribution to society lies in its
aggravating habit of keeping on whatever happens."

"You mean, *l'art pour l'art*?"

"Now you'll come up with that quotation from Jean-Paul
Sartre about the starving child."

"Sartre was quite right."

"What if Chaplin achieved nothing at all, in spite of the fact
that millions and millions still laugh at his films?"

"I consider myself to be a political man, you're quite right,
and that's precisely why I object to politics as a literary fashion."

"I'm just reading Neruda."

"Philosophy for philosophy's sake—you consider that wrong?"

"I'm asking you."

"What Sartre forgot to say is that in the face of a starving
child or a victim of napalm bombing even a simple meal looks
obscene."

"Chaplin was great as long as he remained dumb." (But everybody knows that.)

"All literature deserving of the name is basically subversive."

"Including Proust?"

"Why don't you go into practical politics if you think you're a political person?"

"One day we'll act."

"When?" (The speaker laughs.)

"Do you accept that literature is dead?"

"As far as I'm concerned, I've been acting for years."

"I know these people who go about saying that literature is dead. One of them writes poems he's not going to publish yet, and the other is at least prepared to accept Samuel Beckett."

"But now really to come back to Chaplin . . ."

"Fame has abandoned poetry for scientists and acrobats. It was Apollinaire who said that."

"When one is talking about Peter Weiss and Jean-Paul Sartre, shouldn't one perhaps make a distinction between a writer who produces an ideology of his own and one who makes literary capital out of an existing ideology?"

"And what do you do yourself?" (It is a student speaking.)

"Was Chaplin a trained Marxist, do you think, or a Marxist *par génie*?" (This from a speaker who has hitherto been silent.)

"What do you mean by that?" (This from the lady with him.)

"Everything is permissible that succeeds—and there's little enough of that."

It is now midnight. Out in the street I say: "I really only wanted to talk about Chaplin. I've just been to see *The Circus* again. . . ."

BERZONA, March

Conversation with two members of the West German Socialist Students Association (SDS) in Canero. Their names are Wetzel and Amendt—one very elegant and cheerful, the other earnest and blond, but sophisticated, too. Luckily I had just been reading about this affair. Belatedly enough, but just in time—otherwise they would not have been able to unfold properly. Their canalized intelli-

gence. Somebody at the table did not conform
in question and argument to the recognized
terminology; he was eliminated. Proper
awareness now has its own vocabulary. The
revolutionary masses, the workers, will have
a lot to learn before they grasp that it
is their salvation that is intended, and that
for their own salvation they are indispensable. Very frank about the Establishment: at
the moment they can still make use of us, but
later on no more. In the evening, long-
drawn-out supper at the fireside with spaghetti and Chianti. Spreaders of enlightenment, prepared to use force if necessary,
but always with the magic formula: force
against possessions, not people. And if the
possessions are being guarded by people?
There will be deaths.

NOTES FOR A MEMBERS' HANDBOOK

C'est ainsi que je fons et eschape à moi.
—MICHEL DE MONTAIGNE

None of us wants to know what old age will bring. Though we see it every day around us, we prefer to preserve a conspiracy of silence, in order to protect ourselves: even the aged themselves are expected to conceal the repulsive aspects of old age. This conspiracy, although to outward appearances in the interests of the aging, is in fact harmful, since it prevents self-recognition and delays voluntary death to the point where the aged person lacks the strength to act.

The injunction to respect age stems from periods when long lives were exceptional. (See statistics.) Nowadays, praise for an elderly person is invariably linked with the assurance that he still looks relatively young, indeed positively youthful. Our respect is always based on the word still *("still inde-fatigable," "still worth looking at," "still agile in spirit," "still capable," etc.). In other words, it is not age we respect, but the express opposite: the fact that in spite of his years a person is not senile.*

Self-deception is possible for a time. Outsiders noticing a man's gradual decay will not usually tell the man himself. On the contrary: they encourage self-deception in all possible ways (speeches on birthdays, election to honorary presidencies, etc.), partly out of compassion, partly because it is easier to get on with a doomed man when he himself is obliged to conceal the signs of aging in him. When he can no longer escape admitting that he is becoming an old man—which he has been for years—he will discover that his admission surprises nobody; it simply causes embarrassment.

The doomed man begins to formulate such sentences as: After all, we have already experienced / We, too, once / If you should ever find out what it means to / In my time / In our time / Nowadays everybody thinks / At your age I should have been ashamed / In my experience there is only one / One must give youth a chance / etc.

The doomed man recognizes what he is from the fact that nobody envies him, even when he enjoys fame or possesses a fortune, that is to say, has advantages that younger men do not have; despite that, nobody wants to change places with him.

When hearing of someone who has done or is likely to do something outstanding, the doomed man immediately asks how old that person is (very early stage). The doomed man tends to envy contemporaries less for their achievements than for the date of their birth; for their reserves of future time.

The visible change that most irritates him is not the change in the color of his hair: he knows hair becomes gray—even his own. Yet at the hairdresser's it is still a slight shock: the hair on the tiles, waiting to be swept up, is grayer than the hair on his head: he can hardly believe that these dirty white tufts—no trace now of blond or brown—come (as they must do) from him. And when the hairdresser holds the mirror so that he can see himself from behind (as others see him) and grimace at the onset of baldness (not revealed by the shaving mirror at home) he rises hurriedly to his feet. The visible change that most irritates: wherever he goes, socially or professionally, the majority of his contemporaries are younger than he is; not all are younger, but certainly those contemporaries who interest him most.

His need to offer words of advice.

The doomed man's mania for historical parallels to tropical events: whether or not the comparison is revealing, the past must be brought in, so that the doomed man can shine in conversation.

The doomed man identifies himself through a new kind of boredom. His previous states of boredom were usually connected with his surroundings: school, office, military service, etc. Even then he could always (earlier) imagine a situation in which he would not be bored at all. What is new: the realization of his own wishes now begins to bore him, too.

On social occasions, in order to keep himself from becoming bored, he is apt to behave with exaggerated liveliness; the doomed man parades wittiness as freshness of mind.

It is not only the realization of his wishes that bores him; the doomed man knows which of his wishes cannot be realized. He calls this his experience. What bores him is to find his experience confirmed.

Fading of curiosity.

The doomed man takes interest in others (intermediate stage). He takes every opportunity of inquiring what the others, the younger people, are doing at the moment. Everyone already knows what he himself has done. He is the one who now has to ask. It is touching to see the interest he shows, or tries to show. In doing so, the doomed man, though still capable of discernment, tends more and more to praise. Through sincere praise he can still keep in touch with younger people. Or so he thinks. (It is well known that old men do not like to acknowledge what comes after them: the thing is to show that he is not an old man, by handing out praise.) Occasionally he may venture a criticism, but it is always encouraging criticism.

The doomed man must avoid at all costs showing open indifference toward younger men.

In regard to opinions, the doomed man cannot fail to notice that people tend less and less to argue with him. This makes him feel like an authority—while the others, the younger men, look at the ashtray or stroke the dog under the table so long as he is speaking. The value of opinions is in direct proportion to the share of future time remaining to the person holding them. Realizing that it is now too late to make new friends, and not wishing to arouse pity, the doomed man likes to talk about his friendship with a person now deceased, raising it to legendary heights. The deceased person cannot contradict (unless the correspondence between them has been published), and the younger people can only wonder why there are no longer such splendid friendships as once existed (Bauhaus, etc.).

When something pleasant occurs, the doomed man is conscious how much he would have enjoyed it if it had happened earlier.

Family feeling and senility. It can at any rate hardly be disputed that family feeling grows stronger with senility. Equally, love of one's country (return from abroad in later years). The doomed man, fearing loneliness, accentuates any form of belonging that does not have to be established, but already exists.

His need of tradition.

The fear of one day being dependent on others expresses itself in conflicting ways: on the one hand, the doomed man seeks by kindness to arouse a sense of obligation in those nearest to him; on the other, he tends to make all the decisions himself and to prolong his authority as long as possible over the people on whom he will one day have to rely.

The doomed man likes to complain of his poor memory— even in cases where it would be extraordinary if any human brain, including a seventeen-year-old one, could have coped.

(Coquettishness as an early symptom of senility in more ways than just this.) His memory is not failing—it is simply saturated. The doomed man can recall word for word a conversation during the Second World War, but less precisely one that took place yesterday evening.

A man's natural loss of self-confidence during the climacteric can induce his family, even when he is still providing for it, to make its first efforts to dispossess him. He tries at first not to notice. The fact that he has learned through a lifetime of experience to use a can opener will not prevent someone saying, "Here, let me do it."

Thinking it is Wednesday when it is really Thursday has happened to him often enough before; but now he feels upset when it happens.

The doomed man is always concealing some fear. When his napkin falls under the table he feels he has given himself away.

A doomed man may, for example, know the date of Khrushchev's downfall, but his relatives will tend to doubt it. When he shows them in an encyclopedia that he is right, they give in: he was lucky this time. But the fact that he felt it so important to prove himself right betrays him just the same.

The doomed man sticks to his little whims, if only to prove to himself that at any rate he is still someone; things that do not impress other people he nevertheless does just for spite (late stage). The obstinacy of old age.

The doomed man wakes up before dawn—the hour for executions—with increasing frequency. He wakes because he is not in the least tired. He becomes an early riser—for what?

Much traveled as he is, the doomed man still finds customs control an unnerving experience, though he has long given up smuggling. If his baggage is nevertheless examined, he can become wild with fury: forty years asking the same old questions, and they still don't believe him!

Since he knows how often he has become reconciled with people who behaved badly toward him, the doomed man now tends to be contemptuous when previously he would have exploded with rage.

The doomed man has an astounding memory. Or so it seems. In fact, he is hardly remembering at all. The doomed man reproduces anecdotes of his own making. His wife is most likely to notice it; he repeats himself word for word. Now and again he adds something she has not previously heard, but very rarely. His repertoire is large enough to keep him going in company; he constantly surprises his listeners, but hardly ever himself. He dips into an album of precise souvenirs: the wallpaper in his parents' home; a raging teacher's false teeth lying on the polished floor of the classroom; prisoner of war experiences; the details of an avalanche disaster; the absurd expressions used by his first employer; the weather on the morning of his divorce, etc.—people are amazed how vividly he can recall things, above all his extraordinary memory for points he once successfully proved. . . . The doomed man identifies himself by the fact that he is not really remembering the teacher's false teeth on the polished floor of the classroom, nor the Arcadian weather on the morning of his divorce: he is remembering his memories of these things.

The doomed man is surprised how little energy young people seem to have. As soon as they stop enjoying themselves, there's little to be got out of them; it is only the prospect of enjoyment that can persuade them to give a job their full attention. If the doomed man thinks he possesses more energy than most young people, he is not deceiving himself. More and more things that simply have to be done in order to keep life going the doomed man does—not only without enjoyment, but without the hope of enjoyment—and this makes him aware of his energy (which he takes to be vitality).

How can you, he thinks reproachfully, laze around like that day after day? This is something the doomed man cannot do: just live for enjoyment—his powers of enjoyment are no longer strong enough.

Comfortable living hastens the onset of senility.

Comfortable living conceals it longer.

The doomed man finds himself increasingly dependent on the forbearance of others, though by no means all his errors and omissions are discovered. Did he really, as he claims, close the front door? He can no longer depend on himself.

It happens increasingly that the presents he gives are taken back for exchange: his taste is old-fashioned. But he can always save himself by being generous with money.

Dignity: the doomed man's final refuge.

What is indispensable to a person who is losing the art of spontaneous communication: settled convictions. They reduce things to a common denominator without the need for personal communication. The doomed man betrays himself, not through the nature of his convictions (left or right), but through his increasing need for them.

Now and again (particularly toward dawn) the doomed man experiences moments of very clear insight; then his mind works as in his best years. He realizes it when suddenly, without any visible cause, the thought of his future only fills him with horror.

Fear of strokes.

If he continues to attend social occasions—either because he cannot stop or he feels it to be his duty—the doomed man can identify himself not only by the fact that people make more room for him than a single person needs—he may fail to notice that the people who come to talk to him relieve one another as if on sentry duty, but he will come to realize that there is nobody he really misses.

Often, when we see an old person in his coffin, we feel a sense of shame: the dead face almost invariably reveals that this person must once have been more than he was in his final decades.

Our first reaction is, of course, one of relief: that from now on no more peasants will be killed in their fields or children in their schools. . . . It is hardly a miracle, however, when mass killings are called off because they are not achieving their aim. They are simply not worth the cost, neither militarily nor politically. Another obvious factor is that the daily loss of world prestige, since the world learned what was going on, makes the destruction of Vietnamese villages too expensive. All that has happened is that a mistake has been spotted and put right. Saigon awaits the next attack; in the jungle more and more posts are given up for lost, and we feel sorry for the American soldiers in them. President Johnson's decision is a patriotic one: the partial capitulation, disguised as a peace offer, is necessary to preserve imperial power, which in other places—Latin America, for instance—is maintained without an all-too-open use of war. Cessation of bombing in the north as an American concession calling for gratitude, which should take the form of leaving the American occupation of the south undisturbed. However, the Vietnamese will continue to intervene in their own affairs. So there will be no peace until the invading army sails away. And who will rebuild this Vietnam that has proved too costly for the United States? Since the American invasion of Vietnam was not a personal error on the part of Kennedy or Johnson, but rather the result of a power system that depends for its existence on the oppression of other nations, Johnson's withdrawal will make little difference. A system has been exposed, and the revolutions against this system will grow.

"C'est pire qu'un crime, c'est une faute," said Talleyrand, meaning presumably that a mistake exacts its own penalties, a crime not necessarily so. Today's news shows the war in Vietnam to have been a mistake—the escalation of a mistake inherent in a system. . . . Our relief will be short lived.

—Published in the weekly periodical *Weltwoche*, 5 April 1968

PARIS

Being in Paris is like meeting a former mistress—or rather some one who could have become a mistress, though the chance was missed

at the time. Paris was already the world's
mistress, and full of literature. One nods
as if we were acquainted, but it is simply
not true. Paris has never had any use for
barbarians, and nobody who cannot speak
French properly is anything but a barbarian—
a point every waiter makes clear after only
three words. One makes oneself ridiculous
with one's mute claim for attention, as if in
the presence of a lady who cannot possibly
know that one has been dreaming of her.
What's the man staring for! Much better not
to nod, but to spread out a foreign newspaper, the <u>Frankfurter</u> <u>Allgemeine</u>, like a
white flag. Even when you know the names of
its boulevards, its statues, its Seine in all
seasons of the year, a restaurant or two, its
galleries, its grimy façades with their clus-
ters of tricolor flags, its metro, etc., this
city is perfectly aware that it has never had
the slightest thing to do with you. I can
sit there as long as I like, even dig up memories: that Fourteenth of July shortly after
the war, that clumsy effort to buy perfume
near the Vendôme, rehearsals in the theater,
a meeting with Samuel Beckett, a night in the
Halles, the pair of us wandering among early-
rising butchers in blood-stained aprons—all
of this is no concern of Paris, this city
full of young faces wearied by memories of
greatness. Incidentally, I have usually felt
happy in this city—but that is my affair.
The Place des Vosges, the Jardin du Luxem-
bourg, the Seine, the Arc de Triomphe, the
Goya in the Louvre, the Café Flore, etc.:
these remain its own, its world center.

MURDER AS A POLITICAL WEAPON

The great advocate of nonviolent opposition, the great fighter
against poverty in the richest country in the world and the

champion of civil rights for American Negroes has been shot dead by a white man. It would be irresponsible to say or even to suspect that the American state plotted this murder. Firstly, state murders have a different look; secondly, the state had every reason *not* to want this man, the prophet of nonviolence, out of the way. If there is anything the country now needs it is nonviolence on the part of the oppressed people within its own borders; everyone knows what the Vietnam war costs to run, and the poor inside the country will have (as always) to be patient. The march against poverty that Martin Luther King had planned to lead this spring was to have been as peaceful as all his previous deeds and speeches. His death cannot put an end to the poverty of the American Negroes, but it could possibly put an end to their patience, their hope for a peaceful entry into the promised land, such as the gentle and fearless Dr. Martin Luther King preached. What are the Negroes to do? They should not lose their nerve because a white man—an individual—has fired a gun. Who already made several attempts to assassinate Martin Luther King; who threw those stones in Chicago; who issued threats throughout this vast country, so that every pilot in whose plane this minister sat feared that this time the time bomb was there; who telephoned all the other leaders of the civil rights movement to tell them their time was also coming: was it not always this same individual from Memphis, who is so hard to find in this country where policemen appear in such imposing numbers at race riots? The weapon, since discovered, can be handled only by one man; yet the assertion that Martin Luther King was murdered by one single man would nevertheless be a lie. There was knowledge of the threats in Memphis: forty policemen, experienced in dealing with refractory Negroes, were watching the motel in which the threatened minister was staying—but not, apparently, the house opposite. The shot was heard, yet the gunman, seventy yards away with his telescopically sighted weapon, could not be caught: the back entrances were not being watched. A good country for murderers. The White House warns the nation: nothing will be achieved by violence. Something has been achieved: Martin Luther King has been silenced.

The *Neue Zürcher Zeitung* writes:

"After waiting in vain for implementation of the epoch-making decision of the Federal Supreme Court ordering the abolition of racial segregation in the schools, which was carried out, if at all, only in a symbolic way in all too many places, King, then working as a minister, organized a Negro bus boycott in Montgomery, Alabama. This demonstration, which took place in the late fifties, concerned the Negroes' right to occupy any free seat in public transport vehicles. Up till then it had been the rule throughout the South that Negroes could occupy only the seats at the back, even when those at the front were vacant."

Such is progress. At a party here in Zurich I once heard a lady say; "give them an inch and they demand an ell." There's something in that. Martin Luther King, it seems, also demanded too much when, instead of preaching in Atlanta, he started to interfere in the problems of other ghettos: Harlem, Chicago, Baltimore, Los Angeles . . .

The *Neue Zürcher Zeitung* writes:

". . . the problem of the northern ghettos is much harder to solve, since it is a social and economic problem presenting itself as a racial problem. (. . .) Martin Luther King's success began to dwindle, and increasing attention was paid to the more radical Negro leaders, who started to exploit the smoldering distress in the ghettos."

Which tells us who the exploiters in these ghettos are: not the people who exploit the Negroes' working potential in such a way that it causes distress in the ghettos, but the Negro leaders who want to abolish this distress.

"In Memphis the refuse collectors—all blacks—have long been on strike, and not only because they want a pay raise, but also because they want to be allowed to form a trade union."

The report makes one admission:

"On the following Monday a second protest march was to have been held, although a local court had issued an injunction against it. The way of all American social reform movements, and particularly of the trade unions, is paved with such injunctions. Again and again they have been disregarded."

So Memphis is no special case, but the usual pattern: rights are denied, and since the oppressed, inspired by Pastor King, disregard the disregard of their rights, the oppressors feel aggrieved.

"In the country's present mood of deep disquiet, not to say of bitterness and hate, King's defiance of the white Establishment in Memphis led straight to his assassination." Our correspondent in Washington, who can hardly be suspected of spreading left-wing views, has this to say of the trade union movement in the United States in general:

"It has been a path strewn with sacrifices. It has meant prison and often worse, far too often death for those taking part in these actions."

The Negroes are not the only ones who have suffered. During the twenties two Italian immigrants, Sacco and Vanzetti, were arrested and charged with the murder of some pay officials. During the trial in Boston, which lasted sixty-three days, numerous witnesses testified to seeing Vanzetti with his fish barrow thirty-two miles away from the scene of the crime. Despite this, both were sentenced to death. Sacco and Vanzetti belonged to the political opposition, being members of a workers' movement. There were protests throughout the civilized world. Sacco and Vanzetti were sent to the electric chair nonetheless. As a political weapon neither murder nor judicial murder can be regarded as an American speciality: Stalinism also provided many perfect examples of it. Judicial murder is an unerring gauge; it reveals glaringly that the clique in power finds particularly dangerous and consequently feels obliged to destroy: in the United States this has always been the social reformer, the workers' advocate. Joe Hill, otherwise Hillström, came to the U.S.A. from Sweden in 1907 and soon rose to become the popular voice of the American trade union movement called Industrial Workers of the World. In January 1914 Hill was arrested in the state of Utah, where the great copper mines are situated (still a popular tourist attraction today), and condemned to death for a murder he had not committed. Hill spent twenty-two months in prison, during which time a worldwide protest action raged, and then, on 19 November 1915, the sentence demanded by the copper-mine owners was carried out. There are other methods of a different kind. On 24 April 1963 a postman, William Moore, was walking along Highway 11. Moore, born in Mississippi, was on his way to hand Governor Ross Barnett a personal petition calling for civil rights for Negroes. Moore was a white man. He was shot dead from behind, killer unknown.

> *Oh, Bill Moore walked the lonesome highway,*
> *He dared to walk there by himself,*
> *None of us here were walking with him,*
> *He walked the highway by himself.*
> *Yes, he walked to Alabama,*
> *He walked that road for you and me,*
> *In his life there was the purpose:*
> *That black and white might both be free.*
> . . . .
> *They shot him down in cold blood murder,*
> *Two bullet holes were in his head,*
> *His body lay upon the road-way,*
> *Where lynchers left him cold and dead.*

In Talladega, Alabama, two hundred college students marched on the city hall: they were protesting against outrages on supporters of the civil rights movement and against police brutality toward supporters of the civil rights movement. The peaceful march was stopped by forty state policemen using tear gas; the students came to a halt and sang:

> *We shall not, we shall not be moved.*
> *We shall not, we shall not be moved.*
> *Just like a tree, planted by the water,*
> *We shall not be moved.*
> *We are fighting for our freedom,*
> *We shall not be moved,*
> . . . .
> *We are black and white together,*
> *We shall not be moved,*
> *We will stand and fight together,*
> *We shall not be moved.*

Songs containing no fighting challenge, not even a genuine complaint; the protest is a pure affirmation of faith, sung with hope, and it is fitting that it should often take its melody from

Negro spirituals. Out of a strike in Charleston in 1945 of the Negro food and tobacco union workers, arose a song for decades to come—its keynote, with quiet determination:

> *We shall overcome, we shall overcome,*
> *We shall overcome someday.*
> *Oh, deep in my heart, I know that,*
> *I do believe, oh, we shall overcome someday.*

What happened after the murder of Martin Luther King? President Johnson immediately sent his Attorney General, Ramsey Clark, to Memphis to investigate the murder. We shall not be easy to convince. Not only because of the Warren Report; not only because the police report on the heavy rioting of 1966 in Watts, the Negro ghetto of Los Angeles, contradicted eyewitness accounts—but because even the Advisory Commission on Civil Disorders set up by President Johnson, after examining twelve hundred witnesses, comes in its report to the conclusion:

"Our nation is moving toward two societies, one black, one white—separate and unequal.... What white Americans have never fully understood—but what the Negro can never forget—is that white society is deeply implicated in the ghetto. White institutions created it, white institutions maintain it, and white society condones it."

In 1966 it was established after an official enquiry that fourteen hundred babies and toddlers had been bitten by rats in American slums. A proposal to devote $40 million from federal funds to a rat extermination program was rejected. The cost of fighting the war in Vietnam amounts to $79,795 million daily. In 1964 Congress passed a significant civil rights law, giving Negroes equal rights at the voting booths. This is how it works out in practice in the South: in order to register his vote, a Negro must pay $30; or he must pass an examination, and the people who test his level of education are white men; maybe he will need to use a bus to get to the polling booth, and the people who control public transport are white men. Of course, there is nothing to stop a Negro spending a whole day walking to the polling station if he wants. And what of the level of education? In 1966, twelve years after a basic law was laid down by the Federal Supreme Court in Washington, only 10 percent of the three million Negro children were attending an integrated school. In 1965, signing the Voting Rights Act, President Johnson said:

"Today is a triumph for freedom as huge as any victory that has ever been won on any battlefield. . . . Today we strike away the last major shackle of those fierce and ancient bonds."

What followed this ceremonial signing? Within a year a large number of supporters of the civil rights movement, both colored and white, had been murdered in the southern states; the trials of the murders, where they could be found, were short and often ended in acquittal.

For what should the Negro hope?

SAN BERNARDINO

Seven times in a year we drive along this
stretch, and it happens every time: the feel—
ing at the wheel how good it is to be alive.
It is magnificent country. Particularly in
the curves: the body feels landscape through
motion, attunement as in dancing.

NOTES FOR A MEMBERS' HANDBOOK

When a man at a party asks us to guess how old he is and seems to be waiting eagerly for our answers, I venture: late thirties. His smile is a little disappointed: obviously he had hoped for a more glaring mistake. Somebody else gives him a polite: thirty-five. The man behaves as if at an auction sale: any advance on thirty-five? We could of course reckon it out, but we are not really all that curious, and for most people the late thirties would do. He wears horn-rimmed glasses, which perhaps make him look older; he takes them off. A woman of mature years says flatteringly: thirty-nine. Now it's time to stop, before someone raises the bid; now he must reveal the truth: forty! He says it with an exclamation mark. . . . The foredoomed man enjoys being thought younger than he is, even if only by a year, and yet on the other hand he doesn't enjoy it. After all, he really is forty.

The foredoomed man betrays himself by saying with increasing frequency of this or that contemporary; "He's senile!" Dealing with old people becomes more difficult than it used to be: he can no longer find them comic.

Should he go in for sport (skiing, for example), the foredoomed man catches himself, if young people are present, moving faster than he really wants to.

He does not like having to acknowledge people of his own age, former schoolmates with paunches and bald heads; at such times he feels a bit embarrassed, particularly when he has a girl with him, but not only then.

Sure symptom: alcoholism . . .

Intellectuals discover that their first reactions to growing old are more primitive than their usual modes of behavior: an intellectual is suddenly pleased to find himself mounting public staircases two steps at a time.

The foredoomed man finds it harder than the doomed man to accept the younger men coming up in his profession. He catches himself dismissing everything that comes from younger people as mere fashion. Mere fashion begins for him at the exact point at which, in spite of his efforts to adapt, he can no longer keep pace.

P.S.
The doomed man tends to go in the opposite direction: he immediately suspects something epoch-making in what may be merely a fad, and prides himself on his pioneering spirit.

Premature senility among former child prodigies.

Hypochondriac tendencies: the foredoomed man fervently hopes that some alarming symptom of approaching senility may simply be a sign of illness—curable or incurable, but at any rate physical.

Since at the moment the people among whom he moves are

not making him conscious of his advancing age (unlike later, when every waiter presenting the bill will leave no doubt who is the senior at the table), the foredoomed man treats his aging as top secret. Excuses for feeling low: he is depressed by the political situation, the commercialization of culture, the powerlessness of the intelligentsia in a bureaucratic society, etc.

A forty-year-old who is always looking for haute cuisine (to the extent that he can afford it) and while eating talks incessantly of food: a gourmet—a foredoomed man.

His fear of running out of ideas—in fact, he has as many ideas as ever before, the only difference being that he no longer accepts them without question: the foredoomed man already knows the nature of his ideas.

On no account will he allow anyone to help him into his coat. When at some intimate gathering there is a shortage of chairs, he is among those who sit on the floor. He dives into swimming pools and never uses the ladder. If he has to wear a dinner jacket, he adopts a free and easy manner, hands in pockets. On hikes with younger men he carries the rucksack, etc. At the same time he draws attention to his first gray or white hairs: as if a natural process were in his case some sort of curiosity.

The relationship between a doomed man and a foredoomed man is easier for the doomed man. The foredoomed man is allergic to all attempts at familiarity on the part of his elders, however distinguished, and the foredoomed man emphasizes the distance between them by an assumption of modesty.

He cannot bear old men's jokes. That is not new. But now he begins to think of them himself.

Watching his first bullfight for many years, he forgets himself in the excitement of the moment: the matador falls amid cries from the crowd—the foredoomed man has jumped to his feet like all the rest; but, as they all sit down again, he says, "Once, in Bilbao, I saw a matador," etc.

His stimulant: activity.

The future ... For the young man: a collection of vague possibilities (one day he will marry, perhaps later in life or perhaps even never, one day he may become a star, or maybe not, perhaps he will one day emigrate). ... For the foredoomed man the future is also uncertain, but within the bounds of the foreseeable, by no means hopeless, a collection of calculable possibilities (he can still get a government appointment, but it will have to be soon). ... For the doomed man the future is everything for which he can no longer be considered, a collection of definite impossibilities (he will not become a glider pilot, he will not see the first landing on Mars, not even the new railway station in Zurich, etc.). ... The foredoomed man speaks most about his future, his plans. He betrays himself through occasional tactlessness; in the presence of people years older than himself the foredoomed man stresses the fact that he is no longer young, whereas to younger people he likes to lay stress on what he has already achieved. The foredoomed man is always the first to introduce the subject of age.

He acquires an eye for age differences in others. Up till now an old man was simply an old man, but recently he has begun to feel, looking at an old man, that he has a fair idea of how that face must have looked thirty years ago. ... He does not like looking at pictures of himself as a student, an apprentice, a recruit, etc.

Long before there can be any question of senility, the foredoomed man betrays himself by wondering how he will appear in the memories of others. Previously he didn't care a damn what people said about him. The artist who keeps in mind his posthumous image while still working is a foredoomed man.

In his profession he knows more and can do more than before: new possibilities are opened to him and he wins promotion. At the same time he realizes that he can learn from younger men. This is something he had not reckoned with; up till now he had always learned from older men, which is easier to bear. ... The foredoomed man does not resist novelty, but he is aware that it is not his own.

After a severe accident, from which he was lucky to escape alive, he describes his experience again and again in precise detail. The foredoomed man knows that in a few years things will have changed: our chances of a tragic death are subject to a time limit.

In most careers the period of presenility is that in which the best work is done ("maturity," "command of resources," "mastery," "complete grasp," etc.)

He makes a discovery. During a conversation in the street or at a party where there is dancing, or hearing some bad news, he suddenly finds himself thinking of old O——, long since dead: how, when hearing bad news, old O——would not react at all, but would continue with the conversation (at the time he, the younger man, had been impressed by that); how old O——, at parties where there was dancing, would keep one chained to his side by special marks of interest so as not to be left alone, and would promise his full backing (which at the time seemed to him, the younger man, magnanimous); how old O——, while talking in the street, would frequently stop, thus maintaining his domination of the conversation. ... The discovery: that what he thought characteristic of a person is in fact characteristic of a time of life. He himself now does exactly the same.

As a father the foredoomed man is well aware that his children are new adults, one might almost say contemporaries. Consequently he expects them to regard him as a contemporary, too, and he no longer claims to be the teacher-who-knows-best, but simply (what else is left?) a friend—until he notices that they do not see him as a contemporary, but as their father.

Since his wife is also growing older (he does not notice it at home, though he does at parties) the foredoomed man prefers to attend parties by himself, when he feels freer, ageless. ... True, she dyes her hair (which he doesn't) and is a more lively conversationalist than he is, but she is always mentioning their son-in-law or how they first met (during the Second World War) or the time they were in Cairo, etc. She does it

*above all when younger women are present—perhaps un-
consciously.*

*When he reaches his fiftieth birthday, which he has long
dreaded, he is amazed: he has always imagined that a fifty-
year-old is an elderly man, but he doesn't feel elderly at all.
Funny how all his acquaintances are fascinated by his figure.
Happy Birthday to You, while he himself looks unconcerned.
Maybe it was true once that a man of fifty was elderly. He is
still in full possession of his faculties (not like Michel de
Montaigne:* C'est ainsi que je fons et eschape à moi)*, let's by
all means drink to that. . . . Despite all his secret fears he still
has no conscious attitude toward the process of aging: all he
does is resist all feelings of resignation.*

BERZONA

During a game of bowls a wife says to her
husband: You're no good, as usual. Later on
he says: All I want now is to bash my wife
right out of the way. Of course he only
means her ball in the alley. Everything in a
joking tone. When he misses, she laughs: If
you can! . . . There are two possibilities:
either man and wife play together, or we
split them up, so that man and wife each com-
bines with another partner to play against
the other. As host I leave the choice to my
guests. Most couples, whether married or
not, prefer not to play together, particularly when they know each other's game. They
really seem to enjoy it less as a team; not
even wine helps. He says: Why can't you do
as I say? Or: Sorry, it slipped out of my
hand. And, when she doesn't respond, he says
it again: Sorry. Since we are educated and
adult people, it obviously doesn't matter who
wins. She says: Watch how <u>he</u> does it—meaning the man on the opposing team. He says:
Your bad luck for marrying a dud. It can
happen that the couple, previously on the

best of terms, don't talk together for quite
a while, until she suddenly says: It's your
turn, but don't mess it up this time. All in
a teasing tone. The game permits no serious
conversation. He does really want to do it
well. She says: Good—very good! Whereupon
he replies: Now, don't you go and mess it all
up again. One almost has the feeling they
want to lose; at any rate, winning gives them
no shared pleasure. . . . When they play with
other partners against each other, things
become easier, more fun. She says to her
strange partner: We're winning! He says to
his strange partner: Magnificent! Or when
she misses: The rough surface did that. But
they still talk to each other as husband and
wife, from team to team. He says: Give in,
Helen, there's nothing you can do. All in a
teasing tone. She says to her strange partner: Just knock him out of the way! And he
does, but no one is upset, it's all a game.
They are just teasing one another. She says:
You see! or she says nothing, her ball now
lying exactly where it ought to be, and he
asks: Did you bowl that? Of course she
bowled it; he is only asking. Her partner
gives her a word of encouragement as he hands
her the ball (her husband never does even
that): And now win us another point! Her
husband says: What luck! It really doesn't
matter who wins. She says to nobody in particular: Leo can't bear losing. He doesn't
react to that, but says instead to his partner: Your husband is unbeatable. Meanwhile
they can be talking about their children,
road conditions, the theater in Zurich, etc.;
he says or she says: Come on, it's your turn.
. . . So one team actually wins, and it is at
once forgotten; a pleasant evening, ending in
more conversation, and they go off as they
came—a contented couple, a happy marriage.

INTERROGATION II

A. You have seen the news.
B. The burning cars, the phalanx of students, the clouds of smoke on the boulevard, and so on. Of course the pictures upset me, but I must admit they don't horrify me.
A. . . . watching them on television in your own room.
B. True, I wasn't there, but when I see pictures from a real battlefield I do feel horrified, even if I only see them on television.
A. How do you explain the difference?
B. What is at present happening in Paris is disorder and unrest, violence within a revolt. The pictures from the battlefields, whether in Vietnam or the Middle East, have a more familiar look. *À la guerre comme à la guerre.* Bombed ruins, dead bodies strewn about, prisoners under interrogation, standing barefoot with bound arms among uniforms and helmets and submachine guns: that all conforms to the rules we know.
A. Let us leave war to one side—
B. Why?
A. Students and others who cannot achieve their demands by legal methods are using violence against the state, occupying the Sorbonne, destroying the things that stand in their way, and the police are obliged to use force against them. When you see street fighting of this sort, whose side are you on?
B. The uniform makes a difference. I find it easier to sympathize with an individual than with a company, which of course consists of individuals, too, though only really when one of them is wounded. . . . I don't know how I would react on the spot.
A. Do you identify yourself with the students?
B. I am too old for that.
A. Even at your age one still takes sides. I assume you do not see yourself as one of the policemen.
B. I am a civilian.
A. How did you hope it would end?
B. I admit this question never really arose once I had seen the water cannons at work, then that barrage of paving stones, the truncheons, and the stretchers. The end was a foregone conclusion—even to the demonstrators themselves, I should

think. They demonstrated that there is nothing to wish for.

A. Do you feel the police were being brutal?

B. There was something professional about their behavior. Something rehearsed. And then they were not on horseback today, which makes a great difference: the mere fact of them being on horseback degrades the ordinary civilian. . . . Maybe I laughed because the policemen with their round shields reminded me of Shakespearean productions, where battles look so decorative that they become ridiculous. Of course it isn't a laughing matter. Violence frightens me.

A. Describe your feelings.

B. Suddenly a boulevard filled with students—

A. When they—the students—suddenly began to attack, did you think of the Bastille, or did you now and again feel: This is how Fascism starts?

B. Where?

A. Among the students.

B. The thought never occurred to me. Fascists do things better— *with* the military and not against them. That is no reproach against the students—rather the military.

A. The fact remains that students, or whoever those people were filling the boulevards and calling themselves pro-gressives, started it all by disrupting the traffic, occupying the Sorbonne and hoisting flags as if victory were already won. Aggression against the guardians of the constitution— in other words, violence. Do you disapprove of that or do you not?

B. What struck me was that it all began in a lighthearted sort of way, with young people singing arm in arm—chatting rather than chanting, enthusiastic but unorganized. Any-way, there was a sort of lightheartedness about it that you don't see in a battalion going into action in the Mekong Delta. One didn't feel these people were out to kill.

A. All the same, they started throwing paving stones.

B. Most of them looked very young, and at the time tired. They gave the impression of not knowing what to do with their youth in our present society.

A. They have got pretty well everything.

B. . . . that their parents think important.

A. What haven't they got?

B. For instance, that boy in the leather jacket who ran toward

the water cannons—I don't know what he was expecting
beyond a thrill. At one point I found myself wondering what
would really have happened if there had been no policemen.

A. What do you feel about damaged property?

B. As I said, differently from in ordinary theaters of war. The
damage, as we saw, was considerable, and yet there is a
certain irony about it: why should one not be allowed to
destroy men's work, particularly in one's own country? The
damage appalled me far less, quite frankly, than what we
see daily in pictures from the battlefields. The whole thing,
even when blood was drawn, had an element of a practical
joke about it—like those dreams one has of shooting up a
candelabra or driving a steamroller through a supermarket.
The only people who looked really in earnest were the police,
and that was all the more comic, since they could easily have
mastered the situation with machine guns and flamethrowers: frustration made them more stubborn than their
weaker opponents. Obviously they had been told to avoid
any show of violence as long as possible. They assumed the
role of guardians, though the people they were guarding
remained invisible. All of a sudden they cordon off a boulevard. Why exactly? To show where the state begins: at the
point where the police squadrons now stand. The borderline
could have been somewhere else: an odd mile or two is
neither here nor there. Up till now we had seen only young
people arm in arm, singing, but somewhere the state must
begin. Before you can start hitting out you need an act of
disobedience, and that can be obtained by cordoning off a
boulevard. Not that the police seemed very happy about it.
Every intervention from them is a dent in their reputation
as guardians. We were shown that paratroopers are not only
better versed in the use of force and better equipped than
the students and all the other people filling the boulevard;
each one of them, so it seemed to me, was stronger than the
whole boulevard; each one of them, so it seemed to me, was
stronger than the whole body of students put together—because he was acting under orders. That enables a man to be
uninhibited in his use of violence: he is not shooting or beating up in a personal way, and the state can always find a way
of squaring its conscience.

A. So you are taking sides?

B. Experts on revolution say this rising lacks the support of the masses, etc., and so the venture is bound to fail: that is no way to make revolutions.

A. They are obviously right.

B. Yet possibly the venture still has its significance for the society now in power: it sees it can maintain its position only by force—something the ordinary citizen likes to forget.

```
ROME, June

The man at the newsstand, Piazza di Spagna,
had forgotten me entirely.  Not so the wait-
ers: Come stà!  The tattered old beggar woman
is still there, cigarette in mouth.  Via
Giulia.  As always, returning to a house in
which one used to live, one feels unreal.
In the Via Coronari they are still polishing
and upholstering antiques: Settecento chairs,
chests from the Abruzzi, tables from Tuscany.
Via Margutta: now with Beat shops.  Via Della
Croce, which hasn't altered: fruit, eggs,
vegetables, wine, pasta, flowers.  A Roman
friend still has his owl.  Another, a Sicil-
ian, is still a professor.  Sperlonga: one
can hardly expect the sea to have changed,
but all the same a slight feeling of sur-
prise that it hasn't.  The same waves.  We
sit on the same chairs and eat the same fish:
dentice al forno.  Cerveteri: the Etruscans
are just as dead as ever.  Piazza Venezia:
only the policemen have grown younger, the
traffic even more chaotic.  Gianicolo, view
over the town: everywhere one stays too
long . . .
```

QUESTIONNAIRE

1.
Are you sorry for women?

2.
Why? (Why not?)

3.
When a woman's hands and eyes and lips betray excitement, desire, etc., because you touch them, do you take this personally?

4.
What do you feel about other men:
a. when you are the successor?
b. when you are the predecessor?
c. when you are both in love with the same woman at the same time?

5.
Did you choose the woman who shares your life?

6.
When years later you meet (on friendly terms) women with whom you used to live, can you understand your previous relationship or does it puzzle you? In other words, do you have the impression that your job and your political opinions must once really have interested them, or does it now seem to you that you could have spared yourselves all those arguments?

7.
Are you disconcerted by an intelligent Lesbian?

8.
Do you profess to know how to win the love of a woman, and, if you eventually find out what it really was that won you a particular woman's love, do you doubt her love?

9.
How do you define *masculine*?

10.
Have you any convincing proof that women are particularly suited to certain jobs a man feels to be beneath his dignity?

11.
Which of these has most frequently seduced you:
a. motherliness?
b. the feeling of being admired?
c. alcohol?
d. the fear that you are not a man?
e. beauty?
f. the overhasty assumption that you will be the dominant partner however lovingly protective?

12.
Who invented the castration complex?

13.
In which of these cases do you speak more fondly about a past relationship; when you have left the woman or when she has left you?

14.
Do you learn from one love affair things of use in the next?

15.
If with women you are always having the same experience, do you think this is due to the woman? That is to say, do you in consequence consider yourself a connoisseur of women?

16.
Would you care to be your own wife?

17.
What has taught you more about intimate relationships between the sexes; conversations with other men or conversations with women? Or have you learned most without the use of words; from women's reactions—that is to say, by noting what women are used to and what not, what they expect from or fear in a man, etc.?

18.
When a conversation with a woman stimulates you, how long can you keep the conversation going before you start thinking

of things that you keep to yourself because they have nothing to do with the subject?

19.
Can you imagine a woman's world?

20.
What do you find a woman incapable of:
a. philosophy?
b. organization?
c. art?
d. technology?
e. politics?
and do you in consequence feel a woman who does not conform to your male prejudices to be unwomanly?

21.
What do you admire in women?

22.
Would you care to be kept by a woman:
a. on money she has inherited?
b. on money she has earned?

23.
And why not?

24.
Do you believe in biology? In other words, do you feel that the existing relationship between man and woman is immutable, or is it, for example, the result of a historical development covering thousands of years that women have no language of their own for their thought processes, but have to make do with the male vocabulary, and thus remain subservient?

25.
Why must we not understand women?

MOSCOW, 17 June

Stroll round Red Square alone. Summer night. Many people

taking the air in a metropolis; countryfolk. High-rise buildings now as in the West. Girls in skirts not too short, but shorter than two years ago; men in white shirts and no jackets. Sunday. Not a single open-air café to be found. One can only walk about. Here and there lovers on a public bench, silently holding hands. No illuminated advertisements, but the streets are brightly lit; a pity I am so thirsty. Only a barrel on wheels with a donkey in front and people queuing for kvass. The smart uniforms of young soldiers with Mongolian faces; they also are not at home here.

18 June

For protesting against the writers' trial L——has been expelled from the Party, deprived of his teaching post, and censured by the Soviet Writers' Union. The same with K——. Tightening up again—a reflex action following Prague? We dine publicly in a restaurant where both punished men are known, and we speak in German.

HOTEL ROSSYA:
View of the Kremlin. Hilton-type comfort—except that the wall-to-wall carpets have waves in them. Breakfast: I sit down at a table. I am not a delegation, and waiters do not tell one what to do when one is not a delegation. It does not worry me. After all, I didn't come to Moscow just for breakfast.

SOFYA:
Her German is perfect, she deals with everything; I see the worth of the Writers' Union card: we don't have to queue. But not even Sofya can get the people behind the counter to be helpful: one doesn't expect subservience, but they could be polite, at least not so surly. Sofya seems used to it. She doesn't ask whom I saw in Moscow yesterday. I am of course completely free to do as I please. We drink (when we finally get it) a beer; I praise Russian beer. What cannot be discussed: Paris, the situation after the street fighting and the strike. The moment foreign countries are mentioned a curtain falls. So I ask what the position is in the Soviet Union regarding tips. Sofya tells me no tips—they do not depend here on patriarchal whims. An hour later my friend gets into an argument with the taxi

driver, and I'm told the driver was not satisfied with his tip. At supper in my friend's kitchen: what do you have to do to be expelled from the Party? This time without jail: to that extent an improvement, he says. Little bitterness, plenty of patience.

A piece of paper with the address of the Swiss Embassy written on it in Russian script. I show it to a taxi driver, who says: *Nyet.* He doesn't know it. Second taxi driver: *Nyet.* Third: *Nyet.* Only the fourth takes the trouble—with a long-suffering air—to look it up in a street directory.

HOTEL FOYER:
It could be in Milan, Hamburg, Geneva, the same architecture, but the elevators disgorge workers, not gentlemen. They see nothing special about walking on marble. Bourgeois luxury as something to imitate: we can do that too! No architectural style of their own . . .

RIVER TRIP TO GORKI:
A ship full of writers, but: a ship is always something special, and this is my first journey by ship on a river. Hot summer evening. I know nobody on board except Günther Weisenborn. I say good evening to Christa Wolf (GDR) and sense mistrust. The loudspeaker pours out music from a French film. Seagulls. We glide along . . .

VOLGA, 19-20 June
I am sharing a cabin with a Finnish writer who speaks Russian; no language common to both. He wakes me and points a finger first at the ceiling, then at his open mouth: breakfast time.
  Volga . . .

Writers from all over the world, but no familiar names except Alberti. Unfortunately, no list is available. One laboriously asks one's way around. No one from France. A Gorki translator from Italy; no Moravia, no Pasolini, no Sanguinetti. An old literary factotum from the U.S.A., another from Norway. No young people. Nobody from England; a poet from Iceland who speaks not a word. No writer from Czechoslovakia, only a cheerful female Gorki translator and an elderly man from Prague—a critic, I believe. Indians in their beautiful costumes—their dignity, the earnestness of their dark eyes. A writer from Australia, who sticks by me, since I understand English. One from Uruguay; a small Spanish-speaking group sticks together and seems very lively. Hungarians offer invitations to Hungary, Bulgarians to Bulgaria. Loudspeaker announcements all in Russian. Sofya arranges introductions to Soviet writers—they are Party officials. The Soviet writers whose names we know are all missing. . . . Company outing: the firm requests individual contacts, but a common language is lacking; people assemble in language groups. The chairman of the Weimar branch of the Writers' Union, who speaks only German, is nevertheless delighted to be there; he hands his camera to someone to photograph him together with some Indians, and I have to join in, too—writers from all over the world.

VODKA EVENING.

The Volga is brown and slow and broad, its banks hardly inhabited, fields, plains, forests, now and again a group of log houses. I enjoy the wide open spaces. At one point a reservoir: for hours no land visible; then a lock; then river banks again, apparently uninhabited, a flat solitariness with churches from sunrise to sunset, many unused churches, land and sky, the almost soundless gliding over the brown water, seagulls; it isn't boring, as one sits on deck and watches.

CONVERSATION:

Mihalkov (publications totaling 75 million copies) tells me how Soviet writers are paid. I am given to understand: Soviet literature is not manipulated according to capitalistic profit motives; the number of copies printed is determined not by demand, but by the authorities. In the West, he says, the writer is always dependent on the public—but not here. Mihalkov is a genial man. Not a Soviet child that does not read his children's books. Mihalkov also writes for the stage and for television. And on top of that to have an official position, as he has—but it is of course a burden to which the Soviet writer cheerfully submits: service to the community. Mihalkov speaks German. Paper is still too scarce to permit large editions of every book. The Soviet writer is paid according to the size of the edition, which, as already stated, is fixed in advance by the authorities; it doesn't hurt him if the public prefers another book. I see. Mihalkov is chairman of the Writers' Union in Moscow. I keep nodding . . . There is no point in arguing. I have tried. I just praise what is praiseworthy—and there is some of that, too. I give no answers that I wouldn't give anywhere else. Falsehood begins with silence. As a foreigner I can, of course, say what I please; but gradually one gives it up. The correct line is the official one, and, since it is familiar, there is nothing left to discuss. The best thing in Russia is simply to enjoy oneself. I praise the broadness of the Volga and take care not to bring up memories of the Mississippi: comparisons vex them. At lunch, seated among officials, I praise the Georgian wine, which is very good; I never stop showing that I am enjoying myself. I am not asked: What do you think of the disturbances in Berlin, the situation in Paris, the incidents in Rome? Nobody is interested in information. I praise Soviet cucumbers. One may also praise old icons. If one doesn't beat them to it, they praise their cucumbers themselves, and that is also irksome. Naturally I keep silent about the things I miss: after all, I didn't come here to hurt feelings. My poor Sofya: she abbreviates my questions as she translates them in order to take out any sting there may be and suffers in front of her superiors like a mother with a bad-mannered child. It hardly matters who eventually replies to my questions: they never contradict one another. They know criticism only as criticism of the West, and this is uninhibited and simple, untroubled by facts; criticism of Soviet conditions is no concern of anybody's—they never practise it themselves, anyway not the Party functionaries.

PLENARY SESSION on deck:

One sits with earphones on; gulls; every speaker says the same thing about Maxim Gorki, one doesn't need the translations in thirteen languages. Maxim Gorki the proletarian writer, the master of social realism; I soon begin to understand it (without earphones) in Spanish, Rumanian, Portuguese, Finnish—even when I can't guess what the language is. Maxim Gorki and his conflict with Lenin, his exile following the revolution, Maxim Gorki and Stalin, writers and the power of the state—no word of that. When I go off to the forward deck I am not the only one playing truant; even some of the functionaries find the plenary session a bore, but the firm insists on it.

VODKA AGAIN IN THE EVENING.
Talk with Christa Wolf and her husband till four in the morning; outside, a clear night sky over Volga and land. Solace: that one can agree to differ. For a long time a Soviet comrade sat with us, listening, but he did not worry me. He has apparently made his report; today my functionaries know that we seem to have had a very interesting conversation.

RECEPTION IN GORKI:
Children with flowers lining the pier, a gay scene in festal white with red ribbons. Each progressive writer from all parts of the world is given a bunch of flowers; I get one, too, peonies, and also a sore throat.

GORKI, 20 June

Yesterday on our arrival a Russian student was waiting to ask me for personal advice on her examination—a childish, somewhat too large face with bright round eyes. She had come all the way from Moscow. The extravagance of her hopeful journey; there I stand with feverish shivers and peonies. Why didn't I at least give her the peonies? Sofya has ordered her back to Moscow: the girl has no place in the program.

21 JUNE
I now have three Russian mothers: the fat chambermaid and a hotel nurse and then a woman doctor, who sits on my bed and sounds me, all of them tender in their concern, a roomful of plump mothers. No common language. They wash my neck, and I have only to stretch out a leg to get my feet washed. Later the chambermaid brings me a present: three Russian dolls. The Soviet Writers' Union is also becoming motherly: my Party official says; You're missing nothing by missing the plenary session. Sofya also pays frequent visits and brings me greetings. The plump chambermaid tells me a long story, of which I understand not a word, but she doesn't mind. Herr Wolf brings me something to read, *Sinn und Form*, and I read some prose

by Christa Wolf. A Soviet critic (the one who listened in to that night conversation with Christa Wolf) visits me, together with a woman: both very well up on the literature of the capitalist world. All of a sudden a frank discussion. He tells me I ought to see Novosibirsk, the city of scien⁺ists, progressive Russia. He speaks German, while she speaks English; at the same time he pretends not to understand English and she pretends not to understand German; thus each of them has a sort of tête-à-tête with me—off the record. They stay a long time; I have the feeling they are enjoying this hour away from the Union. When Sofya comes in the conversation becomes official again. I can't deny, unfortunately, that it hurts me to swallow.

22 JUNE
Tour of Gorki with the city's chief architect. A lot is being built, but I should like to ask questions. Instead, I am shown the same things, over and over again. I see: apartment blocks placed side by side like hives for bees, an endless desert. I ask: What do you think of high-rise buildings? Oh yes, high-rise buildings very good, certainly, of course. Why do I not see any? I obligingly admit that I myself live in a high-rise building and am not very happy in it; but the suspicion remains that I, a guest from the capitalistic West, think socialism incapable of erecting high-rise buildings. So there are many high-rise buildings in the Soviet Union? But of course, much high-rise building. Meanwhile a building of the city architect's own: a school; he is still using pilasters and Ballbek columns. Another lesson: high-rise buildings offer the advantage of better views combined with the same living density. I know that, it is the same in the West, but I say nothing—what's the use? A fine view of the Volga while I am being told for the fourth time about something familiar for decades: the prefabrication of building parts. I feel annoyed. When I was shown the first example, I nodded, so as not to deprive the man of his pleasure; hearing the second explained in the selfsame words, I nodded again to save him a third explanation; on the third occasion I reminded him through the interpreter that I had myself been an architect. In any case what this city architect is showing me as socialist achievements are not even variations of known building processes, they are exact copies. So, shown yet a fourth example, I turn away and look at the Volga. I nod and keep on nodding

I am not all that keen on old churches, but there is one here, and I am shown it both outside and in: they are proud of their beautiful old Russian churches. Rightly so. We drive on: housing developments as before, both completed and under construction; I obediently gaze—silent, though I should be saying something occasionally. I find myself sweating. What I am seeing is unfortunately not worthy of praise—dull, hideous, and unimaginative. No student submitting it on paper would get his diploma with it, yet here it is—built. I praise the trees on the roadside and am told they were planted, all planted. We come to a large factory: so this is where Volga cars are made. A building is pointed out: Laboratory! And, since I show no surprise, once again: Laboratory! I learn that before a model goes into production Soviet engineers carry out many tests, calculations, etc. When on the return journey they once again say Laboratory, I feel embarrassed: silence is construed as suspicion, perhaps even concealed envy. I ask what a Volga car costs: 5,200 rubles. Since I am expected to show amazement how much cheaper cars are here than in the capitalist West, I do a few calculations. At the unofficial rate of exchange: 6,000 Swiss francs, which would buy me a Volkswagen. But this rate, as I know, doesn't apply here. The official rate is 22,000 Swiss francs: a Porsche. But I know what Volga cars are like, we are riding in one, and I confess my amazement at how expensive it is compared with the wages here: 100 to 170 rubles a month. Yes, I am told, but gasoline costs only a fourth of what it does in the West. . . .

ATTEMPT AT A DISCUSSION:
Living in green surroundings has been proclaimed as the ideal ever since the beginning of this century, and indeed has been put into practice all over the world on several occasions: Is the idea valid, or does it lead to the disintegration of the city? The vitality of former cities: place of residence, place of work, place of relaxation all in one; whereas today residential centers and cultural centers are separated. What do Soviet sociologists have to say about that? The satellite town, even when it has its own cinema, school, and so on, can never become a social nerve center; while the city—no longer lived in, but only visited —inevitably loses in intensity. This is the experience, hence the question: Is the town still viable in an industrial society in which the working place can no longer be in the city and the

place of residence no longer where the work is? If not, with what can we replace the town as a social nerve center? I ask. No discussion. Here there are only solutions; what has already been done is the solution.

In the evening a great banquet at long tables, bottles everywhere within reach, toasts that despite loudspeakers nobody hears, everyone drinks without waiting: the city of Gorki and the Gorki branch of the Writers' Union greet the writers from all over the world. The hall gets hot, we take off our jackets, caviar, aspic melting, five hundred people or so in a mood of boisterous cheer, myself among the Germans, who are quieter, the Georgians humming with life, embraces, an eager Rumanian reminding us once more through the loudspeakers that Maxim Gorki was and is and always will be a proletarian writer, the old gentleman from Prague assuring us of the same, and an Indian confirming it. Self-service, a band playing old Vienna, my Party official raises his glass to my recovery, applause for the Indian, people wandering about clinking glasses, the man from Weimar wants the microphone for greetings to our brother nations, but has to wait till the factotum from the U.S.A. is finished. The Georgians singing among themselves, A Hungarian sits down beside me, but we can't understand one another, clink glasses instead, the man from Weimar reaches the microphone: greetings to our brother nations. One can't understand a word, but he returns to the table, satisfied; he has spoken in Gorki's birthplace. My lady guide drinks, Weisenborn surreptitiously substitutes water for vodka in his glass, I watch Christa Wolf, who occasionally droops, then gives herself a push, we raise our glasses to each other without drinking. A children's carnival, but we are not children, we are bears, toast after toast, vodka good, human beings on holidays from the state, you human, I human, it is not just a booze-up, but a let-off from the catechism, all nice people, then all of a sudden the question: What is a decent person? I suggest: A decent person is a brave person, one who is true both to himself and to others, that is a brave person in this country. Agreement, we empty our glasses and a Party official fills them up again, comes around the table while the others continue talking and mentions a certain name: yes, we both know him. The Party official says: A decent person! We drink to a man who has fallen into disfavor by speaking up for Daniel and Sinyavsky, who has been expelled from the Party and deprived of his teaching post and severely reprimanded by this same Writers' Union which is now gaving a good time here. The Party official: Your friend, my friend, too. . . . It is incongruous. I return to Moscow ahead of the others to see a theater production. Sofya hangs on my arm. An elderly female comrade, traveling in the same night train, takes care of my caretaker, leads the reeling girl into her own compartment, and fills her right up with vodka.

MOSCOW, 23–26 June

Rumor: A Soviet physicist has written to the Kremlin criticizing the status quo—the danger of neo-Stalinism, the need for cooperation between East And west, the hindrances caused by Party bureaucracy to science and intellectual life generally, the insanity of nuclear rearmament, etc., the need for reform.

Production of *Don Juan or the Love of Geometry* in the Satiric Theater without blatant misrepresentation. Mirinov a first-rate actor. Full house stifling—95°—audience mostly young people. Afterwards get-together with director and three of the main actors; these people, unlike the Party officials, are greedy for information. The production, first scheduled eighteen months ago, is frowned on in official circles.

Elections in France, but one can find out nothing. Foreign newspapers for sale only in the three or four major hotels. I buy *L'Humanité* and *Paese Sera*, but they are respectively nine and eleven days old.

Journey to Siberia approved.

The student girl who followed me to Gorki turns up again: her German is self-taught, she has read a lot, her questions are precise and sensible, consequently difficult. Unfortunately, Sofya is present, but the girl is quite unperturbed when Sofya translates her questions with an air of disapproval. Sofya is not stupid by nature, just well-trained; questions about Kierkegaard or the Second Commandment (graven images) or Pirandello are not on her wavelength; the name of Sartre is distasteful. Obviously the student girl is repeatedly being told that I am in a hurry, which—as she can see—is not the case. On the contrary: we would have time for tea. But where? Natasha (that is her name), given some corsets, could be a character from Chekhov: one of his Russian souls, waiting and languishing.

GORKI INSTITUTE:

German scholars ask questions, till one begins putting questions to oneself—other questions of a kind that really concern a writer. But they are not to be provoked. A heresy, which they are quick to perceive, is headed off with a quotation from Mayakovski. But if a comrade should say that today? Afterwards a walk around the museum; documents from the life of Maxim Gorki. The miseries of czarist Russia: they explain the revolution better than comparisons with the modern West; the need for this revolution—but also its cruelty.

Relaxation in a public park: when one cannot tell from the trees or clouds exactly where one is—respite from a phantom.

Library for foreign literature: women in charge of the various departments. Pick at random among subjects I know; no attempts to pull wool over anybody's eyes (how suspicious one becomes, unfortunately). Banquet at the Swiss Embassy: three literary functionaries and three men in disgrace shake each other by the hand. The men in disgrace seem freer, more relaxed. Only Lyublinov, who was recently warned that his theater is to be closed (they are playing Brecht there) finds it difficult to be sociable. Reunion with Tamara, my translator. Aksionov in melancholy mood: an unhappy love affair, so I gather. My Party official: In these surroundings we always feel at home. This time I can't escape proposing a toast; in it I mention my friend who has been expelled from the Party, and Party functionaries raise their glasses to him; they seem quite moved—at any rate not hostile. They like him, I know. Even when called on to pass or approve a much severer sentence, a totally destructive one, against a former comrade, they do it only because they must. I ask Andrei Voznesenksy why he was not with us on the Volga trip; he smiles noncommittally and asks in English: "How did you enjoy it?" A young man of the world, rather too elegant.

Then talk about Beckett's *Happy End*. Afterwards, alone with Lindt, the ambassador. "Bring your glass, it's better to talk out in the garden."

I ask my guide why Voznesenski and Yevtushenko are at the moment in disgrace. Reply: they are not in disgrace, they have simply been abroad too often and must learn to understand their own country properly again.

The evils: Fascism, Maoism.

My impressions differ from my first journey (1966: Moscow, Leningrad, Odessa) hardly at all so far. Without knowing Russian the journey has little point: a silent film with captions supplied by Party officials. In the end one simply trusts to one's eyes, knowing one is not getting beneath the surface; that makes one annoyed with oneself, and the annoyance gets carried over on to the country. One condemns more than one perceives. Since they immediately attribute all the good things to their system, one falls into the countererror of silently attributing all the bad things to the same cause.

Departure for Siberia by air, alone with my guide. Flying is very cheap for the Russians themselves: five hours in a jet for 48 rubles. Many people in the huge airport lounge, workers and countryfolk. Journeys with official approval.

NOVOSIBIRSK, 27–29 June

The Siberian writer who meets me at the airport despite the early hour is hard of hearing, hence his overloud voice as, without looking at me, he tells me all about western Siberia: its size, length and width of the rivers, height of the mountains, temperature in winter, temperature in summer, rate of population growth, mineral resources, length and width and depth and capacity of reservoirs, etc. It is all quite enormous. Width of the Ob in the north: forty-five kilometers. My reply to his question about the width of the rivers in Switzerland needs no translation by Sofya: it is the smile of defeat. We cross two rail tracks: nothing special to look at, but in fact the lines of the Trans-Siberian Railroad. On with the lesson, which I welcome; the accent lies on quantity, as always with pioneers. Hotel room like a dance hall. Breakfast (fighting against sleep) with vodka and handover by escort, then drive to the city of Soviet research. The Ob's industrial landscape: impression of a sky even wider than above the Volga. My new colleague-escorts: two Siberian lyric poets, one elderly, the other young and obviously still enjoying his official position (unpaid), both in dark suits with white shirt and tie, the young fair-haired one with the face of a bird and always bolt upright, whether sitting or walking, always cheerful and pleasantly taciturn. A reservoir (length two hundred kilometers) in pale morning light, its banks covered with birches and firs: how I imagine the countryside in Scandinavia to look. Military trucks. The elderly poet asks me the length of military service in my country. He is the first to ask about our affairs. . . .

Campus surrounded by birch woods. Scholars' houses in fenced gardens. Apartment blocks with nursery schools attached. Quiet, few cars. Center with cinema and restaurant, hotel, shops, etc., many low buildings. No university here—just research. Most people aged between twenty and thirty. No signs of rush, a monastic air. A stroll, while waiting to visit two or three institutes, down to the large lake: people bathing—the very sight makes one shiver—ball games on the beach, girls, too, athletes in blue track suits in the woods, some wearing spectacles.

No pictures of Lenin here.

Lunch in a sort of cafeteria or snack bar; for the first time Russian waitresses who don't look grumpy when one orders. No word of propaganda for the Soviet system from the two poets. It's unnecessary here. Institute of Genetics. Information on gene research—in English. The moment one can get on without interpreters an easier atmosphere emerges. Information about a new virus treatment; as a layman I think I understand the principles, at least.

No East-West hysteria here.

Evening stroll with my guide through the old town, but hardly any of the old wooden houses remain. Opera house fronting a square that is much too large. A desert of arc lamps. A wall of photographic portraits: male and female workers who have received decorations. Theater posters of touring productions from Moscow; pictures of a local production, obviously a play about Hitler. Actors in swastika uniforms, Hitler himself in realistic, melodramatic makeup. People in the park. It is still light at midnight.

GEOLOGICAL INSTITUTE.
Siberia's mineral resources: coal, oil, natural gas, copper, silver, gold, diamonds, etc. Problem: transport.

MATHEMATICAL INSTITUTE.
Their way of discovering talent: Schoolchildren throughout the Soviet Republics can take part every year in a competition, solving mathematical problems which the teacher receives from Novosibirsk; they are also published in the newspapers. The correct solution is less important than the way in which one arrives or fails to arrive at it. Anyone showing talent is invited to Novosibirsk, where he is given new problems to solve and has to demonstrate his answers in a public auditorium and discuss them with the scientists and other candidates. Those who pass this test are taken by the elite school in Novosibirsk and later by a university. The best of them end up at the Research Institute.

VODKA INCIDENT IN THE HOTEL:
Some road machinery delegates from the German Democratic Republic invite me to their table: I don't know what I said; Sofya takes me to my room, she doesn't like these people. . . .

MOSCOW, 30 June

Saying good-bye to friends.

> BERZONA
>
> Somebody tells a true story of a meeting be-
> tween Lenin and the poet Robert Walser in the
> Spiegelgasse in Zurich in 1917. Robert
> Walser asked Lenin only a single question:
> "Do you also enjoy eating this <u>Glarner</u>
> <u>Birnbrot</u>?" I do not doubt the authenticity

of this anecdote even in my dreams, and wake
defending Robert Walser. I am still defending him as I shave.

ZURICH MANIFESTO (signed)

WE NOTE:
There has been fighting in Zurich between young people and the
police. Thus the conflicts at present occurring in both East and
West have come to a head in our city, too.

WE CONCLUDE:
The events in Zurich should not be judged in isolation. They are
the result of shortcomings in the social system. To dismiss them
as rowdysim and to describe the persons taking part simply as
hooligans and loiterers is too superficial.

WE ARE CONVINCED:
One cause of the crisis is the inflexibility of our institutions. This
inflexibility is detrimental to human beings. It hinders adaptation
to the changing needs of human beings and the development of
creative minorities.

WE CALL TO MIND:
Significant changes have always stemmed from minorities. It
was particularly among the young people that the liberal ideas of
1848 found passionate support. This minority was responsible for
the preservation of Swiss independence and for the establishment
of our federation.

WE SOUND A WARNING:
A cultural conflict can be settled neither by blows and bans nor
by appeasement in the form of patronizing offers. "Benevolence
is the drowning of right in the cesspit of mercy" (Pestalozzi).
Suppressing the conflicts will drive the young people on to the
barricades.

WE DEMAND:
1. A discussion forum for young and old, to be set up at a central
   point and independently conducted.
2. Such reprisals as relegating students and schoolchildren,
   withdrawing scholarships, deporting foreign subjects, dismissing employees, should not be resorted to unless serious of-
   fences against the law have been established.
3. Restitution of the constitutional right to demonstrate. (This
   demand has since been met.)
4. Continuation of talks with all minority groups.
5. Invitation to all parties involved to present their points of view
   in the press and on radio and television.

6. The immediate setting up of a working group to investigate the underlying causes of the conflict and to put forward practical suggestions.

FOR THE RECORD

My youngest daughter was there, but was not beaten up or arrested. She says: "It was meant as a lark, everybody was happy; we sat down in the middle of the street (Bellevue)—that was the lark."

"One two three, make Globus free!" This is what the young people chanted in front of the empty building where the Globus stores used to operate. An official notice: "Persons unlawfully entering this building or abetting others to do so will be prosecuted." There was, however, no plan to enter the building, only to demonstrate in front of it as a protest against official delay in setting up the promised youth center. Police pickets. What the demonstrators could not have foreseen: the police blocked the sidewalk in front of the building, where they were to assemble, thus forcing the demonstrators onto the street. Traffic holdup. The police (Dr. R. Bertschi) ordered them to disperse within a few minutes, which with the best of intentions would have been impossible; in any case, the organizers could not make themselves heard above the police loudspeakers. Result: rising indignation. Police action, supported by water cannons. Retaliation with paving stones, beer bottles, and wooden slats. Truncheons drawn, arrests, injuries on both sides. The arrested were taken to the Globus basement, where they were beaten up again with truncheons, even when offering no resistance. Unconscious men were kicked in the testicles. A policeman decided that an injured man must be taken to hospital. His comrade in uniform exclaimed; "Let the swine die." Later, at the police station, the arrested people were again greeted with truncheons. The cases were dealt with by police magistrates.

Death of a child. Headlines and radio reports immediately blamed the demonstrators for the fact that a six-year-old boy died in an ambulance caught in the traffic holdup. Three days later the authorities were obliged to issue a statement that went some way toward damping down public indignation: "The accounts on television and in various newspapers were incorrect. . . . The ambulance driver stated that the detour had slowed him up by five to eight minutes. . . . It must once again be emphasized that the death of this child cannot be directly ascribed to the demonstrators."

At the first special meeting of the city council the mayor, Dr. Sigmund Widmer, considered calling in the army.

The young people (university and high school students, apprentices) wanted to call a meeting to discuss the situation. The city refused them the use of a hall. Even private landlords with large halls of their own refused to rent them to such despicable outcasts. Eventually they were able to hire the Volkshaus on condition that they pay a deposit of 10,000 francs to cover possible damage. We have the guarantee with three checks. Teach-in, people sitting on the floor, discussion lasting till midnight, with guitar music in between. Then they cleaned up the hall and went home. The city detectives too. Not even a chair leg to pay for.

Youngsters (with beards) report that police officials had said to them a week before the disturbance: "You'll get what's coming to you on Saturday." Their rioting has been programmed.

A student named Thomas Held, known as spokesman of the Progressive Student Group in Zurich, but not arrested since he had committed no real or alleged breach of the peace, has been summarily dismissed from his teaching post. An anonymous threat to kill him obliges him at the moment to remain in hiding.

In collecting signatures (for the ZURICH MANIFESTO), the frequent reply was: I am entirely in agreement, but I cannot take the risk—I am a civil servant/an employee of the university/ on a newspaper/on television, etc.

The police now going around in civilian clothes. When five people are seen standing together on the railroad bridge, a detective tells them what they should do: disappear. A small group, promising to offer no resistance of any kind, tries to march into a district where no traffic disturbances will ensue; they allow detectives to confiscate their banners right away.

A civilian entering the main police station was immediately struck down; afterwards he turned out to be a lawyer, a car driver who had come to pay a parking fine.

An apprentice who was not even there has been ordered to have his hair cut if he wishes to keep his job.

Arrested people are not allowed during interrogation to describe events happening after their arrest; they must confine themselves to answering questions: whether they belong to a society, a club, etc.

A young woman coming from Frankfurt, a stage designer, knew nothing of what was going on when she got in the way of the water cannons near the station. She ran away, was struck down by three policemen and dragged into the Globus basement, where she was hit between the legs with a truncheon.

A foreign student was at once deported; no investigation of what he had really done or not done.

Doctors confirm that many of the injuries they have had to treat "certainly did not result from the fighting," but could only be attributed to "systematic beating." The chief of the criminal police, Dr. Hubatka, has denied eyewitness reports that he stood by while people were being mistreated without putting a stop to it.

An adult civilian (but wearing short pants, since he had just been sailing) intervened when, on the bridge by the quay, he saw a prostrate young demonstrator being kicked on all parts of his body; he demanded the names of the policemen concerned, was at once struck down with truncheons and taken to police headquarters, where he was later discovered to be a doctor.

Neue Zürcher Zeitung: "Traffic holdups, damage to property on a large scale, and in immeasurable loss of faith in their young people by the citizens of Zurich." / "Those taking part in the brawl were nothing but a brutal rabble." / Appeal by the mayor: "The vast majority of people in Zurich are filled with indignation by the disturbances caused by young people last night. I, too, am filled with indignation. . . . If necessary, the instruments of law and order will be strengthened. . . . Finally: Young people will not achieve their aims by defiance and violence. . . ." / *Neue Zürcher Zeitung:* "The methods of the police were harsh, but correct." / *Vaterland,* Lucerne: "In our view the Zurich police were right to intervene so severely. Let those brawlers who receive corporal punishment howl and gnash their teeth all they like. . . . They had better watch out! We now know the methods they use, these people who are eternally talking of rights and reforms, yet basically are nothing but evil agitators and brutal anarchists." / *Zürcher Woche:* "One cannot ban this group, but one can boycott it." / *Die Freisinnige Partei:* "This party calls on the authorities to take the following measures in particular: . . . The whole force of the law should be applied against these brawlers and their ringleaders. . . . University and high school students condemned in a court of law must be expelled by the Zurich educational authorities. . . . Foreigners who took part in the disturbances must be deported." / Statement by the City Council: "The allegation that individual officials were responsible for certain excesses will be investigated. The City Council stands for law and order without regard to person." / Police report: "In the course of the street fighting on Sunday night 41 people were injured, comprising 15 policemen, 7 firemen, and 19 demonstrators. With the exception of one fireman and one policeman all the injured have been released from hospital. Arrests totalled 169. Of the demonstrators 55 were under the age of twenty. Of the juveniles arrested 19 are still under arrest." / State of emergency: The Zurich City Council bans all demonstrations "until further notice." Contraventions will be punished in accordance with the provisions of Swiss criminal law. / *Neue Zürcher Zeitung*: "Mob rule in the streets of Zurich." Caption to a picture of a young man: "The powerful water jet leaves no more room for heroics." To another picture: "An injured policeman being assisted by his comrade." Government: "At its meeting on 4 July the Regierungsrat was informed by the representatives concerned of the situation arising from the disturbances in Zurich. Numerous prosecutions have been prepared by the legal authorities, and guilty persons will be brought before the courts for punishment. The police aliens department has been instructed to deport all foreigners who are proved to have taken an active part in the disturbances. The university and schools authorities have been instructed to take disciplinary measures against all university and

high school students liable to punishment. The Regierungsrat, together with the authorities of the city of Zurich, will employ all means open to them to maintain law and order and protect their citizens. The canton police has been alerted." / *Neue Zürcher Zeitung*: "Stop the rot!" / "Positive effect of the ban on demonstrations." / "The rules of democracy." / "A tiny minority and an overwhelming majority." / "Juveniles and the people behind them." / "Their manipulators in foreign lands." / "Misled youth." / "The weight of the evidence will be assessed by the judges, who will make their judgments in complete independence, undisturbed by pressures from the street outside." / "It is to be hoped that the law will reach out beyond the stone and bottle throwers and call to account the actual people behind these acts of violence, whose names are known." / "Demonstration of sympathy for the city police. A girl came to police headquarters with a bar of chocolate. A farmer from Herrliberg offered to help mobilize all the farmers in the district to fight the demonstrators wherever necessary. An academician applied to become a nonparticipating member of the police athletic association. A male chorus from District 4 announced that the whole music society would give its help as required. A telephone caller offered the voluntary services of himself and his butcher colleagues."
P.S.
Special edition of the *Neue Zürcher Zeitung*, 24 September 1933, with headlines: "Torchlight procession of patriotic parties falls victim to organized Marxist attack. Night fighting in the streets of Zurich. Social Democrats and Communists taunt and attack the civic torchlight procession. Hail of stones. Appeal for calm." Slogan of the patriotic demonstration 1933: "We must save our city from the ravages of a class-conscious Social Democratic clique intent on gaining its own ends." Speakers at the demonstration: Niklaus Rappold, *Freisinn* (Progressive Liberal), Robert Tobler, *National Front* (which supported Hitler). "The Fight for a Patriotic Zurich."

REMINISCENCE

In 1936, when I was planning to marry a Jewess, a student from Berlin, and went to the City Hall in Zurich to collect the necessary papers (birth certificate, certificate of nationality, etc.), I was handed unasked an official certificate of Aryan origin, bearing the stamp of my native city. Unfortunately I no longer possess this document, since I tore it to pieces on the spot.

Switzerland was not occupied by Hitler; it was what it still is today—independent, neutral, free, etc.

NOTES FOR A MEMBERS' HANDBOOK

The doomed man sees more desirable women than formerly, though he changes the object of his admiration several times daily. He no longer confines himself to a single type. A tendency towards paneroticism (all stages from early to late.) The number of women arousing his desire stands in direct opposition to his true chances.

The foredoomed man who genuinely falls in love again seeks ruthlessly to overcome all obstacles in the way of fulfilment: he cannot resist the miracle.

A longing for desire . . .

Yet the doomed man goes through long periods of complete indifference to sex; he sees the sexual act (when he happens to think of it) as absurd.

The doomed man, watching a movie, finds lovers' embraces especially boring—and always too long.

Long before his chances become completely hopeless (the doomed man underestimates them at times for fear of looking ridiculous if he has made a mistake), he hesitates—even when the prospects look favorable. . . . He sees a tennis player tossing back her hair or exaggeratedly shaking her head when she serves a double fault, and knows that she is conscious of him. He stays a while to watch—not for the first time. He finds her attractive. On one occasion he throws a ball back to her over the high netting, only then to walk away. In the elevator he knows which button to press for her, but he does not speak. When in the evenings he sees her in the bar, he takes a seat some distance away, though he has spotted what she is reading: there would be something to talk about. The doomed man is familiar with the sort of talk necessary to establish the existence of common interests, but he is now wary of such long dialogues, for they take time and he knows his own lines will bore him (intermediate stage). If he is in love, he knows himself by the fact that he still has the power to choose; he packs his bags and leaves.

The foredoomed man, failing to achieve his object, at once blames it on his age—as if he had never, as a young man, been turned down by a woman.

Unlike the foredoomed man, who fears the final release from virility, the doomed man knows that this release never comes. He wishes it did.

Bachelors keep going rather longer.

Members who rely on commercial preparations to preserve them from aging only aggravate their fear of aging. The bed as reassurance, yet there is a danger of becoming more interested in the proof than the deed.

The doomed man tends to recall women whom he could have had thirty or even only ten years ago; he regrets all of his lost opportunities, of which he now believes there are many. But he forgets what it was that usually held him back at the time: his own taste.

The reason why the doomed man finds many things becoming a bore (a walk through the city, shopping, parties, bus trips, waiting at airports, etc.): his presence arouses no feminine responses; it is as if he were not there. . . . When a young woman passes him in the street, she no longer gives him the impression of looking away from him—she really doesn't see him. There is nothing coquettish about it. He can turn around, and she will not notice; he can see by her walk that she has not noticed. At the newsstand he is treated simply as a customer: the assistant looks at the journals he has chosen and then at the money. Nothing else. In a plane things may be different. The stereotyped smiles of the air hostesses begin to give him pleasure, but not even that lasts long; he asks the time of arrival and they immediately become like mothers to him, even like nurses. If the doomed man should find himself alone in a railroad coach with a younger woman, there will be no feeling of constraint. In earlier days she would have looked out of the window or hidden herself behind a magazine in order to avoid being spoken to. But now she just sits there, as if he were nothing more to her than simply a part of his unoffending luggage. When he stoops down in a bus to recover a lady's dropped glove, she seems surprised to find that there was somebody sitting opposite her. The waitress condescending at last to notice his presence comes to the table to change the ashtray, taking his order by the way, unseeing; when she brings his beer she looks over his head, and later makes out the bill, unseeing. The doomed man asks himself what else he expected besides the beer. Afterward, in the rest room, he catches sight of himself in the mirror as he dries his hands. Then he understands, and puts his coin on the plate. When a woman (actress) tells a man (director) he is gaga, the man has nothing equivalent to answer back with. ("Cow" or "bitch" cannot be considered equivalents, since cows and bitches can also be young.) The "gaga" epithet is her revenge on him for seeing the woman merely as a sex object, and as such she is judging him now.

The doomed man has already stopped kissing his daughter, or at least he gives his kiss an ironical air. He is equally shy of kissing other young women when the social occasion (birthday, New Year's Eve, etc.) would permit it. He considers his lips an imposition. If on such occasions a young woman kisses him artlessly along with everyone else, the doomed man betrays himself by feeling disconcerted.

Cases of old men's charm: it does happen that a younger man can be made to feel jealous, even when he knows there is nothing to fear. For the doomed man it is enough to have made the younger man jealous.

Through discoveries that now, because he is no longer so confident of his powers, he has become more attractive to women than he used to be, the foredoomed man discovers his former mistake: he had thought he understood women, but he had ascribed to them only the expectations he felt able to meet. Now he has begun to get some inkling of all the other things women might expect from a man—things he never gave them. This feeling alone makes him more attractive.

In a taxi with a young woman he may desist from suddenly, on some pretext or other, putting his hand on her arm or shoulder. Rightly so. But the fact that he desists shows that the thought is in his mind. And because the thought is in his mind, he feels constrained. Should she become conscious of it, she moves politely to one side, although she knows he will do nothing. The doomed man is still free in the sense that he is not in love—he simply finds the woman nice to look at. His awareness that he would be an unsatisfactory partner in bed irritates him for the very reason that he knows there is nothing to suggest even the slightest prospect of it. She gives him a glance and he feels embarrassed, as if caught out in a fraud. He is still thinking of bed, and yet he is really quite happy simply to be sharing a taxi. He knows his hand would not send shivers through her. And for him, too (he decides as he looks out of the window), it is not absolutely necessary (intermediate stage). He is glad when this taxi ride ends. . . . Even until quite recently the doomed man had felt it absolutely necessary to put a hand on her shoulder—with the result that he might suddenly find her head against his chest. His experience when this happened: that anticipation vanishes with actual contact (early stage). Later the doomed man will no longer try to spare himself even this experience.

Senility is no proof against subjection.

When he remembers a particular man-woman episode— house, surroundings, weather, time of year, a particular dish, her clothing rather less, her body only in general terms—the doomed man catches himself remembering most of all the incidentals, and often very precisely: the loggers who surprised the pair, and the exact spot in the woods. The rest is now legend.

```
21 August
The rucksack is packed, the white wine
```

cooled, all now ready for the outing. Our
actions remind me of another day, also immediately recognizable as historic: Hitler's
invasion of Czechoslovakia. I was at a swimming pool with a friend when the news reached
us—we were just about to take off our
clothes. A quarter of an hour later we went
into the water—not unconcerned, simply
helpless. Today Golo Mann wants to show us
the Valle Verzasca, and we might easily have
started out without knowing what had happened. I do not listen to the radio in the
mornings, but a friend rang us. What do we
know at this moment? Only that the Russians
marched in during the night, a bit about the
way it was done, airport occupied, etc.,
Dubček arrested by the Russians and deported.
Of our friends in Prague we know nothing: it
did not occur to me to phone them. It would
still have been possible.

Our outing, long since planned, seems the
only thing we can do on this day—a walk with
a little transistor radio in our hands. Golo
Mann, the professional historian, is reluctant to speculate; he tells us about his recent visit to Czechoslovakia to do some
research on Wallenstein. I explore the Valle
Verzasca—cliffs, stream, flora, butterflies
—a succession of unforgettable irrele-
vancies. The little transistor is no use; it
simply crackles.
P.S.
Rereading Kafka's diaries: "2 August (1914):
Germany declares war on Russia—Afternoon,
swimming class."

QUESTIONNAIRE

1.
Do you usually know what you are hoping for?

2.
How often must a particular hope (say, a political one) fail to materialize before you give it up, and can you do this without immediately forming another hope?

3.
Do you sometimes envy other living creatures who seem to be able to live without hope (for example, fish in an aquarium)?

4.
When some private hope is at last realized, how long as a rule do you feel it was a valid hope, that is, that its realization has brought you as much as you had been expecting from it all these years?

5.
What hope have you now given up?

6.
How many hours in a day or days in a year are you content to live with only modest hopes: that spring will come again, that your headache will disappear, that something will never be found out, that your guests will leave, etc.?

7.
Can hate breed hope?

8.
In regard to the world situation, do you hope:
a. that reason will prevail?
b. that a miracle will occur?
c. that everything will go on as before?

9.
Can you think without hoping?

10.
Can you feel affection for a person who sooner or later—because he professes to know you—expects little from you?

11.
What fills you with hope:
a. nature?
b. art?

c. science?

d. the history of mankind?

12.

Are you content with just your private hopes?

13.

Assuming that you distinguish between your own hopes and those that others (parents, teachers, friends, lovers) place in you, when are you more depressed: when the former or when the latter are not fulfilled?

14.

What do you hope to gain from travel?

15.

When you know that someone is incurably ill, do you arouse hopes in him that you know to be false?

16.

What would you expect in the reverse situation?

17.

What strengthens you in your personal hopes:

a. encouragement?

b. recognition of some mistake you have made?

c. alcohol?

d. public honors?

e. a run of luck?

f. a horoscope?

g. somebody falling in love with you?

18

Assuming you cherish the Ultimate Hope (Brecht's vision of man as a man's helper: *Wenn es so weit sein wird, dass der Mensch dem Menschen ein Helfer ist*) and have friends who cannot share your hopes, does this diminish your friendship or your hopes?

19

What is your feeling when the situation is reversed, that is, when you cannot share the ultimate hopes of a friend? Every time he is disappointed, do you feel wiser than he?

20.

In order that you may think and act in accordance with it, is it necessary for you to feel a hope to be realizable?

21.

No revolution has ever completely fulfilled the hopes of the people who fought it. Do you conclude from this that it is ridiculous to have great hopes, that revolution is useless, that only people without hope are spared disappointment, etc.? And what do you hope to gain by being spared that?

22.

Do you hope for an afterlife?

23.

On what do you base your daily actions, decisions, plans, thoughts, etc., if not on a vague or specific hope?

24.

Have you ever genuinely been without hope for a day or even an hour? Even the hope—at least as far as you are concerned— that things will one day end?

25.

When you regard a dead person, which of his hopes seem vain to you, those he realized, or those he left unfulfilled?

Seven weeks ago there was talk in Moscow of a letter that a scientist had addressed to the Kremlin. It was not published at the time, but its contents were apparently known to a number of intellectuals. Now the full text, hitherto only the subject of rumors, has appeared in translation (*The New York Times, Die Zeit.*. The author, Andrei D. Sakharov, a Soviet physicist, member of the Academy of Sciences, is a Communist. In his letter he condemns the Stalinist period, those victims he estimates to have amounted to at least ten million people, and examines the aftermath, which is the situation today. Sakharov describes the sterile bureaucracy, which now masquerades as socialism and is consequently regarded as sacrosanct. He speaks openly of the idiotic dogmatism of the party officials: this is incapable of solving the world's problems, and it consequently represents a deadly threat for the future, both for the Communist countries themselves and for the world.

Zakharov's criticisms, well founded as they are by virtue of his position, strike a warning note in both camps: it is high time that both East and West abandon their rigid lines of thought and initiate a policy of global cooperation (which means more than mere coexistence as it is presently understood—an agreement between the great nuclear powers to maintain their interests at the cost of third parties). This is the only hope for the future of mankind. Zakharov points to Prague, and his hopes echo ours: that socialism may at last begin to move in the direction of its great promise.

Has this experiment failed?

The Soviet tanks in Czechoslovakia remind one, it is said, of Berlin on 17 June 1953 and of Hungary in 1956, but the comparison is false: there was no uprising in Prague—the Communist Party there was itself making an effort to democratize socialism, and the Czech government did not for a single day lose control of its experiment. Soviet troops are not, as is being claimed, defending socialism against a counterrevolution. They are simply protecting the present-day Soviet Establishment, which fears the evolution of Socialism—an evolution that is ultimately inevitable, in the Soviet Union as well. The Soviet military intervention is a manifestation of this fear, which is not, however, the fear of the Russian people, but the Soviet Party officials' fear of their own people. The Czech experiment has not failed: it has been suppressed.

—*Weltwoche*, Zurich, 30 August 1968

Hispano—Suiza is now selling guns, which Hitler ordered but did not collect, together with substandard ammunition to Africa. Switzerland is offering its services, with Ambassador August Lindt from Moscow as go-between. Newspapers report an illegal arms traffic on the part of Bührle—Oerlikon. Headlines: "Government Calls for Investigation." At first there was talk of 10 millions, then 90 millions, for weapons to Nigeria, Israel, Egypt, South Africa. Documents falsified in order to obtain official consent to the export of weapons. Dr. Dietrich Bührle knew nothing about it; two assistant directors accused. The government and Bührle, a colonel in the Swiss army, to

which he delivers supplies, are agreed on one
point: without arms exports the Swiss army
could not be maintained. A few weeks following the scandal, which dismayed the public as
if such things had never happened before, the
government ordered military supplies to the
value of 490 millions from Bührle—Oerlikon.
Where else could it order? Nationalization
of the arms industry is out of the question;
it would mean sacrificing the freedom our
army is there to defend. Posters call for
aid to Biafra. The government donates 1 million francs for Biafra. Children are collecting in the streets for Biafra.

MEMBERS' HANDBOOK (Correspondence)

Dr. U. B., fifty-three, Berne
The layout of the life pyramid as depicted in ancient scrolls
("a child at ten," etc., "in the grave at one hundred") should
not be taken too seriously. The fact that according to this you
are now in the prime of life can be ascribed only to the drafts-
man's naïve desire for symmetry.

A. W., fifty-five, Lucerne
There is no reason to question the picture you enclose, show-
ing yourself riding the waves behind a motorboat. This is very
gratifying. . . . Our handbook has never suggested that sport-
ing activity is not to be recommended; the more healthy the
doomed man is, the better will he feel.

G. U., seventy-six, Asconda
Death can take place at any age, which means that a doomed
man cannot necessarily be identified by an increased fear of
death; in old people's homes this fear tends rather to diminish
(late stage).

M.S., forty-five, Zurich
You are not the first to be preoccupied by the thought that you
are now ten years older than Mozart was at his death—that
has nothing to do with senility. As you will discover, it is when

you are comforted by the thought that a genius is ten years older than you are that senility sets in.

Professor O.P., sixty-five, Basle
You write that you find gratification in the fact that in retirement you now have time for your magnum opus. In this handbook it has never been disputed that in old age all gratifications are particularly welcome.

O.S., sixty-three, Melbourne
Our handbook has never implied that love of one's homeland is a symptom of senility (you are a Swiss living abroad). This must be a misunderstanding. Patriotism, like chauvinism, is equally prevalent among young persons; and, conversely, we know of cases where devotion to one's homeland vanishes precisely in old age. . . . You have now been living for forty years in Melbourne; your undiminished love for the land of your birth has less to do with the question of age than with the fact that you are living in Melbourne.

H.H., thirty-seven, Stuttgart
Your attitude as a priest is irrefutable. ("I myself look after an old people's home. While in no way denying the imbecility of its inmates, I care for these people in the certain faith that on the Day of Judgment they will not appear before Our Creator as imbeciles.")

Frau Dr. A.S., age unknown, Konstanz
It is not true that in the passage to which you refer I was thinking in particular of you and your respected husband. A man cannot be regarded as doomed simply because on social occasions he allows himself to be overshadowed by his wife. In your case there might be other reasons. As far as I am aware, you are, though somewhat older than he, simply a lively personality, and I never get the impression that your husband feels himself overshadowed. Perhaps he thinks you get on our nerves, but I can assure you that this is not so. The passage you mention refers in fact to an industrialist from Pittsburgh in the United States, whose wife says to him, "Don't speak, but think, honey!" and with that she, too, is not

entirely wrong. Once again let me assure you: I have great respect for your silent husband.

A.G., fifty-five, Herrliberg
The words "senile" and "senility" are not terms of abuse, but descriptive epithets. It is simply because the condition they describe is something you prefer not to think about that you react as if they were terms of abuse—in which sense they are, of course, also used in ordinary conversation, and for the same reasons.

Professor C.V., forty-seven, Princeton, U.S.A.
I find your remarks extremely valuable. A scientific handbook would certainly be of use to our members. Most of the relevant publications that I know have been written by sociologists; and, though understandable to many of our members, I have noticed that no member takes sociological arguments as applying personally to himself. They are more open to medical arguments, though then usually only in the sense that they conclude they must take greater care of themselves.

V.O., sixty-eight, Berlin-Vienna
The connection between senility and occupation requires investigation. I have not seen you on the stage recently. You say that the daily confrontation with an audience keeps one young, and as proof you mention that you still experience stage fright before every appearance. Our handbook has never claimed that a doomed man who is obliged by his occupation to make public appearances will cease suffering stage fright, or have any reason to cease suffering it.

H.P., twenty-three, Frankfurt
Experience makes people stupid. . . . This saying, popular with students, has a certain validity—as experience has shown.

Mrs. C.G., fifty, Kilchberg
Of course I believe in the equality of the sexes. The fact that the aging problems of women are not dealt with in this handbook is certainly not due to negligence or reasons of tact,

but simply because I (as a man) can see women only in their aspect as sexual partners to men (not only in relation to their actual husbands, but to men in general). A man therefore becomes conscious of a sense of loss, to the same degree that a woman not only loses the ability to maintain a pretense through cosmetics but also begins to acquire an identity of her own—hitherto kept under for the sake of the man himself. Her late emergence as an individual shames him. There may still be times when she reminds him of the girl she must once have been, but he now finds himself confronted with an asexual partner who responds hardly, if at all, to his gestures of authority. The level of intelligence being equal, she is now the dominant partner. Women age better than men.
P.S.
But not always.

P.P.S.
When one says that a woman ages earlier, one only means that she has an earlier release from sexuality. The man, on the other hand is obliged (or seeks) to persist in his sexual role, and he ages within the context of it; the old man is therefore a more ridiculous figure than the old woman (intermediate to late stage). The power of the matriarch over the aging gallant.

Monsignore G.S., sixty-nine, Rome
You will find the quotation from Michel de Montaigne in the Essay on Experience, not in that on Age, though the initial sentences of that would also have done; "I cannot accept the manner in which we determine the duration of our lives. I see that, compared with the common opinion, wise men shortened it very considerably. What, said young Cato to the people who wished to prevent him from killing himself, am I now at an age when I could be reproached for abandoning life too soon? And yet he was only forty-eight." (Montaigne himself died at fifty-seven.)

H.A., eighty-one, present address Bad Ragaz
Of course there are always exceptions.

The manifestos, the inscriptions on the walls
of the Sorbonne, the posters, the caricatures

drawn with chalk or ballpoint pen, the
slogans of the French students in May, the
pamphlets—these are now printed in a book.
I can page through it at home in comfort,
admire the color prints out of context, art.
<u>Bourgeois</u> <u>vous</u> <u>n'avez</u> <u>rien</u> <u>compris</u>. Sitting
with my legs crossed, I read: <u>Feu</u> <u>la</u> <u>culture</u>.
Or; <u>L'art</u> <u>c'est</u> <u>merde</u>.

TOVARICH

"It's not possible," I say to my interpreter. "It would be too absurd—ask him if it's really he." Of course I can understand her reluctance to translate my question; he (if it is he) was once one of the two most powerful men in the world. "Why don't you ask?" I say, thinking it might just be possible after all. "I think," she says, "we ought to be getting on." Always this motherliness! Then she tells the elderly comrade that we have no time (at least I suppose this is what she said). All the same, her cold respect toward him contradicts her next words to me: "He's just an ordinary peasant, I tell you, a lot of them here look like that." All I know for certain is that the old man possesses no gas and doesn't know where it can be got in this place. . . . Days ago, in Moscow, I mentioned his name and learned from Sofya that respectful remarks were not encouraged, were indeed out of order: it was tactless even to mention his name. I can understand that this meeting over a garden fence must—if the old man is really he—be very unwelcome to my interpreter, in fact not even true. But what can I do about it? If it is he, he is behaving magnificently: he must have seen at once that I recognized him, but he understands Sofya, too, and has no wish to embarrass this good and conscientious young citizen, who is presumably telling the old man yet again about our mishap. "He says he doesn't know where we can get gas, but there is some somewhere," as if I doubted it. Although he cannot understand our language, he nods. He stands there in shirt sleeves, leaning on his rake, an old man in retirement. Once more I kick myself for not knowing Russian. I would swear to him not to reveal a single word outside the country; I haven't even a camera with me, only an empty container. No idea why Sofya is laughing now, but I'm pleased. When we came to the garden fence, and when the old man saw how much we were sweating in our search for gas, he offered us something to drink. Sofya declined at once. Why? Now she is at least laughing; and I see the old man glancing at me. The Russian word for foreigner is (as far as I know) "dumb man." And the way he looks at me, almost as if touched. "He asks where you come from," Sofya says conscientiously. "I told him you were a writer." What then caused the laughter I am not told. I smile just in case. Another question put to the "dumb man" by him is not translated (Sofya often does that) and so remains unanswered. I do not discover whether he understands English; at any rate, he doesn't react when I venture to ask in English, "Do you have many visitors?" A silly question, God knows; it is lucky Sofya doesn't understand English. I get the impression that he is not under guard, looks quite content with the place where he is and in good health, though old. I stand there trying to recall when the Cuban crisis actually occurred, the threat with the rockets, while he is obviously still wondering what a Western writer is doing in this district. "He has great respect for writers," Sofya says and adds, so that I shan't again imagine that isn't true, "Our peasants have great respect for writers." Each time she makes a slight grammatical error; usually her grammer is remarkable correct. When he evidently asks her what she has just said to the foreigner, she does not answer, but looks at her watch, while we, the old man and I, look at each other, two helpless people. I now praise the flat countryside, the lusciousness of his lettuces, a birch tree, etc., in order to get Sofya interpreting again. He is incidentally smaller than I expected, not fat but compact, his round scull almost without hair. The more convinced I become that it is actually he (at the start I had simply wanted to tease my Sofya), the more constrained I naturally find myself becoming. "Tell him, Sofya, that I am a guest of the Soviet Writers' Union," I say, so that he (if it is really he) will not think I am a spy. "Tell him that, please. It doesn't appear to surprise him, nor to disappoint him, nor to please him; whether a peasant or an initiate, that remains unclear. "We must be going now," says Sofya again, and the old man, who perhaps once decided between war and peace, shows no particular desire to detain the young lady from Intourist, whose job it is to protect the Soviet Union, and the foreigner with the empty container at his garden fence. He has no gas station. He once allowed

Solzhenitsyn to be published, in *Novi Mir*, and he had Stalin's body moved from the mausoleum. Seeing him standing there, his rather stubby hands resting on the handle of his rake, one can hardly believe it of him. "Tell him," I say, "that we have unfortunately lost our way." We have no authority to be here, and yet here we are; I feel sorry for Sofya. She has eyes like a bird, and I am not always sure where she is looking. Sometimes she translates, even when the old man has said nothing. "He wants to know if this is your first visit to the Soviet Union," she says, "but I have already told him." All the same, I say, "My third," which isn't true. Why do I say it? Sofya doesn't translate it either, but points to her watch, and I understand. When we first arrived and spoke to the old tovarich we had shaken hands, a nation of brothers. Now it is more difficult. "Go on," I say, "ask him if he is Nikita Khrushchev." He must surely have understood the name, in spite of my pronunciation. A difficult moment for poor dear Sofya: she now pretends not to have understood the name herself. I take her to be in her middle thirties, which means that as a schoolgirl she would have waved peonies at him, doubting him not at all. "Why don't you ask him?" I say softly; it's not Sofya's fault if he is who he is. As the old man regards me, I hesitate to stretch out my hand. "Tell him we are grateful," I say, "we'll find a gas station some-where." Now Sofya seems confused. "Is there anything else you want to know?" she asks me, instead of translating. The old man (whoever he is) would certainly know about events in Czechoslovakia, Vietnam, as he plants his lettuces; he doesn't seem decrepit, nor (if he is Nikita Khrushchev) embittered by the knowledge that he can hardly count on a state funeral. "What did he just say?" I ask Sofya, but she finds it too trivial for translation, mere chat over the garden wall. "Let's go," she says, "he can't help us." She is getting more and more agitated at our continued lack of gas. "Tovarich," she says to the old man with the bald peasant's skull, but the rest I again can't under-stand. He laughs as he used to in press pictures throughout the world, with eyes half closed. As we shake hands, I don't really believe it could have been he. . . .

BERZONA

Swiss television, wanting my opinion on the

new Education Act, comes along with its
equipment and films me without offering a
fee, can't however use the film, that is, unless the minister I criticize is willing to
reply, and the minister (a Social Democrat,
incidentally) is not. For this they now send
me 100 francs. . . .

REMINISCENCE

One of our principal teachers of architecture, a Swiss, was a
declared supporter of National Socialism. Corbusier he mentioned only as an instance of proletarian art. Switzerland, he
would say, was a natural part of the German Reich, and, on the
subject of the Jews: Jesus could not have been a Jew, read
the Bible again (New Testament, of course) and you will see
how wise and profound it is, and Jesus was fair-haired, the son
of a carpenter who probably came from the north. This jolly
person, Professor Friedrich Hess, was not unacceptable: that
was what the Bundesrat decided on a proposal from the Universities Board, which was appointed by the Bundesrat. Another
teacher at that time, Professor Hans Bernouilli, taught town
planning, which leads, as we know, to sociological and economic
problems; a former supporter of the theory of free money, he
once voiced an opinion critical of the Bundesrat. This man was
considered unacceptable and dismissed.

22 December

Apollo 8 on television: the three men on
their way to the moon. At the moment they
are about 200,000 kilometers from the earth.
Picture: our earth as a bright ball, unfortunately blurred. Then a bunch of small mete-
orites, with it the voice of Borman talking
to the people in Houston, Texas. No reason
in that to stop smoking my pipe. Their slow,
fishlike movements in their state of weight-
lessness. One of them, looking like a white
embryo, waves a hand. They have no sense of
above and below, that is obvious: it makes

the television viewer feel slightly giddy,
simply because he has firm ground under his
feet. Everything technically in order so
far. One of them feeling sick: his doctor
gives him advice from the earth. After the
transmission one tells oneself: For the first
time in history, etc., then watches the
sports program.

23 December

Good earth pictures today. Just as one might
imagine: our earth is a planet.

24 December

They are in orbit around the moon. Very
clear close shots of the surface: craters,
easily discernible because of their clear-cut
shadows, glide slowly across the TV screen, a
constant succession, till one comes to feel
it is all rather dreary. Excitement comes
only from imagining one were there. What one
sees again just confirms one's imaginings.

25 December

The engine firing that takes them out of the
moon's gravity and puts them on their way
back to earth has now taken place. More pictures of the moon, by now familiar, so to
speak. The whole household plus neighbors
watching, but nobody has much to say. Relief
that the operation has succeeded, but no
clear knowledge of what one hopes to gain
from it. Prestige for the U.S.A. One tells
oneself again: For the first time in history,
etc., but already we know it all.

26 December

Social activity indoors, winter outside, I
sit regarding the year's unanswered mail and

declare an amnesty.

27 December

Apollo 8. Successful return to earth, the
three men in white safe and sound on television. On the aircraft carrier they walk on a
red carpet; watching them, we think of
science and technology, of the computers that
brought the enterprise to a successful conclusion, but not of heroes. The television
commentator (Monte Ceneri) works hard to im-
print the three names forever on our memories
and those of our children's children: Borman,
Anders, Lovell. No human being has ever
flown farther than these three tough men; we
feel they deserve a rest and good health and
promotion. The difference between Borman,
Anders, Lovell, and (for instance) Nansen.
The expedition we have been watching with
bated breath has little to do with personalities. And, in fact, the three men in
white do not behave as if they were heroes:
they just seem glad to be out of that cap-
sule at last—three technicians who in the
anonymous adventure were cast for the most
dangerous job. It could have failed, and
then they would now be starving to death as
they circled the sun; but, since it succeeded, it is not they who orbited the moon,
but (as the commentator rightly says), Man
himself.

DREAM OF THE LOCARNO DRUGGIST

"That is a scandal," he says evenly, but aloud, so that he is
awakened by the sound of his own voice saying, "Scandal"—
then in Italian: "*Una vergogna! È una vergogna!*" ... All
he recalls of his dream at this moment is a quavery old bishop,
limping on both legs, maybe an actor playing a bishop, but a

cripple, and everything in a gymnasium.

. . .

At that time he is a country physician, *il dottore*, as if they didn't know his name; everyone in the village calls him just *il dottore*, though his name has for years been in the telephone directory, on the letterbox, etc., *il dottore*, while he of course has to know all their names and even the first names of their children.

. . .

The scandal must be something else.

. . .

After being awakened by the sound of his own voice, as—though still sleepy—he sits bolt upright in the dark on the edge of his bed in order to break the dream, then turns on the light, he is no longer the country physician and for a while uncertain if he ever was one; but soon (it takes only a very few minutes every time) things become clear again.

. . .

A scandal in the village, no need to worry about that, nothing ever really happens there, no murder for years past. During the day they seem friendly enough. Doing scandalous things to one another, that's what keeps them together, apart from the landscape, which gets little sun in the winter. But one doesn't need to worry about that, if one wasn't born here. Incidentally, the village has no gymnasium.

. . .

Il dottore! How politely cynical it sounds.

. . .

He is a drinker: that he knows every time he wakes up and has forgotten what is not clear, and just now it was still clear, completely clear. A happy dream, really.

. . .

That quavery old bishop, who wants nothing from him, and the gymnasium are a sort of joke, then, an incident having nothing at all to do with him; this dotty old man is no concern of his, a bishop limping on both legs. It is gruesome and ridiculous—a disturbance, so in that sense a scandal.

. . .

He is a nonbelieving Catholic.

. . .

The evening before, he thought the villagers had been cheating him, had in fact been cheating him for years, beginning with the bill for his water. He always takes these green forms on trust, just to save bother. They're incomprehensible, but probably correct and (by punch-card standards) fair—they have his name on them.

. . .

She's no longer a girl, of course. Her cheekbones, her stiff hair just as twenty years ago. She seems in high spirits, as he has never known her, and she is up to something or other. She shows no fear. She talks, but they are not alone, surrounded by a disorder for which he apologizes: there are a lot of children lying about, not her children and not his either.

. . .

He slept with her only twice.

. . .

She seems to know what he has become, a country physician, but it is not important. She is very confiding. What she is saying has nothing at all to do with him. They are somewhere. He doesn't know the place, the strange house. It is absurd of him to apologize for the disorder. But they don't touch one another.

. . .

He has woken up with a headache.

. . .

The village knows exactly what he really does. *Il dottore.* Perhaps they talk behind his back—so what? For instance, he has been trying to get the factory (a tannery) to build a purification plant—so far in vain. The place still stinks. Maybe they tell lies, but that doesn't bother him. That's not the scandal that matters.

. . .

As the quavery old bishop suddenly limps into the gymnasium and seats himself on a splendid ornate seat, she disappears. Pity: he might have wanted to ask her something that only she could know—something of some relevance to him, and to him alone.

. . .

His headache comes as always from drinking *grappa.*

. . .

It is years since he last saw her, and he has never thought of her since. All he knows is that she is married and once had a baby, stillborn. That is all. Years ago he happened to meet her in the Bahnhofstrasse in Zurich: a lady, middle class in origin and still just middle class.

. . .

It is the first time he has dreamed of her.

. . .

Mostly, after waking up, he remembers only the stupid outer lineaments of his dream, and for a while feels defeated. Then he goes about his daily work: *il dottore*, who has taken to drink, as the village also knows.

. . .

In what way a happy dream?

. . .

During the day in the drugstore, thick horn-rimmed glasses on his narrow face, he recalls the actual events that the dream had made use of but not meant. The gymnasium, for instance. As schoolboys they once performed a play in a gymnasium, but that is all.

. . .

The water bill is probably correct.

. . .

He has never in his life been a country physician, and the knowledge that for a while after waking he could imagine that he once really had been one worries him. It is simply not true.

. . .

On the other hand it is true that he, *il dottore*, has for years been campaigning for a purification plant. Everybody knows that— not only in the village, but in Bellinzona, too, where he and his clumsy way of speaking Italian are notorious. He comes from Winterthur.

. . .

The tannery did not figure in his dream.

. . .

"*Una vergogna!*" It was not until he heard the sound of his own voice that he said that. In the village they speak only Italian.

. . .

Later he recalls a walk with Leny, or, more exactly, he recalls a memory he once described: how he saw a woman with a rickety old pushcart, and in the pushcart sat a crippled, half-witted child, and the student girl he was with laughed at him when, with appalled seriousness, he remarked that the child had his face or something like it. He never describes what happened afterwards: in the woods he had the student girl, for the first time, and it was ridiculous.

. . .

During the day everything seems quite normal again.

. . .

It was a happy dream until this bishop came in and swept it all aside, this quavery old ham in his purple robes, with his shepherd's staff and his public, the tourists of Locarno.

. . .

Yet he knows very well that he'll never get anywhere with the tannery, though it is polluting the little river. He has demanded an expert analysis, *il dottore*, but they know it all without that; their children swim in the river. What business is it of his? His children don't swim in the river.

. . .

It is a sunny day, winter.

. . .

It all has some other meaning, or it means exactly nothing; it is clear, fully clear, only when he is actually dreaming. What he reads into it when he wakes up is not right at all; everything is different from and truer than what he thinks up in his drugstore.

. . .

When he sees that quavery old bishop, limping along on both legs, then of course he knows he was only dreaming. That was the scandal.

. . .

When he has stopped thinking about it (having in the meantime driven to Locarno and spoken to his assistants, before that breakfasted with his family—now he is dictating orders), he suddenly thinks of Erler, whom he has not seen for a long time. That is probably the way it began: E. sitting on asphalt, thus on the ground in public, his legs crossed Buddha-fashion, wise and witty as ever, but naked, much smaller than a real person and without any arms. It is touching, not horrifying: the well-known revolutionary, but smiling, a tiny cripple.

. . .

Around midday it all crumbles in his mind.

. . .

When his wife asks him what the scandal in his dream was (she heard him say it aloud), he replies, "They are all swindlers, the whole village, just plain swindlers."

. . .

E. doesn't believe in reforms. That was always their bone of contention. But the way he sits there on the asphalt without any arms—without any pretensions, naked and lovable.

. . .

The middle of the dream remains empty.

. . .

Once the children have to go to school they will leave the village, that has been more or less decided for some time; it is not urgent, yet all the same he speaks of it at breakfast. There's no life here.

. . .

He loves the student girl who has become a lady in his dream for the first time; she now knows all. No caresses, though. On the other hand he is aware in his dream, not for the first time, of a secret love affair that, every time he wakes, seems never to have been. That is what he would like to ask her: if she remembers it. Then it would have been she.

. . .

Il dottore: that's what they call all learned professions here; if he were a physician they would say *il medico*.

. . .

Gradually everything shifts its place.

. . .

For example, it now occurs to him who can really be called a swindler: the accident insurance company, which for years has been refusing to pay up. But he didn't dream of that.

. . .

There still remains the student girl with the cheekbones and the stiff hair. A boring face, actually. She is sitting at a long table in a tavern, wearing a brown silk dress, a middle-class girl, incidentally tanned; only later does it become a house with strange children on bureaus, untidy but middle class; she has nothing to do with any of it. She talks only to him. It doesn't matter that he is married. She assumes it is his friends who keep wandering in and out and interrupting. But it doesn't worry her. They must be his friends, of course, though he doesn't recognize them. She says she is now very strong, very strong.

. . .

He has a vague memory of corridors.

. . .

That affair long ago had been very unsatisfactory.

. . .

Animals in the corridor, but indistinct.

. . .

Some days before he had been explaining in a tavern why he had stopped pestering the tannery—roughly: one can't change the world, at least he can't, it's not his job, etc., he's not a complete idiot.

. . .

His sexual dreams are usually anonymous. (He is in his middle forties.) He is very happy when he recognizes her: her boring face has a certain resemblance to his Danish assistant's; but it is Leny.

. . .

Incidentally, he doesn't care for the Danish girl.

. . .

E. knows all, too, and there is nothing more to be said. A happy and unhoped-for-reunion. E. doesn't seem to mind having no arms, hardly any arms. Not an accident—but it is the first time he has seen him naked. Everything is easy. The way he sits there on the asphalt (sit-in) and grins: one would like to stroke him. Actually he isn't grinning, or hardly. He is like a child, that is all, lovable.

. . .

Perhaps the television also played a part.

. . .

It isn't as if the following day is affected by the dream, so to speak: he doesn't have to forget any of the dream; it just doesn't hold out against the day (at any rate the day in the drugstore), it simply dissolves into a sphere of private ridicule—a happiness that can't stand up to the light of day.

. . .

Why is he not a country doctor?

. . .

Only the bishop remains repugnant.

. . .

Sometimes he begins to drink toward evening (and tells himself every morning that this must now stop)—first wine, then *grappa* —because the only thing he knows is that it is all wrong, what he thinks, what he says, what he does, what he knows.

1969

BERZONA

Once from a plane I thought I recognized the
house: a little gray block in a side valley.
I felt sorry for it, standing there so long
without a tenant, just looking after our
books, our official papers, letters, notes,
crockery—and also our wine. When we one day
return, it wears a very factual air. Everything still there. Nothing to report. Presumably the telephone has rung now and again.
It has not fallen down, and after an hour it
is no longer unfamiliar: this is where we
live. Winter south of the Alps: melted snow
flowing over granite turned deep purple by
moisture; round about, faded ferns, the
trunks of birch trees, snow-covered peaks,
and beyond them the Mediterranean. On walks
one meets nobody, just now and again a goat
or two; the streams are still frozen over,
but it is warm in the sun. Nowhere now
could one find a lovelier place. Without
guests, who have eaten at our granite table
and slept in our beds, it would not be ours:
it would remain just a landscape—very beautiful on a day like today.

LETTERS FROM READERS OF MY ARTICLES

"Do you perhaps believe that the Vietcong commit no murders?" /
"If you consider it necessary to criticize the U.S.A., why don't
you go and live in a Communist country, if you find everything
there so wonderful?" / "Are you really a Swiss?" / "Is the author
prepared to enlighten us neutrals in another article about the
true conditions and activities on the other side?" / ". . . I know
only one of Lenin's sayings, but it is right: useful idiots. That is
exactly what you are. How much longer?" / "It is the so-called
young people who support people like you, criminals, ex-con-
victs, homosexuals, outcasts, idlers. It is for people like this that
we have to pay taxes." / "That you also put in a word for conscientious objectors was only to be expected in the circumstances." /
"Your whole article is a load of muck, but it earns you a pile of
money, and for you that is the main thing." / "You swine! You are

a rotten swine! They should cut off your cock and feed it to the gulls on the Globus roof! You disgusting lunatic, but your pigsty will soon be in flames! Swine!" / "Why always only criticisms?" / "The American soldiers in Vietnam are dying for you too, Herr Frisch, as you have obviously forgotten. As neutrals we therefore have no right . . ." / "One cannot resist the feeling that you are an intellectual scoundrel, however much, in view of the good qualities you also have, one would like to think otherwise. With the world in the state it is now, it is simply irresponsible to be so negative and destructive. . . . Your offensive, insidious, corrosive manner suggests an ignoble character, making one feel: This man is incorrigible."

HATRED

If I had now to draw up a balance: there is nobody at the moment whom I hate; only a few I should prefer not to meet in case I should find myself hating again. My hates are not rare, but short lived. Perhaps it is mostly just anger. No instance of life-long hatred. Above all, I feel fairly certain that my hatred harms me more than the people whom I hate. Hatred as a flash of flame, leaving me afterwards feeling stupid. Due perhaps to the fact that the hater is more eager for reconciliation than the hated. When I realize that someone hates me, I can more easily evade the issue: I simply stay among people who do not hate me. Despite a natural dose of self-hatred in my makeup, my first reaction when I find myself hated by somebody without provocation is irritation. Had I been reckoning on sympathy? No, not really. The irritation is due to the unexpected intensity of a one-sided relationship. The reaction to it is not counter-hatred, rather dismay, and, above all, self-awareness (and I have the feeling that this helps me to a certain degree)—or I can forget my hater. Not, however, the other way round: when I am the hater I cling to the person I hate, and it does not help me at all when he takes evasive action. On the contrary: the less I see or hear of him, the more thorough my hatred becomes —that is to say, the more harm I do myself. Another point: hatred toward a person obliges me to exercise a certain degree of justice, which I never achieve and which exhausts me. Usually there is no need for a definite reconciliation: my hatred eventually becomes too expensive for me, stands in no sort of relationship to the person concerned, who, whatever he may have done, eventually becomes an object of indifference to me. . . . It is otherwise with hatred that is concentrated on a group rather than an individual, or on an individual who is simply the representative of a group. My only lifelong hatred is a hatred of certain institutions. Then hatred becomes itself an institution. Even in that case hatred harms me more than the object of it, but I accept this, because here hatred can be seen as conviction, which permits neither indifference nor reconciliation. . . .

```
One feels concerned, gives advice and fur-
niture and money. The awareness of individ-
ual helplessness in the course of events
causes one to seize whatever opportunity one
has of doing something: one goes to the tele-
phone and conjures up connections, achieves
something, too, though promising no miracles.
But one is available, and that always deludes
refugees in the early days. They now have a
place to live, even a job, but in six months'
time they begin to feel lonely: their prob-
lem does not remain our problem.
```

First performance of Brecht's posthumous play *Turandot.* Director: Benno Besson. Why in Zurich? The parable is not particularly apposite either to West or East, but, like all parables, it gives the impression of hitting some nail or other on the head. Where Brecht goes astray in his picture of the West: we cannot be summoned to conferences—to give our blessing to the war in Vietnam, for example. We can even protest against it without fear of losing our heads. Our real trouble is that our protests have no effect; on the contrary, they simply serve to convince our rulers how tolerant they are. How true of the East is this parable of the Tuis, who are obliged to assemble in order to provide ideological applause for the invasion of Czechoslovakia? One knows that Brecht was thinking of intellectuals under the Fascists when he began the play; why didn't he finish writing it and then work it out on the stage? His China-Chicago is set as usual in a period just before the dawning socialist era, and it is thus as innocent as the old peasant in the play who, with the cunning of common sense, understands what the little red book demands. (So it was originally in the play, though the producers, no doubt in deference to Chairman Mao, thought it best to cut the "red." . . .) The play permits no doubts: Truth comes, Truth conquers, curtain—as if the intellectuals could no longer come into conflict with Truth after the curtain. Unfortunately, the audience has learned too much in the intervening years. The proverbial breadbasket that, the moment you stop bowing down to the rulers, is whisked up to the ceiling—how true! how true!—but the withdrawal of a passport, the expulsion from the Party, the banishment to a prison camp or the sending to a lunatic asylum (because you don't bow down to the rulers) could not be presented in quite such simple allegorical terms. Oh, these children's plays for intellectuals! When I see the severed heads on the battlements I, of course, know exactly whose heads are not meant; but I think of them just the same. And there's no point then in projecting posters of the Matterhorn on the wall, as Benno Besson does, to prevent misunderstandings. But Zurich cheered—something no society does when it sees itself unmasked. It was altogether wrong, a theatrical "occasion." The very confidence with which it was asserted that under socialism there would be no more Tui problems made everything look antiquated. You have to be very careful with parables. . . .

Zurich, February

Arson in the Hottingen telephone exchange.
The culprit, named Hürlimann, knew the building, having been employed for years with the post office, and he placed his inflammatory materials so carefully that the fire brigade could do little: the building has been saved, but most of the switchboards are destroyed. Headlines report tremendous damage; it will take weeks to restore the exchange to working order. The culprit, who immediately gave himself up to the police, seems happy with

his deed; a preliminary psychiatric report
describes him as a hitherto trustworthy mechanic with a grown–up family, but few
friends. He admits that he found his work
boring, and recently he became embittered by
being passed over for promotirn: a younger
mechanic was put above him, thus blocking
any prospect of a change. The question
whether the existing working conditions are
satisfactory, or perhaps not, is not touched
on in the psychiatrist's report, which is
content merely to label the man a psychopath.
The technical outcome of this technically
accurate revolt: thirty thousand telephones
have been struck dumb. Conversations with
people in bars: even those who are now suffering a lot of inconvenience are not without sympathy for Hürlimann.

QUESTIONNAIRE

1.
If you cause someone to lose his sense of humor (for example,
by arousing his shame), and if you then conclude that the
person concerned has no sense of humor, do you find the fact
that you are now laughing at him a proof of your own sense
of humor?

2.
What is the difference between wit and humor?

3.
When you feel that someone shows antipathy towards you, do
you find it easier to respond with wit or with humor?

4.
Is it your idea of humor:
a. to laugh at third persons?
b. to laugh at yourself?
c. to bring someone to the point of being able to laugh at himself
without feeling ashamed?

5.

If you discount all laughter at the expense of third persons, do you find your sense of humor often aroused?

6.

What makes you aware in company that you have forfeited all sympathy: when people close their ears to your serious arguments, your knowledge, etc., or when the sort of humor natural to you fails to evoke a response—that is, you become lacking in humor?

7.

Have you humorous feelings when you are alone?

8.

When you say a person has a sense of humor, do you mean he makes you laugh or that you can make him laugh?

9.

Do you know of any animals with a sense of humor?

10.

What suddenly gives you the feeling that you could have an intimate relationship with a particular woman: her features, her life story, her beliefs, etc., or the first recognition of affinity in matters of humor, even when your opinions differ?

11.

What does humorous affinity demonstrate:

a. similarity of intellect?

b. that two or more people can be alike in their imagination?

c. an identical sense of shame?

12.

If you become conscious that at a given moment you really do lack humor, do you then feel that the humor you sometimes possess is a superficial quality?

13.

Can you visualize a marriage without humor?

14.

What more quickly arouses your jealousy, to see the person you love embracing or kissing another person or to see this other person arousing in your partner a humor of which you were not aware?

15.
Why are revolutionaries so averse to humor?

16.
Are you able to regard persons or social groups whom you hate on political grounds with humor (not simply with wit) and still continue to hate them?

17.
Is there such a thing as classless humor?

18.
If you are in a subordinate position, do you consider it humor when your chief smiles at your genuine complaints and demands, or as a lack of humor if you cannot also manage to smile, or do you at such times laugh until your chief stops smiling, and in which case are the results more pitiable?

19.
Does your sense of humor ever reveal you as a different person from what you would like to be—or, in other words, does your own sense of humor never shock you?

20.
Does humor stem only from resignation?

21.
Assuming that you possess the gift of making people laugh, and that you make use of this gift on all social occasions until you have earned the reputation of being a humorist, what do you hope to achieve:
a. communication?
b. the advantage of being popular with everyone?
c. the possibility of passing off a slight on someone by saying it was intended as a joke and the person concerned has no sense of humor, etc.?
d. the satisfaction of never boring yourself?
e. the chance of winning the laughers to your side in matters that cannot be sustained by argument?

22.

What do you bear only with humor?

23.

If you live in a foreign country and find your own particular brand of humor never works, can you adjust to the need of keeping all your relationships on a serious level, or does this make you seem a stranger to yourself?

24.

Does a sense of humor change with age?

25.

Does being in a good humor mean you are:

a. accommodating?

b. free of ambition?

c. unworried?

d. morally uninhibited?

e. rising above yourself?

f. bolder than usual?

g. free from self-pity?

h. more honest than usual?

i. glad to be alive?

26.

Assuming that you believe in a god, have you any indication that he possesses a sense of humor?

5 March

All day watching German television. Election of the Federal President. Fixed faces main-taining their image in front of the cameras: after the first ballot, after the second bal-lot. Christian Democrats with an air of easy relaxation, like bosses meeting on holiday: really, there are more urgent matters to be attended to than this ballot game, but it has to be done today, for the sake of democracy; a crush in the corridors, but don't forget in the crush that television voters may be watching; the fuss of such an occasion does not worry them, the result being a foregone conclusion, God willing, and nothing is known to God's disadvantage. The first ballot goes as expected (though a rather close thing), Chancellor Kiesinger as usual the twinkling father, Minister Heck and the other Christian Democratic bosses showing a tangible willingness to oblige when submitting to a vote. At last, toward evening, the result: the Social Democrat Heinemann after all. After the defeat, a democratic decision which Chancellor Kiesinger categorically declares himself willing to accept (a staunch democrat to the backbone, even when democracy will keep on having its upsets); an embittered Franz Josef Strauss says straight out: "No glorious choice."

OUTLINE OF AN ACCIDENT

He had the right of way, and to that extent was not to blame. The trailer truck came into the highway from the left shortly before Montpellier. It was midday, sunny, not much on the road. . . .

. . .

She has short fair hair, trousers held up by a broad belt with a brass buckle, mauve pop spectacles. She comes from Basel, is thirty-five, witty. They have known each other a year.

. . .

Her question—"Or shall I take over now?"—was not the last thing she said before the accident (as he later perhaps thinks); she had said it often during this trip.

. . .

In Avignon, alone in the bathroom, which he locks though she is still asleep, his mind is made up: It can't go on like this. He will tell her at breakfast (without making a scene): "Let's go back. It would be more sensible."

. . .

She got to know him in hospital—a doctor to whom she (so to speak) owes her life. On his account she is seeking a divorce.

. . .

Nights in bed followed by sightseeing, Roman or Gothic, every day like school examinations: history of the popes, just because they happen to be in Avignon—she has a habit of asking things he doesn't know or only vaguely knows, thus sapping his confidence. If she is really interested in why the Pope emigrated to Avignon in the fourteenth century, she can look it up in a book. But the popes are not the real trouble. Afterward in bed she gives him back his confidence.

. . .

He is unmarried.

. . .

She thinks the trip a success. She has been saying that ever since Genoa, where it poured with rain. Later the weather improved. She says, "You're not even looking!" She is particularly enthusiastic about Provence, and during the drive sometimes bursts into song.

. . .

He is bald, and knows it.

. . .

Aix-en-Provence, of course he finds it beautiful, very in fact. But she doesn't believe him, because they never look at the same things.

. . .

The place famous for its asparagus is called Cavaillon, not Cavillion. She told him so yesterday, incidentally, and she is right. It is really called Cavaillon, he sees it on a road sign just outside: Cavaillon. So he is silent, and shortly afterward drives through a red light.

. . .

Hotel bedroom with *grand lit*, where she afterward reads the newspaper, *Le Figaro Litteraire*, which, as they both know, he doesn't understand. She is a Ph. D., Romance languages.

. . .

In Nice they have dinner with friends, a pleasant evening, though afterward she says that during the whole meal (*bouillabaisse*) he spoke of nothing but food. No reason why a partner shouldn't say things like that. He has resolved never again to speak about food, and now he overdoes it, remaining demonstratively silent when Marlis herself begins to talk about the food, as is quite natural in France.

. . .

It is not their first trip together. On earlier occasions he was in a good humor, as long as he felt sustained by her admiration for him as a doctor. Their first trip after her recovery was to Alsace.

. . .

He has never had a serious accident, but all the same he would be happier if Marlis used the seat belt. She doesn't for fear he might drive even faster. He promises to stick to his promise. And he does. After Cannes. When he notices that she is nevertheless keeping an eye on the speedometer, though saying nothing, he forgets what he was about to say. He is being boring, and knows it.

. . .

In Avignon, after leaving the bathroom, he tells her, "I'll wait downstairs." What is the matter? She really doesn't know. Perhaps he's overworked.

. . .

She admires intelligent people, particularly men, for she thinks men more intelligent than women. Mentioning someone, she says, "He's very intelligent." Or, "I wouldn't call him exactly intelligent." But she never shows it if she finds somebody unintelligent. She takes it as a sign of her love for Victor that she is upset when in company he talks less intelligently than she does.

. . .

He has no intention of marrying.

. . .

"Now you're doing a hundred forty kilometers!" He was waiting for that. "Please don't shout at me!" First of all, he is not shouting, merely saying that is what he was waiting for. Her eyes always on the speedometer. In the second place, as the speedometer shows, he is doing a hundred forty precisely. That's what she said. Yesterday (on the freeway between Cannes and Saint Raphael) he did a hundred sixty, once even a hundred eighty, when Marlis lost her head scarf. After that they agreed: a hundred forty maximum. Now she says, "It's just too fast for me." When even Volkswagens are passing them. She says, "It's just that I'm frightened." He tries treating it as a joke: maximum yesterday a hundred forty, maximum today a hundred twenty, by the time we reach Bilbao we'll be down to thirty. All right, then. Since he himself thought it a poor joke, there's no need for Marlis to think it a poor joke, too. She has stopped singing, he has stopped passing, they are both silent.

. . .

Her husband (her first), was (is) a chemist.

. . .

Because of his impatience, she did not buy those shoes in Marseilles. She is not angry, just says her shoes are pinching, and in Arles, where he is prepared to be patient, that there are no shoes she cares for.

. . .

Actually, he would prefer to breakfast alone. He doesn't really know either what the matter is. He knows no woman he would rather be waiting for at breakfast time than Marlis. She knows that.

. . .

How intelligent is Marlis?

. . .

He knows the fault is his.

. . .

Later he may perhaps think he woke up feeling the day would end with an accident; beneath the plane trees in Avignon he was already practically convinced of it.

. . .

Her naïve delight in shopping: even when there's nothing she needs she stops in front of shop windows, breaking the conversation. But with other women it was hardly ever different, either.

. . .

He comes from Chur, the son of a railroad employee, got his degree with honors, is shortly to be promoted to senior surgeon.

. . .

The famous place where the gypsies gather is not called Saintes-Maries-sur-Mer, but Saintes-Maries-de-la-Mer. She does not tell him so. She even avoids the name, so as not to have to correct Victor before he perhaps finds it out for himself.

. . .

She calls him Vic.

. . .

She has no wish to be the dominant partner. No man can stand that, and least of all Victor. He is a surgeon, thus used to having people trust him, and Marlis, too, trusted him before.

. . .

Marlis has a habit of saying, "Are you sure?" She wanted to know whether C.——, a mutual acquaintance in Basle, was a homosexual. He has hardly stated his opinion when she says, "Are you sure?"

. . .

In Avignon, waiting for her under the plane trees, he suddenly feels as he used to when he was still in a good mood. It seems unfamiliar, like a ghost. The sunshine in the plane trees, the wind, probably mistral. Perhaps things will go better today. He will not suggest breaking the trip off. An absurd idea, really. He sits at a little round table beneath plane trees and studies the *Guide Michelin*, so afterward he will know the best road to Montpellier.

. . .

He is forty-two.

. . .

Once in his student days Victor spent a week in Provence. He thinks, driving toward Arles, that he remembers the amphi-

theater in Arles. Marlis is reading out details from the *Guide
Michelin*: diameter of the amphitheater, number of seats,
height of the outer façade, year of construction, etc. She reads
it in French. It is written in French, and it's not Marlis's fault
if, the moment he hears French, he feels as if he is taking an
examination—even though he understands it. While she is
reading the *Guide Michelin* she is not watching the speedometer. On that previous visit to Provence he had been with a
girl from Hamburg; what he remembers of it is sitting with her
on top of the outer wall, a very precise recollection of this amphitheater in Arles. He describes it in advance. A pleasant evening
in Arles, Victor lively and talking more than usual. She enjoys
it when he talks like that. They drink (something he does not do
when he is on duty). Next morning they visit the amphitheater
in Arles, and he realizes he had been thinking of the amphitheater in Nîmes. Marlis doesn't notice, but he does.

. . .

She is slim. She has large teeth and full lips that always leave
them showing, even when she is not laughing. Tell her she is
beautiful and you are out. On the other hand, she goes to a lot
of trouble to look beautiful to the man who considers her intelligent.

. . .

An hour after leaving Arles he admits to having confused its
amphitheater with the amphitheater in Nîmes.

. . .

She knows Victor is waiting. She feels there is no hurry. Why
does he always go on ahead, so that then he has to wait for her?
She can't go any faster. It is always the same. Sitting at the little
round table beneath the plane trees, he admits to himself that
the fault is his, because he always goes on ahead. She is right:
he can surely enjoy Avignon. And he does. The sunlight in the
plane trees. When he sees that Marlis has stopped again in
front of a shop window and can't tear herself away, though
she knows Victor is waiting, he resolves: Patience. She says

there are no shoes for her in Avignon either, as she has just seen. Then adds that she is much too lightly dressed. Does he think it will be warmer in Spain? He suspects it will be, but says nothing, so he won't be proved wrong if this journey does in fact bring them into Spain. Instead, he says, "Will you have a brioche?" But what he offers her is a croissant. He realizes just in time, but doesn't correct himself, since she did not hear him. He now notices every mistake he makes. So he thinks. But he doesn't, for instance, notice that she is waiting for a light for her cigarette. "Sorry," he says, and holds out his lighter. Then, "Sorry," again—overdoing it.

. . .

In Basel she no longer lives with her husband, but neither does she live with Vic; that would make things difficult for her divorce.

. . .

The sudden way in which, after giving her a light for her cigarette, he looks at her—not nastily, just impersonally, as if she were an object. She asks whether he perhaps doesn't care for her pendant. Then, all of a sudden very determined, he calls out: "*Garçon!*" He brushes a hand across her cheek, but it is not clear what the gesture is supposed to mean. Unfortunately, the *garçon* doesn't come, though he is wiping a table only five paces away. His gesture has confused her. He is resolved to remain cheerful and relaxed. He says, "A glorious day." She asks: "Haven't you paid yet?" A question is no reproof; he taps the tray with a coin until Marlis calls out, "*Garçon?*" Then he comes. No need for him to feel vexed because, while he is paying, Marlis asks the *garçon* the best way of getting to Montpellier; she can't know that he has already worked it out exactly on the map. When the *garçon* at last takes himself off, she says, "You understood, of course?"

. . .

What is he afraid of?

. . .

Once (not on this trip) she said to him, half joking: "You are not my doctor now, Vic, you must get used to that."

. . .

Alone in the garage with the man who has washed the car, he says *benzin* instead of *essence*; it doesn't matter when Marlis is not there. He gets what he wants.

. . .

In Basel everything is different.

. . .

Only once during the whole trip, in Cannes, did she say, "Idiot!" because he did not follow her instructions and drove into a one-way street. Why does Victor take it seriously? Now he waits for the next bad mark.

. . .

She is looking forward to Spain.

. . .

After all, she is an expert in Romance languages; if now and again she corrects his French, Victor ought to be grateful.

. . .

In Avignon he waits in the open car, smoking, for there is something she has to buy. Plenty of time. We're on vacation. He smokes, he will make an effort. When at last she comes, he receives her like a cavalier, gets out to open the car door for her, says, "I've found your sunglasses." They were under the seat. Marlis says, "You see?"—as if he had mislaid her sunglasses, the second pair on this trip. Marlis didn't find what she wanted, another nail file, but she has got some beach shoes, which he finds amusing. Why is she cross? She always has the feeling Victor is so impatient. Like in Marseilles. She has half a suitcase full of shoes, and he can't understand why ever since Marseilles she has been wearing only the shoes that pinch. His suggestion that they should make another detour via Marseilles was not meant sarcastically, but she doesn't believe him. Now they are both cross.

. . .

A pity about the nights in bed.

. . .

Everybody knows La Mancha doesn't lie to the north of Madrid, as Marlis claims; all the same, before she comes down to breakfast, he checks it on the map. Not to bring the matter up again—just to make sure.

. . .

They drive in the open car, once he has promised not to speed. There is a difference, after all, between driving and being a passenger. The way he never passes at all (as between Cannes and Saint Raphael), but sticks behind every truck, is, in fact, ridiculous: afterward, he himself thinks how impossible he was.

. . .

He hates his name, Victor, but does not like it either when she calls him Vic, especially when the people at the next table can hear.

. . .

It is his opinion that Europe must and will one day introduce a common currency. Marlis is not convinced, but listens to his arguments and says nothing. Why does that irritate him? It is not the arguments that fail to convince her.

. . .

She has completely recovered her health.

. . .

If she keeps silent, he gives himself another bad mark. Why is he now talking about the asparagus in Alsace (food again!) instead of watching out for the road sign to Montpellier? She puts on her sunglasses, says, "This is the road to Lyons," then, since he doesn't reply, "I thought you wanted Montpellier." He hangs his left arm out of the window to show his unconcern. Shortly afterward a road sign: *Toutes les Directions.* In Alsace, on their first love trip, she had trusted him completely. Another road sign: *Toutes les Directions.* No mistakes yet.

. . .

When he thinks he is being humorous, she usually does not respond; at other times she might suddenly laugh at a remark of his, and he doesn't know why.

. . .

She knots the head scarf, a new one bought in place of the nail file, under her chin; Victor does not notice it till she asks, "Do you like it?" He suddenly says, "You're right," as if she had said something in answer to his remark that he had once driven without her through the desert from Baghdad to Damascus and found it. Now he says, "We're right up shit creek," which surprises Marlis, for it is not the way he usually speaks. He laughs, as if they had come to a halt at the break in the middle of the famous Pont d'Avignon; they are, in fact, in an industrial area confronting a sign: *Passage Interdit.* He changes into reverse, she says, "Don't get jittery." When, after a series of errors (betrayed by the gearbox), he eventually regains the road, which any idiot could have found, Victor has still not said whether he likes her new headscarf.

. . .

She is just naturally intelligent.

. . .

If he could now put on his white hospital coat, things would be different at once; the idea of driving through Provence to Spain in a white hospital coat . . .

. . .

Why is he not talking?

. . .

It is not true that he has never had an accident, only that Marlis doesn't know about it—it was a long time ago. He had been very lucky. He had more or less forgotten it himself. Remembering it now, he looks sideways at Marlis, as if she had just reminded him of it by keeping silent when he passed a *deuxchevaux*.

. . .

What does "plexus" actually mean? He is a surgeon, and it would be funny if he didn't know. All the same he waits for her to say, "Are you sure?" But she is silent. Only when Victor remarks that the shortest route is via Aigues-Mortes does she say, "Are you sure?"

. . .

Marlis is sitting barefoot in the car, since her shoes pinch, but she doesn't mention it. He feels sympathy—instead of just talking.

. . .

Why does he put a hand on her thigh?

. . .

In Antibes he did shout at her, but he can no longer remember

why. Later he thought he had apologized by saying, "All right,"
then—white with rage and not believing himself in the wrong—
"I beg your pardon."

. . .

Whether the flat countryside that so delights Marlis should be
called Provence or Camargue is really neither here nor there.
Why does he insist on Camargue? He could, of course, be right.

. . .

Silence till Aigues-Mortes.

. . .

He manages to park the car in a very narrow space in spite of
her warning, which he does not acknowledge with even a nod.
Without scraping, and at the very first go, too. Without a word.
A hundred yards farther on, nothing but empty parking spaces,
some even in shade. Though Marlis can't have known that,
either. And she says nothing.

. . .

Apéritif by himself beneath plane trees while she looks around
the little town. He suddenly feels as if he is on vacation. This
light beneath the plane trees, this light, etc.

. . .

He has never felt that she owed her life to him. It was an operation that is usually successful. But perhaps she felt it. . . .

. . .

This would be a place to stay in. It's eleven o'clock, too early
for lunch. All the same, a place worth staying in. The old fortress
walls keep off the mistral. When Marlis returns, he will be a
changed man—cheerful, relaxed; it is all his fault, his alone.

. . .

There are times when he would like her to bear his child.

. . .

She can't understand why Victor does such things as in Antibes. First he shouts at her, then suggests a restaurant (three star), Bonne Auberge. She is not impressed by these stars. He insists. Irritable again because his suggestion doesn't thrill her, he leaves her to wander about Antibes by herself for a full hour. What is he doing? When they meet up again, the same old palaver about where they should eat, she pointing out that there are restaurants nearby, why bother about three stars, etc. The district to which he drives her doesn't look like restaurant territory. When she at last asks, "Are you sure?" he drives on without a word, turns off, turns off once again, and there it is: Bonne Auberge. The head waiter leads them to the table on the terrace that the gentleman had personally chosen an hour before. Unfortunately, it is now too cool on the fine terrace. Inside there are painted landscapes, waiters in folk costumes, the food all right though dear, but it doesn't matter. Marlis is nice to him, although he shouted at her an hour ago. She feels sorry for him.

. . .

Mistral is also the name of a poet—Victor knew that. On the other hand, the wind they call "mistral" doesn't come from the sea, as Marlis believes. But never mind. On the other hand, she is, of course, right: *Lettres de mon Moulin*, which he once read in school, is by Alphonse Daudet, not Mistral. But never mind. All she had in fact said was, "Mistral is a poet, you know that."

. . .

His car is a Porsche.

. . .

Beneath the plane trees in Aigues-Mortes: feeling in his jacket to make sure he has not lost his passport. Victor has never lost his passport in his life. The shock of not finding it there . . . but in the same moment he remembers: it is in the car. He is sure of it, remembers exactly where he put it in the glove compartment; but he will check. He is not sure.

. . .

If he had carried through his resolve in the bathroom to end this trip today, they would now be in Lyons, by evening in Basel, though it is so lovely here: this light beneath the plane trees, this light, etc. When she returns he will suggest a walk down to the sea.

. . .

He hopes she will find herself some shoes.

. . .

Beneath the plane trees in Aigues-Mortes: an hour before the accident he wants another coffee. Is he too tired to drive? He praises the light beneath the plane trees, this light, etc. Doves cooing around the statue of Saint Louis. Marlis wants to go on, she is really not hungry, she doesn't even want an apéritif. Now it is Victor who feels there is plenty of time. An old man with three long French loaves under his arm.

. . .

Spain was her idea.

. . .

He doesn't consider himself an egoist. He is only happy when he feels he can make someone else happy. If he doesn't succeed, he is dismayed; he takes everything personally.

. . .

Nobody seeing them from the outside would find anything odd

about her reading *Le Provençal* while he, his long legs stretched across the sidewalk, drinks coffee and waits for the miracle, which would have to come from outside, from the cooing doves perhaps. . . . He would be prepared to marry. Just a question of humor. She asks, "How much longer do you want to sit here?" He replies, "Sorry—you're reading the newspaper, not I." He doesn't mean it quite as it sounds, and the fact that he then, the compulsive cavalier, takes her handbag—well, she is accustomed to that. So no miracle.

. . .

For the first time it is Victor who wants to visit the cloisters. Romanesque. She is not keen.

. . .

They walk arm in arm.

. . .

For the first time it is Victor who keeps stopping. Market with fruit and vegetables. It is touching when Victor says, "There are shoes here"—and obviously still has no idea of what she is looking for.

. . .

Why must one go to Spain?

. . .

He waits in a narrow street. Marlis has forgotten her head scarf, but he is not really waiting for her. What would he be doing if he were alone? When he sees her coming, then again stopping in front of a shop window, he buys a *Herald Tribune* to see what is going on in the world. When after a while he looks up from the newspaper, Marlis has vanished. . . .

. . .

Tourists at lunch.

. . .

Later she says, "Sorry." She has bought an amusing cap. "No," she laughs. "It's for you." Marlis in the best of spirits. When he opens the car door her question: "Or shall I take over now?" He drives. Why always only he? He begs her urgently to let him drive. No way of explaining that now. "Don't you like it?" She means the garish cap. For the first time he is nervous of the road.

. . .

She is a child.

. . .

His passport *is* in the glove compartment.

. . .

"You look so funny!" She has put the cap on his head to stop him looking so serious. He is surprised that Marlis has fastened her seat belt. Without being asked. He leaves the cap on his head as he puts the car in gear, a glance back, so as not to bump into anything. Make no mistakes now . . .

. . .

So that's the last of Aigues-Mortes.

. . .

She has a son who goes to school; she has studied in Paris; she is getting a divorce; she is a woman, not a child.

. . .

The horses in Camargue. Sometimes she says something, sometimes he says something. Luckily little traffic. Then he tries thinking professionally again: When is a person dead? The problem with heart transplants. He catches himself saying, "I must get the oil changed tomorrow," when he should be saying what he is thinking. He is making it too easy for himself.

. . .

As a child she used to ride.

. . .

Driving behind a Belgian trailer without passing: when he does at last pass, he just has time, but it was risky. She says nothing.

. . .

Patients like him: his calmness, his sureness, his confidence, etc.

. . .

Now she is wearing the funny cap. "Everything suits you," he says, but he is looking at the road. Is he even listening? She reads aloud from the *Guide Michelin*, to make him look forward to the cave paintings in Altamira, to stop him thinking only about oil changes, to show him why they are going to Altamira. She means it nicely.

•

. . .

He has always been lucky, compared with other people: in his health and in his profession, in everything, in fact, and not only as an Alpine climber (Piz Buin). . . .

. . .

She says, "Thinking of food again!" He wasn't in fact thinking of anything at all, but watching the road; he was only going to say something or other about Montpellier, because he saw a road sign: Montpellier 12 Km. Better if he'd said nothing.

. . .

Victor escapes with light injuries, cuts on the temple, but has
no memory of a trailer truck. She dies in the ambulance on the
way to the hospital in Montpellier. He cannot even remember
the highway where it happened, where the overturned trailer
now lies between the plane trees; at the inspection he has the
feeling of being here for the first time, at this highway junction
where he is questioned by the police (in French) and learns that
he had the right of way, was therefore not to blame.

. . .

Later he is appointed senior surgeon.

. . .

For a full ten years he never speaks of the accident near Montpellier; he doesn't know how it happened.

. . .

A few acquaintances know something about it.

. . .

He becomes head of a clinic, father of two children, travels a
lot, but never to Spain.

. . .

He knows a doctor shouldn't speak about himself on the eve of
an operation, but all the same he suddenly mentions his accident
near Montpellier in France: "I had the right of way, as I said,
and to that extent was not to blame. . . ." Afterward he says,
"How did we get on to this accident?" The patient doesn't know,
either. Why doesn't he just say good night, then the usual thing:
"You'll sleep, otherwise ring for the night nurse." But he has
already said that, then takes up one of the books from the bedside table, but reads no more than the title. He puts it back on
the bedside table. What he had really wanted to say: Nothing

to worry about, he would be there in the morning, wouldn't operate himself, but he'd be there, no need to worry, etc.

. . .

He never had another accident.

. . .

The patient, obviously disappointed, does not dare ask why the head isn't doing the operation himself.

. . .

Her question: "Are you sure?"

. . .

He never says anything more about the accident.

. . .

Marlis saw the truck, she warned him; he saw the truck, but didn't brake—he had the right of way. It is possible that he even stepped on the gas, to show he was sure. She screamed. The Montpellier police agreed he was quite correct.

VULPERA—TARASP, June

The things one does on a cure! Reading the Neue Zürcher Zeitung (one hundred ninetieth) every day for a week. . . . Can one accuse such a newspaper of lying?

Hotel in the good old style. Nothing extravagant. Elevator too small to take an elevator boy as well, with wooden grill. When you press the button nothing happens for a while, then, when it does get going, it

wobbles. A technical factotum: one can
assume that it has wafted many a highness up-
ward. But bath and toilet are modern. Not
like Hilton Hotels for large wage earners--
these hoteliers know how aristocrats live at
home--like they do here: with simple, reliable, and deferential service, without pomp;
used all their lives, however, to having
carriage doors opened for them and pajamas
laid out on the bed with folded arms, as if
already praying.

Not immediately apparent on the first day:
what they do for a living. Immediately apparent: that they belong to the propertied
classes, even when talk is confined to the
weather, to diet, a son-in-law in Lisbon,
dogs, dead people, etc. The signs: their
right of choice is taken for granted, they
demand without hesitation--nothing unseeming,
just attentions for which they pay suitably,
friendliness makes them friendly; their
certainty that they can only be asked about
what they want. Their air of unquestionable
right. . .

Young people smearing the Zurich court of
justice with red paint, having already succeeded in disrupting the traffic in the
streets. (11 June) The press very grave,
warning the authorities. Only resolute
action by the police can stop the public taking matters into their own hands (against the
young people). "Civic guards." Not a word
about the cause of it: the fact that the
young demonstrators of summer 1968 are being
brought before the courts, whereas the police
culprits of summer 1968 are not to be brought
before the courts, since they cannot be
found. It is something that the mistreatment

of arrested persons is no longer denied—but,
according to the Neue Zürcher Zeitung, enough
has already been said about that.

Walks in the National Park.

One cannot say that their newspaper tells
lies; it just manages three times a day to
get in the way of understanding. Its particular trick is to present the propertied
classes as the people with a sense of responsibility. Not only in finance and industry, but in the army as well. The proprietors are dependent on the workers' strength,
but not on their opinion; on the contrary,
the majority is dependent on the opinion of
the propertied classes, which is what gives
the proprietors their sense of responsibility. It can be seen in practically every
NZZ article, sometimes between the lines.
The page layout is as boring as possible:
that gives the newspaper a serious look,
which is transmitted to the readers—they
feel serious the moment they pick it up.
Their expression as they read it—even more
serious. And afterward they know how un-
serious any report to the contrary would be;
consequently, they have no need of it. Now
and again a bit of character assassination,
humorous or thorough in its condescension,
its nastiness obvious only to those in the
know. The better writers keep strictly to
the facts, so long as these confirm the
paper's opinion, that is to say, they let the
facts do the talking. Particularly in
foreign affairs. Swiss neutrality does not
inhibit the individual citizen's thoughts,
but it does oblige the nation to be careful
in its utterances—and thus to some extent
this newspaper, too, since it is the mouth-
piece of Switzerland. Its stylistic neutral-

ity (Ulbricht is not handled differently in
the reports from any colonel at present in
power in Athens; Brezhnev is never defamed as
an individual; Kiesinger and Strauss are
quoted without comment; some understanding is
shown for the problems of the Italian Communist party; Nixon is not reproached for a
minor withdrawal of troops from Vietnam,
etc.) does sometimes give the reader an idea
of what politics is about: a struggle between
spheres of interest—in foreign countries—
whereas at home it is more a matter of public
ethics ("Stop the rot!") Since local matters, possibly familiar to the readers, are
not necessarily suited to the objective style
that allows facts to speak for themselves,
opinions must now and again be steered in the
right direction by adjectival constructions:
"irresponsible," "left-wing intellectual,"
"similar to methods abroad," "wire-pullers,"
"brawlers and the brains behind them," "so-
called progressive," "those secretly pulling
the strings," "mischief," "hooligans and
loiterers," "intriguers," "at the taxpayers'
expense," "the seeming innocuousness of the
well-known left-wing intellectual," "destructive," "un-Swiss," etc. An account differing
from the newspaper's own bias is "biased."
Frequently, too, an amusing passage: "Unfortunately, it has been shown that with tolerance and patience—contrary to original
expectations—the desired goal can in fact no
longer be achieved." This not only defines
the nature of tolerance, but also lets one
know exactly what is considered desirable.
The art of the refined lie consists in con-
veying that the opinion which three times
daily confirms the power of the proprietors
is not a class opinion—it is the only possible ethical standpoint, and consequently in
the interests of the majority.

National Park: though the human beings stay
on the pegged-out paths, the marmots whistle
and take cover, the stags keep to the other
side of the valley, the chamois only in
telescope range.

Daimler-Benz announce huge profits. Bonus
shares (quite legal) for the shareholders:
one major holder gains 140 million. To maintain the industrial peace that has made this
profit possible, the employees are also to
benefit: a single payment of 320 marks for
each worker.

Belles lettres: when people whose social
opponent one is find it possible to introduce themselves unreservedly as admirers.

The ancient Greek idea of Hades: an elderly
couple from Zollikon playing checkers, somewhere else a family with a chaste daughters,
in the corner a fat Finn (reading Malraux),
always on his own, others being brought together by boredom, drawing their chairs close
after a few tentative bows. What do they
talk about? From the next table I hear the
best place to go shopping. While they drink
coffee as in life. Later in the bar: the
best place to drink in Hong Kong. But then a
lady knows a Jewish joke: laughter as in
life. The wives get along better: their
sexual attraction has deserted them, too,
but they talk more and are livelier, sitting
up straight in their chairs. A man without a
cane laboriously dragging one shoe after the
other; one is constantly on edge--what if he
meets a step? A wife, tending her life's
companion after a stroke, is wearing jewelry
like loot, pounds of it, and now and again
telling him things he used to know. The
couple from Zollikon, having danced a slow

waltz together, have gone off to bed. Con-
noisseurs at the next table: I hear they
collect Persian carpets--valuables that
retain their value. It is ten o'clock. Tomorrow is also another day. Nothing will
change.

The way they listen to the news before dinner, the men in dark suits, the ladies with
fur wraps, not listening: Brezhnev curses
China, Husak is still purging, but the Czech
writers still hold firm, even the Czech
workers seem to be on the side of freedom,
Pompidou is forming his cabinet, Israel goes
on retaliating, in the Rhine fish are dying,
the Swiss government to investigate, and
finally the weather--not all good news, but
on the whole a confirmation: Such is life.
In principle carrying on as the proprietors
want it.

"The City Council is not prepared to tolerate
further transgressions. . . . The people's
right to express their opinions freely and to
hold demonstrations will not be affected. . . .
A directive from the City Council gives the
police precise instructions on their method
of proceeding." Beside that an agency
report: "The motorized water cannons will be
filled not only with ordinary water, a chemical substance will be added that will make
the water even wetter. If the situation
becomes more serious, flamethrowers as used
by the army will be brought in. These,
carried by policemen on their backs, will be
filled with water and liquid teargas. According to the police, the chemical addition
to the water has already been tried out in
Germany."

Ofenpass: where in 1945 I had to keep a hut

warm for German deserters, tails low in
capitulation. Schuls railway station: the
truckloads of survivors from Theresienstadt
concentration camp. These souvenirs everywhere, even when I don't mention them.

How does a majority come into being (not only
election majorities, but public opinion in
matters never put to the vote)? It is not
only the mailman, a state employee, who has a
family; the professor, a state employee, also
has a family, and in addition to that a
social task—research, depending on financial
aid. Should he run the risk of losing this
aid through a signature or a speech? One
can't expect it. Yes-men? The individual
reacts to the prevailing social climate; it
is risky, at the very least, to go against
public opinion. Usually there is nothing to
be gained by it, little chance that more will
come from personal intervention than reprisals against the one who intervenes. However, the greater the number of grovelers in
a country, the more pampered and touchy the
ears of the rulers; a legally valid referendum of students is already being described
as "coercion" (NZZ). Anything that runs
counter to prevailing opinion is scandalous.
In consequence, I become more cautious. Why
make life more difficult for myself? In
consequence, I give in to social pressure; in
doing so the individual easily falls into
the error of imagining that what in himself
is caution and compliance (or at best apathy)
is in everyone else an honest view. The sum
total of all yes-men, trying not to make life
more difficult for themselves, produces the
bogey of public opinion, which the rulers
then put into words. They have the instruments: schools, press, television, university, church. Just because it is basically

not the expression of an individual conviction, but the result of social pressure, public opinion reacts indignantly to any contrary conviction; the very idea of the
conviction seems to the majority basically
subversive: "Stop the rot." Once the grovelers find themselves in the majority, they
no longer need to grovel and become collec-
tively aggressive: civic guards. Under-
standably, they do not want to lose the
reward of their lifelong cautiousness.
Public opinion, as the consensus of everyone
corrupted by social pressure, is always moralistic: it must compensate. That is inherent in any system. The fear of reprisals
molts into a point of view. The majority
does not, of course, take over power: prevented by its very point of view, its understanding with the people in power, it simply
relieves the people in power of the responsibility for reprisals. Law and order, that
can be left to the bars. If some teacher
with different ideas needs to be thrown out,
the rulers need hardly worry: the majority—
that majority which the rulers built for
themselves in a democratic way—will take
care of it, through reprisals. One likes to
call the people in Switzerland "sovereign,"
because the majority decides. But how
sovereign is the majority?

A walk through the National Park.

Much to laugh at, as usual, when Friedrich
Dürrenmatt prepares the conversational menu.
. . . Recently it was Genghis Khan, fresh from
the library, lavishly garnished with Chinese
dynasties: history spiced with tall stories
and grilled on wit. Today we had The Naked
Ape, equally delicious: man on the spit of
zoology, roasted on facts (blood pressure

during coitus: 200), and larded with home-
grown speculations. It is unwise to come up
with conversational wishes of one's own:
the chef's own choice is always the most
delicious. Not long ago, in the hospital in
Berne, it was Proust, soaked in bitter,
sleepless nights, served with fresh memory
and carried cheerfully flaming to the bedside. That was four-star stuff! Such things
can't be repeated subsequently for the benefit of one's wife. So no Proust today--not
even served cold--but The Naked Ape again,
this time boiled with jokes about doctors
and tidbits from Konolfingen (Dürrenmatt's
native village), artfully arranged, and with
it a calf's head of relevant literary criticism, peppered with quotations. With Veltliner to wash it down. Afterward he gave me
the pocketbook to which he owes all his
knowledge. I shall take care not to read it.
Firstly, because what he makes of it is
always better, and secondly, because he is no
longer fascinated by things that others already know. Recently the conversation turned
to a Godard film that he had not seen; he
brought it around to another film that he
had seen, but, when he found out that we knew
it, too, he abandoned it and began to describe a Japanese film that nobody but himself had seen. He must always be one step
ahead, then he is invigorating company indeed. In earlier times it was astronomy
with which for years he held me fascinated.
I took a fat book he lent me to a tent in
Corsica and read nothing else for three
weeks. When I next saw him I had at least
mastered the vocabulary, and felt better
armed for conversations on astronomy. He
said, "What I find really interesting is bio-
chemistry." He needs my ignorance, and there
is no lack of that. I have retained my

interest in astronomy, as he has, too, of
course, but we hardly ever talk of it. By
the time I've reached the supernovae he is
long past the pulsars. Once in Neuenburg
Theo Otto, the scenic designer, began to
display a detailed interest in architecture.
Friedrich Dürrenmatt listened for a long
time, but then became gloomy: he suggested a
game of bowls, and won hands down. Next day,
when he again suggested a game of bowls, he
was less lucky, and the match was abandoned;
he wanted an apéritif, and had much to say
about dramatic techniques. He is always the
giver. As recently, too, in Berne, with a
very old bottle of Latour Bordeaux, which
the nurse uncorked for me, the visitor, I
preserving, as she did, an earnest hospital
manner, while Friedrich Dürrenmatt laughed.
Over a doctor's mistake, for example: he
told the story without complaining, in a
spirit of pure comedy. This is more than
mere humor. We have known each other over
twenty years. It is not true that he cannot
listen. When the landlord in Schuls sits
down at our table to tell us something (such
as, for example, how the locals fleece someone like the Aga Khan) and then stays on just
to chat, Friedrich Dürrenmatt is a herculean
listener; it all depends on whom he is with.

THINGS TO BE THANKFUL FOR

No institution (like the income tax authorities) demands a
yearly or half-yearly return of things to be thankful for. . . .
Yesterday on the street, some way off, I saw a man to whom I
owe much, very much, in fact, though it was all a long time ago.
He seems to be aware that I can never rid myself of the feeling
of gratitude toward him; it is really no longer a feeling, simply
an awareness. Lifelong. I had the feeling that he saw me before I saw him, but he kept on walking as if he had not recog-

nized me. What is my awareness of gratitude to him? I could have caught up with him, but I didn't, and felt guilty because I didn't. Not only had he made it possible for me to study architecture: I also owe to him my appreciation of Schopenhauer, Mozart, and Beethoven, Nietzsche, psychology, Riemenschneider, Oswald Spengler, Bruckner, Khmer art and much besides, including the Engadine. True, the suits and coats he passed on when he had done with them, though still in good condition, were always a bit too large, the sleeves in particular too long. . . .

If there were some institution to which one had to submit a return of things to be thankful for within the space of a week, I should add:

a.
my mother

b.
the fact that I very early made contact with a Jewish, a very German Jewish, person

c.
the early death of my father

d.
the experience of actual poverty

e.
that I was not ordered to Stalingrad or to join the Reichsschrifttumskammer (the National Socialist writers' organization)

f.
untroubled health

g.
my meeting with the publisher Peter Suhrkamp

h.
my meeting with Brecht

i.
having children of my own

j.
that I stopped studying German philology

k.
all women—yes, on the whole, all of them

l.
the Zurich theater in Kurt Hirschfeld's days

m.
pleasure in food

n.
having practiced for a time as an architect; what was valuable about it—my experience with building contractors, employers, workers

o.
the tug between the local forms of speech and the formal written language

p.
a Rockefeller grant

q.
my late success

r.
friendships with younger colleagues

s.
financial independence in late years, that is, in the knowledge that it is not the general rule

t.
my neighbors in the village

u.
periods of a bad memory for my own errors and omissions

v.
the companion living with me

w.
the fact that ambition declines

x.
dreams, even bad ones

y.

all sorts of good luck with the car

z.

that I have a passport

There is no institute interested in recording our feelings of thankfulness, their present strength, their increase and decrease, etc. Probably one would fill out the form (A to Z) rather differently every year.

21 July

Landing on the moon (Armstrong and Aldrin).

News of a dog, lost in Calabria, finding its owners in Turin after nine weeks on the road. Somebody from the City Youth Department reports: A fifteen—year—old orphan girl left the village of Cognac, France, in a distraught condition after being raped by her employer; she went on foot to Basel, where an aunt was living; there she was raped by the aunt's husband. A persistent woman, whom I have never met before, asks for advice: her brother is shortly to be sent to prison for robbing a jeweler's shop, perhaps also smuggling drugs, and I am known to be against injustice; her brother, basically an artist, too, will not be able to stand five years in prison. Nina, our cat, has had another kitten—and eaten it.

OUTLINE OF AN ACCIDENT (II)

In the night, great gusts of wind. No rain, but it sounds like it. A broken shutter sounds the alarm. The dry trees rustling. He is awake. No reason to get out of bed. The windows are holding. What do a couple of garden chairs, broken anyway, matter? No lightning, just gusts of wind, probably it is clear and starlit above the sea. What can possibly happen? The car is safe in the garage. No swaying lamps, no earthquakes. Later the electricity fails. A vision of the island being swamped by the sea, the house alone among the olives on the hill. Later he sits barefoot in the living room, where he falls asleep again, alone in the house, which is standing firm. The morning is blue and normal. A parasol has capsized and broken, the island is not swamped. He cannot remember all the things he imagined during the night. Here and there branches on the dry ground. He breakfasts in his pajamas, wondering who can be got to repair the shutter. Later he picks up the branches from the dry ground, before getting dressed, barefoot. The telephone has also been cut off, as he now discovers. Later the mail arrives, showing that life is going on as usual. Solid ground beneath his feet. He has the feeling there are more urgent things to be done. Thoughts of selling the house. He does not know why. Nothing hangs together: his wife, waiting for his phone call, the parasol, the letters, the blue and normal day, his shoes, which he ought to put on. Around noon he goes barefoot down to the beach. Memories of the wind in the night and the highway near Montpellier, the chalk marks on the concrete, the tourists, the village, no cause for alarm. So he goes for a swim. No solid ground beneath his feet, the sky cloudless above the sea. If for once he could only know! He swims out as far as his strength holds, and it holds until the land can no longer be seen.

SPIEGEL, 28 July 1969

"In 1965 there were about 2,380 employers and owners of capital with an average monthly income of 190,000 marks. In the same year one third of all wage and salary earners had a monthly income of 500 marks at most: earning in twelve months as much as the millionaires in twenty-three hours."

ADVERTISEMENT IN A SWISS BANK

"Is it true that it is always only the rich who get richer? This was a theory put forward in the nineteenth century. It has been shown to be wrong. It is a very long time since society was divided into a few rich people (always growing richer) and a host of poor people (steadily growing poorer). Under today's conditions practically every working person can make a fortune—if he has a mind to.

And compared with previous times and conditions practically all of us are rich."

STICKER IN ANOTHER BANK

"Do you hate cash?"

QUESTIONNAIRE

1.
Do you hate cash?

2.
Why?

3.
Have you ever had to live without cash?

4.
If you meet a man in swimming trunks about whom you know nothing, how is it that after a few words (not about money) you know he is a rich man?

5.
How much money would you like to have?

6.
Assume you are poor and have a rich friend who is willing to help you, and he gives you a considerable sum of money (for example, to enable you to study) and now and again some of his clothes, still in good condition, which do you find it easier to accept?

7.
Have you ever stolen:
a. cash?
b. objects (a paperback from a stand, flowers from a stranger's garden, a first edition, chocolate from a camp site, stray ballpoint pens, a souvenir of a dead person, hotel towels, etc.)?
c. an idea?

8.

So long as you have no fortune and only a modest income, rich people will be reluctant to talk about money in your presence, but they will talk all the more readily about problems that cannot be solved by money, for example, art. Do you regard this as tact?

9.

What do you feel about inheritance:
a. if you are likely to come into one?
b. if you are not?
c. when you look at a baby, knowing that, however it turns out, it will own half a factory, or a house, a plot of land that is not threatened by inflation, a vacation home in Sardinia, five tenement houses on the city outskirts?

10.

Have you any savings? And if so:

11.

Explain by what right the state bank decides the value of the money you have earned and saved, and for whose benefit your savings have suddenly evaporated.

12.

Assuming that your background is simple and you suddenly find yourself in possession of a large income, so that money is no longer of great significance to you; do you feel you are the same person as before? If the answer is yes; do your former friends think so, too, or do they feel that money must be of great significance, since it has deformed you as a person?

13.

What is the present cost of a pound of butter?

14.

If you were in a position to live from interest on shares, would the fact that you continue working, even though you could live on your interest, make you feel less like an exploiter?

15.

Are you frightened of the poor?

16.
Why not?

17.
Assume you are a great benefactor, that is to say, you pass on to people whom you personally admire a share of the considerable interest you earn from the work of others: can you understand the public esteem in which you are held as benefactor, and your own easy conscience?

18.
What do you not do for money?

19.
Timon of Athens once placed dishes containing nothing but water in front of his friends, in order to test their friendship; he discovered only what he already knew, but professed to be bitterly disappointed, claiming that they came only on account of his wealth and were no true friends. Do you find his condemnation of others justified? Obviously, wealthy Timon of Athens thought friendship could be bought.

20.
Would you like to have a rich wife?

21.
How do you, as a wealthy person, explain the enjoyment you get from ostentatiously denying yourself something you could easily afford (a yacht, for example), and your almost childish delight when you manage to buy something cheap—so cheap, in fact, that anybody could have afforded it? And why are you at the same time so keen on acquiring unique objects such as icons, swords, Ming porcelain, etchings, the works of dead masters, historical coins, autographs, Tibetan prayer mats, etc.?

22.
What do you dislike about the newly rich:
a. that they get along without a coat of arms?
b. that they talk about money?
c. that they are not dependent on you?

23.
How do you justify to yourself your own wealth:

a. by calling it an act of God?
b. by telling yourself that you owe it exclusively to your own proficiency, that is to say, by assuming that other abilities which do not produce income must be inferior ones?
c. through dignified behavior?
d. by telling yourself that it is only the wealthy who are able to get the economy working for the benefit of all (spirit of enterprise)?
e. by acts of charity?
f. by your higher level of education, which you owe to an inherited fortune or to a foundation?
g. through an ascetic style of living?
h. through conscientious observance of all conventional requirements that do not concern the bourgeois profit system, through an inner acceptance of your position, through artistic sensibility, good taste, etc.?
i. by the amount you pay in taxes?
j. by generous hospitality?
k. by telling yourself that since the beginning of history there have always been rich and poor and that is how it always will be; in other words, you have no need to make excuses at all?

24.
If you were to become poor again, not of your own volition (like Saint Francis) but by force of circumstances, would you— knowing their attitudes from having lived among them on equal terms—be as forbearing toward wealthy people as formerly— disarmed by respect?

25.
Have you ever taken a bank note bearing the portrait of a great poet or a great general—their glory being passed from hand to hand—and set light to it, then asked yourself, as you contemplate the ashes, what has become of its guaranteed value now?

    BERZONA, August

    Visit by two very young girls who, scarcely
    seated at the granite table, ask their ques-
    tion: how to achieve freedom. One of them,
    Barbara, has just been discussing it with her

father (a teacher); the other, Verena, cannot
or will not discuss it with her father (a
banker), "or they will put me in a home."
What both want: "absolute independence, without being a burden to others." The banker's
daughter sees only one way: to go to Amsterdam or London, and disappear without trace,
without father's money or work. The teacher's daughter also wants to repudiate false
values, not to become a slave to money, "but
to do something meaningful"; she wants to
remain at school, to become a teacher, but to
preserve her independence by refusing to be
talked into things she does not need.
Verena: "And that simply can't be done."
Barbara: "But one must have a bit of money."
Verena: "Then you're back where you started."
Barbara: "Not if I don't <u>want</u> to be. <u>I</u> don't
need a tape recorder." Verena: "I can give
up my tape recorder whenever I want." Barbara: "What will you live on if you don't
work?" Verena: "I don't hate my father, but
I must get out. He just doesn't understand."
Barbara: "As you heard, my father is also
against you doing nothing at all." Verena:
"Mine doesn't even know what I am talking
about. He thinks I'm very crazy." Etc.
Discussion over raspberry juice. What would
I think right? Both, different in origin and
temperament, are united in disgust against
the prosperity of a society that forces
prosperity on them. Barbara: "Just doing
nothing, that's no object in life." Verena:
"You know what sort of life my father has in
mind for me." Barbara: "You don't have to
follow that. When you've finished school, do
whatever you think right, but at least you'll
have learned something. You'll go to pieces
if you do nothing." Verena: "I'll work when
I need a bit of money, but I just want to

make do with very little. As little as possible." Barbara: "I, too." Verena: "I asked
her father what's wrong with doing nothing,
and now I ask you too, Herr Frisch." After
my reply: "And if I drive about in a sports
car and learn about art and get married, I
shall still be a parasite and still fritter
away my life. And it is my life, after all.
You said that, too. I feel in a commune one
does at least get to know oneself."

29 September

Bundestag elections and appointment of
Chancellor in West Germany. The so-called
Christian parties, which since the setting
up of the Federal Republic have governed
alone (in the end with a former National
Socialist as Chancellor) have lost votes,
so that Willy Brandt, Social Democrat, becomes Chancellor. Consternation among the
former rulers. Like landowners who can't
bring themselves to realize that divine right
has at last been abolished even in Germany:
lordly in their arrogant assumption that only
people of their sort can rule, then dismayed
by the news that the stable hands really do
want to take over the mansion, subsequently
offended when the attempt at bribery fails
(Kiesinger offered the Free Democrats six
ministerial posts instead of three, the most
they would be entitled to, and, ignoring the
voting rights of the majority, promised rene-
gades that they would be fixed up at the next
election with the necessary constituencies),
then finally the smile of defeat: "The
Social Democrats cheated their way into
office," "greedy for power," "a government
without a policy," etc.

NOTES FOR A MEMBERS' HANDBOOK

If his political outlook has always been conservative, the doomed man feels satisfaction in not being really upset by international developments. The daily news simply confirms his political outlook: he never expected much to change. In commenting on world events, he is never gloomy, age gives him an aura of wisdom. He has never been under any illusions, and consequently he is not obliged to think differently from when he was young forty or fifty years ago: to this extent the conservative retains his sense of youth longer than the revolutionary.

The reason why an old man who has retained his revolutionary fervor seems at most endearing, but never convincing: younger people cannot conceive that their own manner of speaking might one day, in the light of history, be shown up as mere pathos. Better at a meeting concerned with revolution not to allow such apostle figures on the platform; they provide a ridiculous and inhibiting demonstration of how manners of speaking become dated.

The foredoomed man feels a certain temptation to become a liberal—owing to the fact that, unlike young people, he has now learned to live with his mistakes. He does not, however, have to yield to the temptation. The more conscious of his mistakes a man is, the more likely he is to seek political power, which provides him with a mantle of infallibility. The great reformers have nearly always been foredoomed men.

In numerous cases a political outlook has been the result of a natural rebellion against the authority of a father. It is not until this father is in his grave that one can see to what extent a person's political outlook is in line with his true character, that is to say, to what extent it is a political outlook at all. Age sifts.

A doomed man with left-wing beliefs tends to find himself bored by new pamphlets, brochures, manifestos, student newspapers, etc., in spite of his approval from a party standpoint; he feels things that teach him nothing beyond what he already knows by heart to be hopeless.

The difference between a young man and a foredoomed man when they speak in political terms about the future: one gets the impression with the latter that he is really interested in the future.

The political temperament is, generally speaking, far less prevalent than democracy supposes. Most people consider they are being political when, in order to be sociable, they make use of a political vocabulary. As doomed men they are almost certainly disappointed with their lives—not politically, however, only privately.

People who have been exploited all their lives do not on the whole become with age more progressive in their political outlook (though they now have nothing to fear except an old people's home). On the contrary, however much a man may rail against the exploitation to which he has been subjected all this life, one can still detect in him a sort of envy when he hears that the conditions he knew are now about to be changed.

True of the doomed man, though not yet of the foredoomed man: with the disappearance of his capacity for enjoyment, politics becomes the last sphere in which a man can feel superior just because he is old. He is scarcely ever swayed by impulse; his hardened brain is scarcely subject to irritation; political decisions come easily to him—not because he is ignorant, but because he is hardened. He functions like a machine; he neither enjoys risks, nor does he fear them; he has already survived this or that error of judgment; his diminishing imaginative powers permit him to consider things calmly without being fearful of the consequences; he cannot consider the lives of other people so very important, so decisive a factor; he himself has very little life left to lose, and so his suitability as head of state is constantly increasing (gerontocracy).

Old men as heads of state enjoy a conspiracy of silence; though their subordinates may know from their own experience what old age does to a man, they never apply this certain knowledge to heads of state.

In contrast to the worker, whose single asset, his ability to work, diminishes for physiological reasons; in contrast to the intellectual, who early recognizes his regression (and the more intelligent he is, the earlier will he recognize it); in contrast to the artist, who has to face the knowledge that all creative skill evidently has something to do with hormones, the politician least fears the onset of old age. Presumably this is because political power, though no longer creative, can still by its very nature achieve the greatest effect.

1969

"People used to be categorized according to the color of their skin, the width of their noses, the skull formation, and the body build. Modern ethnology is less interested in such outward signs; it has been discovered that people can be far more precisely distinguished through the ideas and values that are particularly important to them. In our case, the idea of individual freedom within a self-chosen community occupies first place."
(p. 15)

"The social defense of our country consists in maintaining healthy social conditions, so that for all individuals within the free state life is worth living, and an opponent seeking ways of rousing the people and undermining political order finds no vulnerable places to attack."
(p. 31)

"In the very midst of peace, long before it comes to a violent confrontation, the enemy works unceasingly to sow suspicion and discord, to destroy our natural self-confidence, and to sap our inner powers of resistance."
(p. 145)

"We have taken all precautions that lie within our power under peace conditions. We can look danger squarely in the face. We are prepared. / Those out to destroy us are systematically attempting to sow doubt and fear. We do not believe them. / We are not alarmed by so-called scientific theories that predict the downfall of nations, civilizations, even the whole world. Nobody can know what the future holds. We remain skeptical. / Our life and our destiny lie in the hands of God. He alone decides our future. Those who believe in him feel no fear."
(p. 146)

"Switzerland reacts as a strong and healthy organism reacts to infection."
(p. 152)

"The enemy uses all means to break down our inner strength. . . . All that we hear, see, or read we examine carefully to see whether there might be something in it. We believe nothing unless we know from where it comes and who is disseminating it. . . . We do not allow ourselves to be impressed by things learned only from certain newspapers or books, foreign radio, films, and television."
(p. 175)

"In times of peace Switzerland has no capital punishment. Since in times of emergency it is a matter of national security and the lives of civilians and fighting soldiers, we cannot in such circumstances do without capital punishment. . . . Only drastic measures can save our country from dire peril."
(p. 186)

"Doing one's duty in the interests of the whole nation means standing firm in times of war, even when many things go contrary to expectation."
(p. 191)

"The aggressor's policy is based on the following pattern: A political party is founded as an outer framework. This does not need to be large. It relies on a small core of reliable and, above all, ruthless members. The aim is not primarily to gain power through democratic elections. When the time is ripe, things can be helped along by means of terrorism and a minor *coup d'état.* The party must retain the semblance of legality. . . . In countries with a high standard of living it is not easy to win the support of the masses; consequently, one must seek out the discontented elements. Intellectuals make good decoys and advertisements. . . ."
(p. 228)

"We respect scientists and artists without regard to their political opinions. We know, however, that totalitarian systems make no distinction between politics and cultural activities."
(p. 231)

"The enemy, who scorns all religious faiths, does not scruple to use biblical quotations for propaganda purposes."
(p. 235)

"The enemy is out to win followers."
(p. 230)

"He is not succeeding."
(p. 231)

"The enemy is trying to lull us to sleep."
(p. 238)

"We are not asleep."
(p. 239)

"The enemy is trying to scare us."
(p. 240)

"We shall give him no opportunity."
(p. 241)
"The enemy is trying to weaken our economy."
(p. 244)
"We are not taken in."
(p. 245)
"He is driving a wedge between the people and the authorities."
(p. 256)
"People and authorities stand shoulder to shoulder."
(p. 257)
"At this stage of the struggle newspapers, radio, and television still remain our most important weapons. But beware! The enemy, if it cannot intimidate them, will try to infiltrate them."
(p. 259)
"A small nation cannot be assailed with the weapons of revolutionary war as long as it remains inwardly resolute and strong. Switzerland reacts to the overthrow of a neighboring state swiftly and firmly, but without panic."
(p. 263)
"He surrounds Switzerland."
(p. 266)
"We curl up like a hedgehog."
(p. 267)
"He draws the knot tight."
(p. 268)
"Switzerland takes no orders from foreign countries."
(p. 269)

"We hold together and remain strong. We place our trust in our Federal Councils for a complete period of office. Government crises such as occur in other countries, destroying the people's confidence and depriving the country of an effective government, are unknown here. There are far fewer weak places to probe. Politically we are a discriminating and valiant people. Each of us has his weapon and his ammunition at home. . . . Bloodless revolution is impossible. We shall fight under all circumstances."

(p. 271)

"Following the occupation of the greater part of our country, Swiss people will come together somewhere in a foreign land and form a Swiss Resistance Movement. Among these people will be surviving members of the government and the confederations, senior army officers who have escaped from captivity, parliamentarians, party and trade union leaders and representatives of the women's organizations. They will form a government in exile, based on an emergency constitution. For the first time people

will listen to Radio Free Switzerland."
(p. 280)

"Shortly afterward, millions of leaflets will be found in Switzerland, having been dropped from rockets. These will say: 'Men and women of Switzerland! We are not yet strong enough, and the international situation does not as yet permit us to pursue active resistance. This situation may last a long time. The watchword meanwhile is: Grit your teeth and keep silent.' "
(p. 282)

"Do nothing foolish. / In Buchgraben drunken soldiers broke into the church and desecrated it. They shouted and bawled, smashed pictures and ornaments and fired at the crucifix. A man living nearby was seized with fury. He fetched his rifle, which he had hidden under a haystack, and fired at the miscreants, injuring one of the occupation troops. One the following day the commanding officer of the occupying unit summoned a police company of the party militia to Buchgraben. All the men were assembled in front of the church and machine-gunned. The women and children were driven out and the village set on fire."
(p. 286)

"Resistance is not served by emotional outbursts of anger; it requires clear-headed, sober planning."
(p. 287)

"Finally they (the occupation forces) go to work on the Church. Religion is not actually forbidden, but its adherents are discriminated against. Religious instruction is banned in the schools. The training of priests is suspended, so that many communities are without a spiritual adviser."
(p. 289)

"Keep the banner of spiritual freedom flying. / Two writers of the younger generation and a woman journalist are the focal point of a massive show trial organized by the occupation forces. Before the invasion they belonged to the avant-garde and enjoyed a European reputation. Because they often wrote cynically about the conditions in Switzerland, they were thought to be in sympathy with the ideological ideas of the present occupying power. After the invasion, the occupying power's head of cultural affairs attempted, by offering them well-paid positions in the cultural commission, to yoke the two writers and the woman journalist to his propaganda wagon. . . . Under the new order they remained true to their mission of telling the truth, as they had also done under the old order. They were found guilty of endangering state security and sentenced to long terms of imprisonment."
(p. 290)

"The example is followed. Everyone knows now what he has to do.

The cultural bait dangled by the occupying power is ignored. Each stands firm for truth: mothers, teachers, churchmen, writers. . . . No one collaborates."
(p. 291)
"Many Swiss men and women are shot or deported to concentration camps. Villages are destroyed. But these sacrifices are not in vain: every blow against the enemy brings us closer to freedom. Every person who falls in the struggle has given his life for his country and for freedom just as much as a soldier on the front line. The resistance government has pledged itself to take care of his relatives—in devious ways as long as the country is occupied, openly once it has been liberated."
(p. 259)
"It may happen that, when the counter offensive is launched from the Alpine regions, the officer commanding the Swiss Resistance Army will issue a leaflet instructing the Swiss population as follows: 'Men and women of Switzerland! The hour of liberation has come. The armies of liberation are advancing from the Alpine regions and from foreign soil. In a few days we shall be at your side. . . . Do not commit any hostile acts against Swiss citizens whom you suspect of collaboration with the enemy. Many of them were our secret agents. . . .' "
(p. 299)
"We have conjured up this picture of war so that we can familiarize ourselves with the realities of it in our imaginations. Only in this way can we become inwardly strong and face danger without fear of collapse."
(p. 300)
EMERGENCY PACK
(p. 304)
In rucksacks, stored at home within easy reach: hard-wearing, warm, and rain-resistant clothing, underwear, spare socks and stockings, headgear, scarf and towel (protection against rays), handkerchiefs, boots, slippers, blanket or sleeping bag, toilet articles, toilet paper, gas mask, goggles, spare glasses for wearers of spectacles, flashlights with spare batteries, sewing materials, first-aid kit, string, shoe laces, safety pins, candles and matches, mess kit, camp stove, pocket knife and cutlery, radio with spare batteries, plastic cloths.
 Emergency rations for two days in air- or gas-tight packs, consisting of:
 Light concentrated foodstuffs such as crispbread, rusks, canned soup, processed cheese, dehydrated meat, canned meat and fish, chocolate, sugar, tea, instant coffee, dried fruit, milk powder or condensed milk.

Small case containing:

Personal papers, ration cards, insurance policies, health card, professional certificates, money and bonds, civil defense book, Red Cross identity badges for children.

SHELTER PROVISIONS

(p. 305)

For use in war and under radioactive conditions:

. . .

Foodstuffs should be stored in the shelter in a dry and ray-proof place, in their original packings, plastic bags, or metal containers. They should be used occasionally and exchanged yearly or according to instructions on the package. The supply of special store packs is at present under investigation. More detailed information concerning these will be given at the proper time in the press and on radio and television.

PATRIOTIC SONGS

(p. 314)

. . .

(From a book entitled *Zivilverteidigung* ["Civil Defense"] commissioned by the Bundesrat and published by the Federal Department of Justice and Police. This handy-sized book, bound in a lasting linen cover, is being distributed free of charge to all Swiss households, in all four Swiss languages. All the same, there have been protests; some people have returned this official attempt at brain softening by mail, while others are driving with trucks to the Bundeshaus in Berne and dumping the trash on the square outside.)

JAPAN

No secret—but how do I explain it exactly? Departure from Copenhagen airport in daylight; Greenland beneath the clouds, one learns it from the loudspeaker; it just does not get dark; an hour in the Arctic Circle; the half light can mean either morning or evening, and I do not know where the north is, or if it is now today or yesterday; the mountains of Alaska, but the sun is never where I expect it to be; on the clocks in Anchorage it is simply noon; then we fly on, but now backwards in time; again hours of nothing but cloud. I write a letter to you until suddenly it is there: Fuji, its white peak in a blue sky as on all the posters; Japan also obscured by cloud; once more fasten your seat belts. . . . A month later, as the airplane flies over Vietnam (they do not announce that on the loudspeaker), it is night, and

night in Bombay, a warm night, still night in Athens, and as we
land in Zurich the sun is just rising—punctually in the east,
from where I have come. Talk about it! That is what I am doing;
the journey suddenly begins to make sense.

Read the newspapers and concluded there was
nothing really happening. Reassured, went to
work: another attempt at a play. . . . In the
evening the TV news confirms that nothing has
happened: more shooting around Suez, some
fatalities; the Vietnam conference in Geneva.
One knows all that. Finally the weather
forecast: warm front moving as usual, forecast for Thursday and Friday. Afterward
again the feeling that nothing is happening,
nothing at least of which I have not the
slightest inkling . . .
  Reading:
Ten years of revolution in Cuba. Dates. It
all begins on 25 November 1956. Embarkation
in the Mexican port of Tuxpan, a yacht with
eighty-two revolutionaries on board crosses
the Gulf completely unnoticed. They land on
the beach of Las Coloradas in Cuba (Oriente
Province) on 2 December 1956. They are
spotted and scattered; on 5 December 1956
there remains only a group of twelve parti-
sans, intent on liberating Cuba. At the
time, presumably, I read newspaper stories of
bandits, of the legitimate government being
in control of the situation; and three years
later, in 1959, almost certainly on the front
page, I read of the flight of Batista. At
some time or other the first pictures appeared of the bearded bandit. (I wonder
while reading what I was doing in 1959.) At
intervals a bit more news from Cuba: executions. Thus the name of Castro became fixed
in one's mind. Obviously a ferocious dicta-
tor, this time a Communist one; hence the

American boycott against Cuba, all made comprehensible through commentaries—Castro
nationalizing everything, but the cultivated
land (tobacco, sugar) belongs mostly to
Americans. Castro talks of long-term com-
pensation, but no guarantee that Cuba will
remain a profit colony; American investments
threatened, confiscations by force, the free
world in peril. Now and again further news,
which confirms rather than surprises: the
catastrophic economic situation due to communism, terrorist acts. Gradually one gets the
picture. Nothing new. Once only do we hold
our breath: Kennedy orders the U.S. Navy to
open fire if the Soviet rocket transporters
continue heading toward Cuba; Khrushchev
takes the pressure off. We breathe again.
But Cuba is now reckoned a danger in the
world. . . . I ask myself how long I have
known what has been happening in Cuba. Certainly not only from today. But in 1956,
when it all started with twelve men in
Oriente, one could have had no idea, not even
in the three years of guerrilla warfare. I
ask myself if anything is happening today of
whose significance I can have no inkling.
Was today a historical date?

1970

BERZONA

Is the telephone being tapped? And if so, is
there any point in it? That is a question
best discussed on the telephone.

LUNCH IN THE WHITE HOUSE, 2 May 1970

The officer sitting watchfully in the anteroom is as friendly as a
concierge satisfied with our passes; we are announced. The
black taxi driver had, on the other hand, seemed sullen when we
told him our destination. We have to wait. The officer looks
bored, his cap on the table, a revolver in his belt. I notice that
I cannot sit down: I am tensed up, though my curiosity, now I
am here, is less than I had persuaded myself it would be. A female secretary goes into the washroom; an old Negro empties
the ashtrays in the corridor. No sign of alarm. Now and again
young men in shirt sleeves go along the corridor to get a Coca-
Cola from the vending machine, talking of nothing in particular.
The atmosphere inside the house is not at all tense. Administration. The daily round of a world power . . .

> Two days ago the Americans marched into Cambodia, the usual
> pictures on television: tanks from behind, swarms of helicopters,
> soldiers with tilted helmets, in full kit, loaded with provisions,
> weapons, ammunition, provisions; working or standing around
> looking lost, waiting for orders where to go in the jungle. Accord-
> to the reporter, they don't yet know they have crossed a border—
> nothing in the vegetation to show it. When the reporter tells them,
> their faces betray no signs of excitement. Only when asked how
> they feel, does one soldier say into the microphone: "This is a
> mistake, I'm sure." Another: "We're going to make history, that's
> all I know."

We wait in the corridor, which is narrow, not to be compared
with a corridor at IBM. No chrome, no leather. We sit in cush-
ioned lower-middle-class comfort. No trace of ministerial
grandeur. It could be a dentist's waiting room, apart from the
photographs: Nixon in Hawaii with a floral wreath around
his neck, he is laughing; Nixon with the astronauts from Apollo

13 after the averted disaster, he is laughing and waving; Nixon
with his wife on a staircase, he is waving and laughing; Nixon
leaving his airplane, waving; Nixon in the garden as family
man, not waving but laughing; then the official Nixon again,
shaking children's hands; Nixon at a gala dinner with Negroes
to his right and left, a bevy of Uncle Toms in dinner jackets;
the same dinner again . . .

Nobody can say for certain how large the Black Panther party
is. "The Black Panther party regards itself as a socialist organization and believes that means of production should be in the hands
of the people. They declare that men only live creatively when free
from the oppression of capitalism." As whites we are warned
against going into Harlem; all the same, we drive to Harlem and
walk around on foot, the only whites in the Apollo Theater. We are
not molested; in the street, as long as the white man doesn't gape,
no hostile looks. Much the same goods on sale, and the same language, too,—but a different continent. No slogans on the walls.
It is difficult to say what has changed in twenty years, but a lot
has. In the movies: the white heroes being laughed at.

Our host sends apologies: it will take him another few minutes.
Easy to understand that, with a new area of warfare only two
days old. I am still wrapped in wonder about this corridor; apart
from the Nixon pictures in frames as cheap as they are taste-
less, there is nothing to suggest we are on the premises of a
firm spending billions a day on war. Not until I go in search of a
washroom do I find, in a side corridor, a picture of Nixon in
Vietnam: soldiers listening solemnly to his fatherly words . . .

I have come here as a tourist, chiefly to see American painting in
its own environment, studios on the Lower East Side. Along the
road one runs into demonstrations: Vietcong flags waving in front
of the Public Library, loudspeakers, a great helicopter circling
over the park, where young people, male and female, are squat-
ting on the ground or on railings, others lying under the trees,
young people with guerrilla beards and Jesus hair, groups with
guitars, policemen stationed around the park. The youngsters
shout: "Peace now, peace now"; the policemen are silent, their
eyes averted, their truncheons hanging from loops around their

hands. "Peace now, peace now, peace now." Nobody is being threatened, the policemen look redundant, the surrounding skyscrapers need no protection. Some call out: "Revolution now," but they are backed by the constitution. Nothing happens to them, but the doctrine urging war has lost its pull. Some call out: "All power to the people," making their two-fingered sign, then suddenly fifteen thousand voices shout: "Peace, peace now, peace, peace, peace."

Henry A. Kissinger, our host, greets us heartily and invites us into his anteroom. We know him from Harvard days; as professor of government he was already President Kennedy's occasional adviser. Now he is at the White House full time, adviser for military affairs. He is in his middle forties, thickset, inconspicuously cosmopolitan; an academician of the German sort, even if he puts his hands in his trouser pockets. The phone call that again calls him away for a while comes from Nelson Rockefeller, and so we wait, not only with understanding but with an embarrassed awareness of how precious his time is. Two secretaries are sitting in his anteroom, just starting on their lunchtime hot dogs. Another picture of Nixon here: the President (seated) listening to Henry A. Kissinger, his adviser (standing), surrounded by flags. Henry A. Kissinger, now free, introduces us to a lady who does not come from the White House, an actress, at the same time referring jokingly to Siegfried Unseld as "my friend and left-wing publisher." Another picture of Nixon here, a portrait with a dedication to Henry A. Kissinger: "Grateful for ever"; I don't get the date, for just then Henry A. Kissinger wants to know what I am working on now, a novel or a play? None of us is actually very hungry, but there are other reasons than that for a meeting over lunch: the task of ordering one's meal is a welcome way of postponing the questions that can't be avoided—questions about the American invasion of Cambodia. We all decide on mineral water. Once the White House waiter leaves us, Henry A. Kissinger starts off with a personal account: he daily receives letters threatening his life. The man from the Secret Service who in consequence shadows him constantly is nowhere to be seen. Is he perhaps the waiter, or are we regarded as completely trustworthy? Then on to the problem of the generation gap: it is all our fault, a failure on the part of fathers and teachers, who yield to every empty threat, capitulate, resign themselves, etc., instead of proclaiming what they themselves think is right and showing the way. Henry A. Kissinger relates how, in one university, where he had gone for discussions with the students, he was accused of being a "war criminal"; around one-half of the assembled students supported the accusation by rising from their seats and remaining on their feet. Henry A. Kissinger was still prepared to go on with the discussion, but, when the appellation "war criminal" was shouted again, he left the room. Quite a few of the students, he says, wrote to thank him for his gesture and to apologize for the incident.

"War Crimes and Individual Responsibility," a memorandum by Richard A. Falk, deals with the massacre of Song My on 16 March 1968, when more than five hundred civilians were wiped out: "The U.S. prosecutor at Nuremberg, Robert Jackson, emphasized that war crimes are war crimes no matter which country is guilty of them." The charter of the Nuremberg tribunal defines not only massacres, deportations, acts of torture, etc., as crimes; it also contains an Article VI: "Crimes against peace: Planning, preparation, initiation or waging of a war of aggression in violation of international treaties, agreements or assurances."

As far as the invasion of Cambodia is concerned, not only are we laymen, but we know it. Henry A. Kissinger has been working on the theory of the subject the layman sums up facilely as war for decades; hence his composure two days after the invasion of Cambodia. The food is good but ordinary, thus providing no distraction. What shall I talk about—simply in order *not* to put to Henry A. Kissinger the question that millions of Americans are asking? He is friendly, perhaps even pleased to be lunching with lay people, and he asks my publisher about his publishing business; but Siegfried Unseld, normally only too glad of an opportunity to speak at length about his firm's plans, cuts his account short in order to put a question of his own, which Henry A. Kissinger (with whom he stands on intimate, first-name terms since the time of the Harvard seminar) answers easily: the action in Cambodia will last a fortnight, till the rains come. Our host's attempt to bring the conversation around to marriage also fails. There is another silence. A President's adviser is in a more difficult position than a publisher or a writer; he cannot, in order to avoid speaking of his profession, switch to a more general and more important topic—for instance, war. For that *is* his profession, and no amount of personal modesty on his side and tact on ours can help out. Henry A. Kissinger says that the Cambodia decision of course gave him no pleasure. It was a case of choosing the lesser evil (lesser for whom?) and—obviously I had heard wrong the first time—the lesser evil would last six weeks at the most. Henry A. Kissinger, who keeps to a diet, talks sparingly and without eagerness: he is under no compulsion. The President is at his country house today. In order to keep the conversation going, I could have told him what the Americans I had met think about it, but Henry A. Kissinger has guessed it even before I speak: they are all students, professors, painters, writers, intellectuals. He says:'"Cynics have never built a cathedral." The protests throughout the country cannot divert the responsible people from their course; they alone know the facts, which are secret. Henry A. Kissinger is an intellectual who has taken on responsibilities, and he relies on the fact that it was not "we" who started this war in Vietnam—by "we" he means President Nixon's administration. A thankless inheritance. To come back to the invasion of Cambodia: the U.S.A. has absolutely no interest in Cambodia; all they want to do is to establish a negotiating position. He asks us what we would like for dessert. According to the opinion polls, 63 percent of Americans today favor the invasion, 25 percent are against. (*The New York Times* is against.) I order fruit salad, and am glad when a young man in shirt sleeves interrupts with a murmured message: "The President is calling." A quarter of an hour on our own, we eat our dessert in silence; what our host can tell us Nixon has already said on television:

No infringement of Cambodian neutrality, for this neutrality has already been infringed by the Vietcong. No aggression against Cambodia, for in the district concerned there are no local inhabitants, only Vietcong, whose bases are being destroyed. The monsoon period will prevent the Vietcong reestablishing these bases for six months. No escalation of the war; on the contrary, it is all part of the preparations to withdraw American troops; after the rains the South Vietnamese troops will be able on their own, etc.

The restaurant in the White House: solidly cozy, like a clubroom —brown paneled comfort. Here there is no picture of Nixon, but four oil paintings of old ships, three of them in distress ... "The President is calling" ... Here I am eating fruit salad in a place where millions of American citizens never get a chance to talk. What is so funny about that? A host in daily peril of his life, but he shows neither fear nor indignation. An occupational risk. Perhaps he even feels flattered: a bit reminiscent of Julius Caesar. What will they be talking about on the telephone? I have a mental picture of Henry A. Kissinger standing with his right hand in his trouser pocket, while we sit eating fruit salad. I wonder why I am reluctant to argue with a man in peril of his life: as if it would protect him, were I to remain silent while he says what he likes. "Intellectuals are cynical and cynics have never built a cathedral." Men think like that in our government offices, too; it is in keeping with this brown-paneled clubroom.

A number of professors from Harvard call on Henry A. Kissinger a few days later to sever their connections with him; they say the Cambodia invasion was irresponsible, and the way the decision was made, undemocratic.

Of course, we should like to be shown over the White House, but we could be taken around by somebody else whose time was less precious. Obviously our host, after we have had our coffee, wants no further table talk about Cambodia, and we are honored that Henry A. Kissinger now offers personally to show us around the residence. (At certain times anyone can view it.) The palace guard, no more numerous than keepers in a museum, give no military salutes; our host, one hand in his trouser pocket, gives some short, informal greeting, and the uniforms subside again in the very act of rising. This gives us, too, a faint aura of belonging. All the same, I don't dare to light my pipe, but hold it in my hand or between my teeth without smoking. White walls, red carpets. I am uncertain what to think. . . . So this is where power dwells; it suggests a being that likes quiet and clean surroundings, beginning with the ashtrays; respects tradition; loves the silent grounds, the green lawns, and the flowers according to season; it probably has no relish for street fights, even when the victims have only themselves to blame, and massacres like Song My must arouse only horror. Even the noise of ordinary street traffic is distasteful: it cares for no noise of any kind that could disturb its meditations; it cherishes the view to a distant obelisk, the splash of a fountain. Whoever belongs in this household of power, whether as military adviser or as custodian, walks without haste, and obviously also without concern, so that one thinks of cries like "Revolution now!" only with a smile. Lincoln and others were shot dead, finally Kennedy; what disturbance has that caused? Their portraits in oil on the walls create a mood that immediately compels the visitor to speak softly; even the portrait of Lyndon B. Johnson, not yet looking down on us from Beyond, makes us feel that here modesty is called for. Only Henry A. Kissinger, who talks less than the usual guide, does not remove his hands from his pockets, thus wordlessly assuring us that everything in the house of power is completely natural, civilized, humane, because informal. He even makes a joke about Jacqueline: that is quite in order. Power, it seems, comes above all of a good family and possesses good taste—in china, for instance, and in furniture. This gives everything that happens here an aristocratic air. Every President has his own china, which later, when he is no longer in office, is put on view in a glass case; thus each succeeding President admires the china of his predecessors, and all are united through a taste for china. We walk along without asking much, less meditative than discreet; as we go up the marble staircase I do not, for instance, put my hand on the banister. The paintings that form part of the furnishings of power keep to the previous century; no Rothko, Roy Lichtenstein or Stella, no Jim Dine, no Calder, etc. A hankering for tradition, but it begins with Lincoln and Washington; there is no knight's armor. Birds are Nixon's main love. There are no Gobelins depicting military victories, or if there are I do not see them; there is no military strutting here, in fact no strutting at all. Power wears a respectable face, and has no desire to shock. Only the reality is huge—not the mansion in which this being lives and entertains. Another view over the park: even the jumbo jet one can just hear does not really fit in. Here history walks on wall-to-wall carpets. There is nothing to remind one of oil, of the computers in the Pentagon, the CIA, the United Fruit Company, etc. Here a large desk, and I take my pipe from my mouth: this—so I believe—is where the President, at the moment Richard Nixon, works. Behind the empty seat stands the Stars and Stripes, to each side of it the flags of all the armed forces. The desktop is empty, everything cleared away, but authentic. The only object that makes it believable that historic decisions are made here is also the only one that is not an antique: a telephone, white. We feel as if we were standing in the Escorial, where one must tell oneself: So this . . . !

Nixon speaking to the press (8 May) on the U.S. invasion of Cambodia: "Decisions, of course, are not made by a vote in the Security Council or in the Cabinet. They are made by the President with the advice of others. I, as Commander in Chief, I alone am responsible. . . . I made the decision. I take the responsibility for it. I believe it was the right decision. I believe it works out. If it doesn't, then I am to blame."

In order not to ask: What help is it to the victims of a catastrophe, a civil war, or a world war, if Richard Nixon, the Commander in Chief, personally takes the blame and possibly destroys himself like Hitler? I ask his adviser what sort of a mind the President has. A very good mind, I am told, better than Kennedy's or Johnson's. But what sort of a mind? I am told it is an analytical mind. The tour of inspection moves on. . . .

Two days later, 4 May 1970, during an antiwar demonstration at Kent State University, Ohio, four students are shot dead by the National Guard, who claim to have acted in self-defense against snipers, an allegation contradicted by all eyewitnesses. Pictures in *Life* show the National Guard shooting into the crowd from a distance of thirty yards, thus not threatened even by stonethrowers. Without preliminary warning. They lost their nerve, it is said, because their supply of tear gas had run out. Nixon says: "The needless deaths should remind us all once more that when dissent turns to violence it invites tragedy," a statement on which *The New York Times* remarks: "Which of course is true, but turns the tragedy upside down by placing the blame on the victims instead of the killers." Nixon is writing personal letters of sympathy to the parents.

We next inspect a little room in which the President can retire for a rest, no larger than an actor's dressing room, with a narrow couch, armchair, closet, and wash basin. The only thing missing: a makeup table. So this is where Nixon rests between appearances. . . . Gradually my inhibitions begin to fade; what we are looking at has nothing to do with reality. Why in fact are we viewing it all? The White House is not all that large, yet our walk seems endless. White walls, red carpets, they give the corridors an air almost of gaiety; what a pity, I almost feel, when our host breaks in with the remark that this is where Chancellor Willy Brandt, for example, was recently received. As he speaks, I am still reflecting on his words at lunch: "What happens in Cambodia after we leave Vietnam is not our problem." I nod: So this is where Willy Brandt had to eat. In front of a colleague to whom he introduces us the joking tone emerges again: "My friend and left-wing publisher." I know now that an open spirit dwells in this house. This colleague, like the young men we saw in the waiting room, is in shirt sleeves, neat, relaxed; the first reports from Cambodia appear to be good, in line with expectations. (At Harvard, in 1963, Henry A. Kissinger could be even more open, an intellectual who did not carry great responsibilities; he showed more concern then.) I wanted to ask a question, but the moment has passed; we are now inspecting a room where Henry A. Kissinger usually sits with the Soviet ambassador. I nod, as if my confirmation were required. The room reminds me of the Tarasp Kurhaus: a lot of easy chairs in little groups, all uncomfortable but solid, stylish, presumably genuine antiques. Now Henry A. Kissinger has both hands in his pockets, as though to show that he is not responsible for the internal architecture. Nor is Nixon. The apartment that the President in office can furnish to his own taste is on the floor above; all we are seeing are the state rooms, which, as I said, are open to all American citizens at certain times. Democracy has no secrets from its voters. . . . This (and now I am already nodding before I know what I am required to confirm) is where the Cabinet meets. A convincing room. Around a long, wide, and heavy table stand leather chairs, not too opulent, just right: chairs that oblige one to sit upright. Here it could be argued whether Cambodia should be invaded or not. But it is only infrequently, I am told, that the Cabinet meets, and then it is just a bore. Henry

A. Kissinger smiles; he only wanted to show us the room. The decisions are not made here, he says. . . .

Walter J. Hickel, Interior Secretary, complains in a published letter that the President consulted him only three times within a year. He writes: "Permit me to suggest that you consider meeting, on an individual and conversational basis, with members of your Cabinet. Perhaps through such conversations we can gain greater insight into the problems confronting us all. . . ."

My question would have been: What does Nixon really want from power? There are aims that can only be achieved by first gaining power (the abolition of poverty in the world's wealthiest country, the integration of the Negroes, peace without exploiting other countries, etc.). What is Richard Nixon's aim? But the question is superfluous; his aim was to become President of the United States, and he has achieved his aim by virtue of having no other—power as the aim of power—and I can believe without question that Nixon genuinely desires peace, if there is no other way of remaining in power. . . .

Everything is getting out of hand: garbage, youth, hair, drugs, Negroes, riots, students, protest in the streets, the fear of America. New skyscrapers, but the guitar is getting out of hand. In the fall, when they once again marched on Washington, there were reckoned to have been a quarter of a million of them assembled around the White House. "Peace now, stop the war, peace now." There were no fatalities; President Nixon had the windows closed and (as he himself later announced) watched football on television. Six months later, on 9 May 1970, they besieged the park again—"Out of Cambodia,"—this time only a hundred thousand (many have ceased to believe they will be listened to), but Nixon had a sleepless night, according to the press: early in the morning the President went to the Lincoln Memorial, where he talked to some of the students and demanded their understanding: it was his responsibility to ensure that the United States remain the leading power. The students say he then talked about sports. According to the press, the President breakfasted on ham and eggs. War helps against crises, but what helps against young people who are getting out of hand? Four hundred universities are staging strikes in protest against the shooting of students at Kent State.

In the park, which—as we have frequently seen through the windows—is very beautiful, but answers no questions, Henry A. Kissinger says he will not remain in office much longer: he has hardly any private life of his own. Now we see the White House from outside: just as one knows it from pictures. Out here in the open I at last light up my pipe, while we walk along, hearing only our footsteps on the gravel. What to talk about? A fine summer day. People who make decisions or advise on decisions affecting millions of human beings cannot afford to ask themselves afterward whether the decision was right; the decision has been made, and we must await what follows. It would really be the opportunity for a joke, but none occurs to me.

> This morning in Jimmy's Coffee Shop: conversation with a cheerful waiter, who takes me for a German and in consequence tells me that he was neither for nor against Hitler, "but perhaps we have to see that Hitler was a great philosopher." Seeing my hesitation, he switches to McCarthy, "who was considered to be a fool," but today one feels that, if McCarthy had been listened to at the time, "we wouldn't have all the trouble with Vietnam." He himself, the waiter, is actually Greek, and a patriot there as well: he finds Pattakos all right, "only some Communists can't stand him." Incidentally, we are not alone: the man selling tobacco next door is for Hitler. Why? Hitler had great faith. What was that? "He believed that the Germans are a superior race." He himself, the tobacconist, is a Puerto Rican with crinkly hair, and he incidentally thinks the United States should have occupied Europe after the war. This reminds me of a conversation I had in 1952 in a California motel. "Depression is worse than war," the landlord assured me, though by that he meant a war in old Europe. Why in Europe? "Because they are used to having wars over there."

In the park there is nothing to see, and our silence is all the more conspicuous; I am glad when Siegfried Unseld begins to talk of his publishing business. Every firm has its problems. Henry A. Kissinger, unassuming, as extraordinary minds usually are, almost vainly unassuming, an expert who has considered all the potentialities of weapons of destruction and only wants what is best (namely, the least possible destruction of the world), he knows what at this moment only a few in the world know (it is only the historians who will eventually know) and prefers to listen, if somewhat absentmindedly, to someone else. I have met no other man whose potential error could have such vast consequences. A surgeon whose knife once slips, an engine driver, even a member of parliament who is not up to his job, a police chief who follows the wrong clue, an air pilot with a hundred sixty passengers, or a Herbert Marcuse, a publisher, etc.—these are responsibilities a single man can assume. But a White House adviser? I begin to understand why Henry A. Kissinger has his hands in his pockets wherever he goes; his responsibilities are in no sort of proportion to his person, which wears an ordinary suit like us. The more disastrous the potential error, the less the individual man can do about it. Without my saying a word of all this, Henry A. Kissinger remarks that he can bear responsibility much better than ineffectualness; then, speaking to the other side, adds something that I do not clearly hear. We are walking very slowly. Henry A. Kissinger has no idea what he will do when he leaves the White House. Return to the university? He feels that would hardly be possible. Our walk on the gravel will soon be at an end, and it seems there is nothing more to ask. Why did Henry A. Kissinger, before the election Richard Nixon's declared opponent, become his adviser? My wife's question is more suited to the occasion, however: How had his scientific theories been vindicated or altered by being applied in practice? That, says Henry A. Kissinger, is a question he is often asked: he has no time to think of it. A terrible remark, but we are now passing through a revolving door. I hear only: "When you are once on the tightrope, there is no way back. . . ." Then (emerging from the revolving door): ". . . no policy without the risk of a tragedy." Tragedy for whom?

NEW YORK, May

Again I have dreamed the ending of a play. Awakened by my delight (even in sleep God looks after his own!), I could easily have written the sentences down--the ending for a

play that doesn't exist, that I have never
worked on and whose plot I cannot even guess
from the ending I was presented with in my
dream.

The thing that nearly always springs first to
people's minds when they discover that I am
not a German writer, but a Swiss one, is "the
gnomes of Zurich." They seem to be pretty
much despised, but there is nothing I can say
about that (it is not my territory). Close
behind the bankers in people's minds as a
symbol of our country comes the fondue, and
after that a long silence. I have stopped
waiting for it. I should be sorry for any of
my respected countrymen who, when that happens, might feel constrained to rush to the
rescue of our national pride. I simply keep
quiet until the subject changes of its own
accord.

Paintings and sculptures at the place where
they are created: one suddenly understands
why pictures are forty or sixty feet long,
why pieces of sculpture are of a size no
gallery could contain. They are less a dis-
tillation of their environment than a coun-
terblast. And no one is obliged nowadays to
go to Paris for his laurels. . . .

Question time at Columbia University, open to
the public. What do they want to know? No
political questions; if the answer happens to
point in the direction of politics they are
silent, politely concealing their irritation.
The older people's questions come from the
region of Freud or C. G. Jung, the younger
people's from that of Lévi-Strauss.

Told me by a teacher in Queens: a schoolgirl
refused to concern herself with the troubles

of Anna Karenina, since she did not want
anyway to live as long as this Anna Karenina
—twelve years or so there would be no oxygen
left in her neighborhood, anyway. . . .

WRITING IN THE FIRST PERSON

Norman Mailer's method in *The Armies of the Night* is curious: he describes his experiences at a demonstration in front of the Pentagon, where he was arrested, in the third person—Norman Mailer laughed, in this instant he hesitated, then Norman Mailer, too, allowed himself to be carried along with the crowd, etc. After his arrest, he expresses his astonishment that the policeman does not know his name and spells it out: M-A-I-L-E-R. This method gives the writer, among other things, the freedom to regard everything, including his own vanities, objectively. The straight first-person style does not permit that without introducing, if the same things are said, a note of masochism.

The first-person narration is perhaps particularly suitable where egocentricity is involved: it facilitates a stricter control. One could, in order to retain this control, write in the first-person form and then rewrite in the third person, to make sure that the latter is not just a camouflage, but, on the other hand, there are sentences that work objectively only in the first-person form; transposed word for word into the ingenuous third person they begin to look evasive. The writer does not get the better of himself in the third person—he simply dodges the issue.

. . .

Do I then imagine that my mental state (how I woke up today, etc.) is of public interest? All the same I note it down now and again and even publish it. The journal as a daily mental exercise in full awareness of what is irrelevant in it . . .

. . .

What is commonly considered indiscretion: information from the writer's private world that is no concern of the reader. And true indiscretion? When one informs the reader of something that does concern him, something the reader himself knows but never admits . . .

. . .

Not even writing in the third person will prevent the reader from suspecting autobiography at the precise point where experience turns into invention.

. . .

The difference between the story-book "I" and the direct "I" in a journal: the latter can less easily be filled in, for the very reason that it provides too little in the way of background knowledge; it is thus an attribution, and not a figure. To have a figure you must also know what it is concealing, what doesn't interest it at the moment, what it is not aware of, etc.

. . .

In soul-baring confessional writings (maximum honesty with regard to oneself), the third-person form is better.

. . .

The third-person form is easier at the start than later, after the conscious or unconscious depositories of the ego under various third-person guises have all been seen through. It is not because the writer considers himself more important that he may feel obliged as time goes on to adopt the simple "I" form: it is just because all his disguises have been used up.

. . .

Unabashed first-person writers like Henry Miller, Witold Gombrowicz, etc., are not writing confessions, and are bearable because the "I" of their works assumes the quality of a role. Writers of this sort give an impression rather of innocence:

they create out of their own selves and live every moment of their creations; one hardly ever gets the painful feeling that they are flaunting their private intimacies. They are simply their own study object, the figure they are writing about, and hence there are no vanities to conceal—these belong to the figure along with everything else.

. . .

Why does resignation always seem indiscreet (in contrast to arrogance, which can get away with anything)? For instance, the older Gide writes no more indiscreetly than the earlier Gide, yet in his mood of resignation he seems more indiscreet.

. . .

A questionable practice in the writing of a public journal is the leaving out of names and personal details for reasons of tact. The Goncourt brothers were not reticent: whoever dined with them came through their journal into the public eye. Why then am I so reticent? It gives the impression that the writer of the journal sees only himself as a personality, and all his contemporaries as an anonymous crowd. There is, of course, no need for reticence when the person concerned is already a public figure; but then it looks as if the writer consorts exclusively with famous people, or considers them alone worth writing about. So why not give names and personal details of all the people the writer deals with in his journal? It does not all have to be malicious gossip—yet even the opposite would be indiscreet. What gives me the right to let out other people's secrets? The price of my discretion: an overdose of egocentricity or—an overdose of politics?

THE ZURICH SCHAUSPIELHAUS

A theater originally founded by German emigrants together with Swiss Social Democrats (above all, Emil Oprecht, the publisher, who in the thirties published the first book about German concentration camps). For near-

ly twenty years it was the place where I felt
at home as nowhere else in Zurich; it gave
the first performances of Brecht's plays,
Mother Courage, Galileo, The Good Woman of
Szechwan, and after the war, in Brecht's
presence, of Puntila. Here, for the first
time in German, we saw the plays of Girau-
doux, Thornton Wilder, Arthur Miller,
O'Casey, Bernanos, Sartre, Camus, and others.
Later it was the parent house both for myself
and for Friedrich Dürrenmatt, where our plays
were awaited and tried out for the first
time. When freedom was restored to German
stages, the Zurich Schauspielhaus became increasingly insignificant. But last winter,
through young Peter Stein, it almost became
an important stage again, a political one,
what it had been once before--an anti-Fascist
theater. But then it turned middle class;
the bourgeoisie speaks of it proudly as "our
Schauspielhaus." And not without cause, as
we can now see. The board of directors was
quick to spot the new slant to the left and,
once box-office takings (with the help of the
bourgeois press) began to drop off, it gave
notice to quit to the manager and his literary adviser (Peter Löffler, Klaus Volker) in
the third month of their first season. The
directors--among them one or two bankers and
representatives of the city administration,
but not a single theater man--were, however,
unlucky in their choice of successor: the new
manager is unable to refute suspicions that
during the Hitler period his record was not
entirely spotless. Nobody knew that, of
course, at the time he was appointed. And,
anyway, a man can change his mind. But that
does not alter the fact that his predecessor
was evicted on account of his left-wing tendencies by the board of governors (they were
supported, incidentally, by the Social Demo-

crat members as well). Our public efforts to
dislodge this body, which spends public money
on catering to the artistic tastes of bankers, have now failed. According to today's
newspapers, Friedrich Dürrenmatt has agreed
to become a member of the board and the
theater's literary adviser.

POSTSCRIPT TO MY AMERICAN JOURNEY

When one says this wasn't one's first journey to America, one is
almost bound to be asked: Do you find it changed? And the last
thing people expect to hear is the answer that it has changed
for the better. I think it has.... Last time the question was
always How do you like America? put in a cheerfully approving
sort of way that invited affirmation; the only thing people
found odd was what had most impressed us. What had most
impressed me was the desert. It was during the McCarthy era.
That type of anticommunism that has no idea what communism
really is, coupled with a repressive type of patriotism (rather
like here at home) has not yet disappeared, but what has vanished is the arrogance of power, even though people still say:
We are the richest nation on earth. And so they are. But they are
scared. Air pollution is only a metaphor for all the other realities
that scare them. At the very least they no longer feel sure that
things that grow bigger and bigger are all necessarily to be
welcomed. Scarcely an evening passes without some expression
of concern, not infrequently the frank question: Are we on the
road to fascism? Some factors suggest otherwise, for example,
the Puritan heritage. The discussions about America that they
hold among themselves grow longer and fail to inspire feelings
of confidence, not even, in most cases, approval of their past
history. The destruction of the Indians no longer seems the
glorious fulfillment of a divine command: it looks more like
genocide. The natural hunting instincts of their forefathers
can, of course, be understood, but the outcome is still, in current terms, genocide. It's true what the President said: The
United States have never, since they were founded one hundred
ninety years ago, lost a war. But there has been no victory,
either. The experience of Vietnam will remain a shock, even if
the troops one day withdraw. They are no longer certain that

they are the great moral power they were in Nuremberg. Things have happened and are continuing to happen of which they previously thought only others were capable. What are we doing in Indochina? say people who have never even indirectly had anything to do with war crimes; they above all are changed, so it seems to me, right into their daily lives. They are surprised that we come here voluntarily. It is a terrible country, we hear more than once, though always with the immediate after-thought: Though we might be the richest nation on earth. Construction workers beat up a procession of flower children: things like this cannot restore the American Dream. And some-thing that was not there twenty years ago: a doubt whether America is on the right path. That former mood of confident self-righteousness is reflected only in advertisements and official speeches (which are advertisements, too), no longer in private conversations. America is frightened. Fear of Russia, fear of China: the rulers propagate fears that will justify their strategies and the cost of these strategies. But in the small bars or in the artists' studios or among scientists or in public parks or wherever else one has the conversations the Americans themselves initiate, the line is different: America is frightened of America. . . . I mean it seriously when I say that it has changed for the better, even compared with 1956, when I visited this huge land for the second time; it is true I have never heard the system criticized, even by people openly opposed to the President and his administration, but their fear of their own selves makes them as individuals more humane.

BERZONA

Meeting with an old colleague from the GDR
whom I have not seen since 1945. Why, with
friendliness on both sides, are we so on
tenterhooks? They are drilled, know exactly
what they will never say, and yet pretend
they are being frank. Their child, playing
with a toy train, can see by the very houses
that Fascists live in them. We talk of other
things. The parents' pride in their anti-
authoritarian methods of upbringing. The

child, who addresses his father by his first
name—which is very touching—suddenly says
he's had enough. He is tired and wants to go
home. The father agrees: in five minutes.
He wants to finish what he is saying, he says
with a gentle appeal for understanding:
another two minutes. The child wants to go
now, not in two minutes—otherwise, he says,
"I'll have you arrested!" We laugh. Out of
the mouth of babes . . .

NOTES FOR A MEMBERS' HANDBOOK

*People who believe that old age brings its own ("spiritual")
rewards tend to base their assumptions on artists, writers,
philosophers, etc., though only, be it noted, the most famous
of them. Public recognition of their work—or even hostility
toward it—can lead us into confusing the person with his
fame, which ages more slowly.*

*What the artist fears in growing old is that he will lose his
creative gifts, and he has usually not learned a profession
or way of life in which this does not matter.*

*Exhibition of an artist's life work in three separate gal-
leries . . . The older the artist becomes, the quicker we pass
from picture to picture; as his skill increases, our curiosity
diminishes, even when we don't admit it—we just praise more
swiftly (starting in the second gallery). Here he is trying to
surprise us, and he almost succeeds; but we have the impression that he is hardly surprised himself. When we get to the
third gallery, we find the painter there in person; now we
are surprised—to find him still living. Not an old man. He is
engaged in lively conversation.*

*Even the foredoomed man at times finds himself taking no
pleasure in his success. In his work he now recognizes more
quickly what cannot succeed, and so spends less time making
mistakes. To that extent he is working more effectively (pro-*

lific period). But earlier, at the start, he felt freer: in his fail-ures there was greater hope.

There are old men's works that are more than a mere extension of something already perfected (Matisse). But they are rare.

How Igor Stravinsky is treated by the people closest to him I have heard only from others who have witnessed it. It sounds incredible, but one believes it without question. It is only at a distance that people are protected by their fame.

There are famous old men who consider everything they did successfully to have been meaningless (Ezra Pound); there are others who bow down to themselves as if to a classic master. The latter attitude can be found among foredoomed men as well.

The foredoomed man likes to imagine that his artistic crises are due to the fact that advancing years and success have made him more self-critical. This is not always so: his urge to create has become weaker than his critical sense, which has remained static and which will not begin to decline until he has reached the doomed stage.

The desire to teach, to have pupils, to be head of an insti-tute, to become an adjudicator, etc., must not necessarily be taken as a symptom of senility.

A doomed man who conducts us around his studio does not notice that everything he so enthusiastically tells us he in-tends to do has already been done—by himself—years ago; he is confusing his passionate desire to copy with the creative urge. He does not feel in the least bit old; on the contrary, he parades his temperament steadfastly before us, his vitality, his enormous appetite, etc.

The doomed man can identify himself by his addiction to fame, which is not the same as his earlier ambitiousness: it is more sensitive than ambitiousness, which is still sustained by our expectations.

Dilettantes age less noticeably.

The doomed man discovers (for instance), that however long he sits in a restaurant, he has no desire to do anything with the beer mats: he does not use them to build pagodas, which then collapse; he doesn't even feel tempted to play ducks and drakes with them on the lake. Beer mats, lake: they arouse no temptations in his mind, so he just crumbles bread and feeds it to the swans, assuming that this tempts the swans. If one were to trace his path through the town with chalk, one would notice that the chalk marks were different from before: not so many zigzags caused by temptation. Even a street accident (glass fragments on the asphalt, policemen, people jostling to see) he can ignore as easily as a shop window. The doomed man is not necessarily tired, nor need he look old; it is just that he feels a diminishing urge to turn his hand to things that do not demand it. For instance, he can look at a Calder mobile without blowing at it or setting it in motion with his finger. Though it pleases him when others do so. He already knows. Even when he sees something he does not know—some curious object in a strange apartment, a piece of material never encountered before—he behaves as if in a museum: Do not touch the exhibits. One must deliberately place the object in his hands, so that his fingers can feel it. Do they feel it? The doomed man has a piece of wire in his hand, copper wire that bends without the help of pliers, and he can just hold it in his hand, without playing with it, without bending it this way or that. He is surprised: he knows what this means and feels upset by it.

There is no doubt that the works of old age can be significant (Theodor Fontane, for instance); the people who find comfort in that fact are mainly those who have no creative gifts to lose, and one should leave them alone.

A doomed man whose pictures hang today in every gallery of note one day decides that he needs a new overcoat. Not feeling able to venture out of doors, he asks for a selection of coats to be brought to his house. He tries on a dozen, but cannot make up his mind, keeps three for a final choice, and then comes to the conclusion that he needs no new overcoat. He

continues to work for a further week, then (aged sixty-six)
slits his wrists and dies at the height of his fame.

Poverty apart, a man whose work is still unrecognized has an
easier time in old age; his continued claim to be regarded as
a coming man keeps him fresh.

Painters or sculptors who have had works destroyed in some
catastrophe (act of God) invariably tend on this account to
feel rather younger than their contemporaries. . . .

It may be generally true that people in artistic professions
(apart from child prodigies) age later than other human
beings. On the other hand, they observe the signs of aging in
themselves earlier—long before others become aware of it.
What others call mastery might already be causing the artist
himself alarm.

When the sense of touch begins to diminish and one hears
and sees less, when the brain absorbs less and works more
slowly, the emotions dry up, curiosity dies or at least narrows
its field, reactions become repetitive or disappear entirely,
the association of ideas falters, imagination withers, desire
of every kind fades, etc.—when all this happens, the doomed
man may find it easier to practise his art: the only things that
occur to him are the things he can do (late style).

Senility can still produce works of art. This is probably why
doomed men not infrequently curse their art—all art, in fact.
The rest is not silence, but art.

The expression on the face of the aged Rembrandt . . .

> The Swiss national drama (during the Second
> World War) was not William Tell—it could
> more suitably have been <u>The</u> <u>Good</u> <u>Woman</u> <u>of</u>
> <u>Szechwan</u>. Only nobody much cared for the
> fact that the Wicked Cousin, who alone made
> the good deeds possible, would then also have
> been Swiss. So <u>William</u> <u>Tell</u> it remained.

QUESTIONNAIRE

1.
Do you consider yourself to be a good friend?

2.
What do you consider to be a betrayal of friendship:
a. in the other person?
b. in yourself?

3.
How many friends to you now have?

4.
Do you think one can measure the value of a friendship (even when broken) by its duration?

5.
What would you find inexcusable in a friend:
a. two-faced behavior?
b. the fact that he stole a woman from you?
c. the fact that he feels sure of you?
d. his irony toward yourself as well as others?
e. his inability to accept criticism?
f. the fact that he respects people with whom you are at loggerheads and enjoys their company?
g. the fact that you have no influence over him?

6.
Would you like to be able to get on without friends?

7.
Do you keep a dog in order to have a friend?

8.
Have you ever been without a single friend, or—in order to avoid this—do you at such times simply lower the standards of what you mean by friendship?

9.
Have you known friendship with a woman:
a. before sexual intercourse?
b. after sexual intercourse?
c. without sexual intercourse?

10.
Which do you fear more; the judgment of a friend or the judgment of enemies?

11.
Why?

12.
Have you enemies with whom you would secretly like to make friends, so that you can admire them with less difficulty?

13.
If someone is in a position to help you financially, or if you are in a position to help someone financially, does this seem to you to jeopardize your previous friendship?

14.
Do you see Nature as a friend?

15.
If you discover indirectly that a malicious joke about you was initiated by a friend, do you terminate your friendship? If so:

16.
How much frankness can you stand from a friend in company, in writing or alone together?

17.
Assume you have a friend who is intellectually vastly your superior: do you feel the fact of his friendship makes up for this, or do you secretly doubt the validity of a friendship that depends simply on your own admiration, loyalty, helpfulness, etc.?

18.
Which of these have you most frequently fallen victim to through your natural need for friendship:
a. flattery?
b. the company of a fellow countryman abroad?
c. the realization that, in this particular case, you cannot afford to make an enemy because it might, for example, endanger your career?
d. your own charm?

e. because it flatters you to be able to call someone who is currently much admired a close friend?
f. a shared political outlook?

19.
How do you speak about lost friends?

20.
When you come to the point of having to do something against your own conscience for a friend and you do it for friendship's sake, has this ever kept the friendship alive?

21.
Can there be friendship where there is no similar sense of humor?

22.
What else do you consider indispensable if the relationship between two people is to be considered friendship rather than a mere identity of interests:
a. pleasure in the other person's looks?
b. the ability to relax when alone with the other person, that is, the assurance that confidences will not be passed on?
c. political understanding on all points?
d. that the other person can give you a hopeful feeling just by being there, telephoning, writing?
e. forbearance?
f. the courage to disagree openly, yet a feeling for how much frankness the other can stand—and hence patience?
g. an absence of prestige problems?
h. an ability to allow the other person to have secrets of his own, thus no feelings of resentment when something emerges of which he has never spoken?
i. a similar sense of shame?
j. when meeting unexpectedly, mutual pleasure as the first reaction, even when time is short?
k. the ability to hope on account of the other?
l. the certain feeling that either, when hearing something unpleasant about the other, will at least demand proofs before accepting it?
m. points of contact in one's enthusiasms?
n. memories that one has in common and that would be less

precious if one did not have them in common?
o. feelings of gratitude?
p. the ability to allow the other to be in the wrong occasionally without becoming censorious?
q. absence of any form of meanness?
r. readiness not to hold the other to opinions that once led to agreement—in other words, neither need feel he must abandon a new viewpoint out of consideration for the other?
(Delete what is not applicable)

23.
How great can the age difference be between friends?

24.
If a long-standing friendship disintegrates—for example, because the friend's new wife cannot be absorbed into it—do you regret that this friendship ever existed?

25.
Are you friends with yourself?

Theater with puppets? Without facial features; they are rather larger than human beings. Their clear-cut gestures are to be adjusted during the scene by a stagehand (nonspeaking, working clothes). At times a gesture that no longer matches the text is left unchanged. For example, the angry accuser pointing with outstretched arm at the accused after he has been proved innocent. Or the other way around: the gesture of outraged innocence long after the text has convicted the accused. It does not matter if the figure falls over and remains lying on the floor for a while till it is needed again: say, for a gesture of great rejoicing. Since the puppets do not move of their own accord but have to be adjusted, their gestures repeatedly lag behind. When the news comes that there is unfortunately no cause for rejoicing, that the longed-for person

will in fact never return, the puppet is
still making that gesture of great rejoicing.
The stagehand works from a visible script,
always detached, unhurried—but exact,
whether preparing a puppet's gesture before
it becomes comprehensible or setting it up
after the moment for it is past. The stagehand as self-effacing as possible: if everything goes smoothly, one should forget him,
like a waiter. The text through a loudspeaker: it should be written in such a way
that we have no trouble in guessing which
puppet is being referred to. While the text
is being spoken, the puppet to which it
refers is not adjusted; the stagehand waits
for the end of a mourning speech before low-
ering the puppet's head and placing its hands
over its eyes. There are also pauses in the
text; all is silence, and various gestures of
silence are set up, for example, a shamed
silence, a demanding silence, a bored or a
stubborn or an expectant silence. Perhaps
the text that has produced these silent reactions could then be spoken once more. A puppet that in accordance with the text has
suddenly assumed a commanding role is quietly
carried to the front or placed on a chair,
its hand formed into a clenched fist, then
the arm raised. It remains in this attitude,
though the words of the others no longer conform to it. This could make the puppet, insofar as we notice it at all, appear extremely comic: it seems not to grasp what has
happened in the meantime. On the other hand,
it could be that a puppet's gesture, for a
long time completely at odds with the text,
suddenly comes back into line with it. The
mourning gesture is justified, the gesture of
rejoicing justified, and this puppet alone is
now at the height of awareness. The text
supplies all the nuances; the puppets provide

basic patterns of reaction, reducing the action to those few twists and turns that are
not verbal, but factual . . .

ALBUM

Here he is on the cover of the album, just as he is known to
everybody who has followed the press in Germany and abroad
for the past decade.

. . .

Here is a list of his works.

. . .

Here, in 1955, he is still young and appears to be wearing a
moustache. The cloth cap he does not, of course, keep on at
the table, though he is wearing an open-necked shirt, the color
of raspberries. It is evening in a villa on the Zürichberg. Here
he is a nephew, not overawed by the comfortably middle-class
china and silver, but taking no part in the conversation; it
doesn't interest him. A sculptor. What he thinks of current
literature has been pretty clear since the soup; he is not going
to see Friedrich Dürrenmatt's new play, *The Visit*. He writes
plays himself. We eat in silence. Since I know this hospitable
house from previous visits, I am wearing a tie, which turns
out to be a mistake when I get to know why I have been invited:
I can put up only a weak resistance to my host when he announces that his nephew will later be reading something aloud.
We are still on the cheese and fruit. The young man, watching
from the sidelines, now seems amused by the older man's embarrassment. (I was at that time about as old as he is now.)
He continues to keep out of the conversation, not questioning
me at all. When we rise from the table and go upstairs for coffee,
he takes his manuscript and waits silently on the elegant sofa
till we each have our brandy. I reiterate my request to be allowed to read the play at home. He agrees at any rate to read
only the first act. There are people who can form an opinion of a
piece of writing on the spot: unfortunately I, as I have already

pointed out to them, do not belong in this category. Since the acts of his play, as I have to admit, are very short, he reads them all. An excellent reader; afterward he feels happy, though I have understood very little.

. . .

This is a year later. He is sitting in my country shack in Männedorf, where I, too, wear no tie. I also have enjoyed the new play he has sent me to read. That's really all he wants to know. He has come from Paris, where he is writing his novel. That morning there had been a military inspection, and my helmet, knapsack, and rifle are still lying in the narrow corridor. Later he amuses his friends in Paris by telling them about this Swiss who always keeps his helmet and rifle ready in the corridor, year in, year out.

. . .

Here he is rolling himself a cigarette, then licking the brownish paper. That was in Berlin. He no longer has to rely on a single admirer. He carries his fame as if he had been sure of it all along.

. . .

Here he is laughing. That does not signify approval or even contentment. His laughter is mostly at people, not with them.

. . .

This is Berlin again. A bar. We are drinking beer with schnapps, then the same again. Conscious of a divided city—Danzig in the background, Mecklenburg, too—the comradeship of adoptive Berliners; literature lives again. Here he is wearing his cloth cap. Whoever doesn't settle down in Berlin has only himself to blame.

. . .

This is 1961, Bonne Auberge, an afternoon alone together; it is here that he speaks for the first time about politics, but in an almost Helvetic rather than a literary way—pragmatic rather than Utopian. However, I have to leave for the Schiller Theater for a performance of my own play.

. . .

Here he is during the intermission, silent in the lobby.

. . .

This is that same evening, Bonne Auberge. The principal actor asks straight out: "You were there?" Actors are natural creatures: from anyone who was there they expect a compliment or at least a critical comment. He rolls a cigarette, licks the brownish paper, etc., but not a word about the production or the play. He can't bear telling lies.

. . .

Here with some Group 47 colleagues.

. . .

Here I couldn't understand his narrow-eyed expression. On a chance meeting in Sperlonga, Italy. Something seems to have come between us; nothing is gained by invitations home or looking at the sea in the night. Here he is playing the judge in a marital dispute that is no business of his, but only briefly, for I tell him to leave. He remains in his chair and says calmly; "Let's at least finish our *grappa*."

. . .

Here we are on the following day, playing ball on the beach.

. . .

This is the Schiller Theater in Berlin again, a dress rehearsal: nobody there except the director (Lietzau) and himself, a lot of cameramen, but not a single one of his German colleagues.

. . .

Here beneath the moustache you can only see his bottom lip: his mouth is visible only when he laughs; he laughs less offensively than he used to.

. . .

Here you see him dancing.

. . .

Here he sits, a renowned cook as well as a writer, at our table, and guesses every spice, showing his appreciation of the cooking by eating and describing recipes of his own. He is particularly fond of variety meats—testicles, for instance, which I have never eaten.

. . .

This must be Frankfurt. Young left-wingers booed his play. There he stands rolling another cigarette, licking the brownish paper, etc. Not defeated by any means: he is not afraid of enemies, goes in search of them, in fact—that's what they're there for.

. . .

This is a New Year's Eve in Tessin. The others seem more cheerful than he. It's not his way to throw off his cares all at once.

. . .

Here he is standing over his own stove, seasoning something. You can see from his back that he enjoys being in his own skin.

. . .

This is in Zurich. He is speaking to some Czech writers, friends from Prague, after the Russian invasion; here you see him in the act of listening, hands in pockets, head bowed, a responsible man thinking of practical ways to help.

. . .

Here at the fireside: not one of the family, just relaxed. Even then he never flatters or holds back. After he drinks he returns to his theme (foreign aid). He is always persistent.

. . .

Here he is speaking to the nation on television, a writer with a sense of personal responsibility. He appeals to the nation's conscience, which he assumes it has.

. . .

Here he is talking about literature: Alfred Döblin.

. . .

Here he is swimming in the cold Maggia. When he comes out of the water, he will talk about Willy Brandt; he knows all the things one ought to know, that is, facts to refute any opponent—though I, of course, am not an opponent.

. . .

Here with Gershom Scholem. When somebody doesn't follow his lead, his wide knowledge of many subjects comes to the fore.

. . .

Should a writer, etc.? His answer lies in his example. Can a man campaign for one political party, yet as a writer remain open-minded? This is in his home: he is reading aloud.

. . .

Here in a car; he doesn't drive himself.

. . .

Here he is in a large hall, arguing with his opponents, used to their boos, firm, but hindered by his innate lack of cynicism. He argues knowledgeably and fearlessly—and always means what he says.

. . .

He is not in this picture, but we are talking about him, and in that sense he is there—strong enough to prevent unanimity, once his name has been mentioned.

. . .

Here, with just the two of us together, he is keeping an impenetrable silence—not unfriendly, but unwilling to stray from general topics; even when the two of us are alone together he asks no personal questions, but stays closed up until I embark on some general topic.

. . .

Here he is asking what I am working on.

. . .

Here you see him wrapped in silence, a man supposedly invulnerable; there are rumors of some calumny against him, but he spares us his personal complaints. He will defend himself publicly.

. . .

Here he is looking pleased. What about? When it is a question of some political victory, he looks different: satisfied, but very conscious of how much still remains to be done. Here he is obviously pleased with some sign of sympathy.

. . .

Here he looks quite tranquil: he is enjoying domesticity. Even with us as guests in the dining room. We eat mushrooms from the Berlin woods. Tomorrow he is off to Bonn.

. . .

Here he is being questioned by the international press: "Germany's Günter Grass." He replies neither as a government speaker nor as a private writer, but as an ordinary citizen with a special reputation. He doesn't put on a diplomat's smile. The questioners do not bother him—on the contrary—and he doesn't evade their questions or give vague answers. His stubborn allergy to German extravagance breeds confidence toward Germany.

. . .

Here he is listening.

. . .

Here he is keeping silence, without rolling himself a cigarette. Afterward it occurs to me: I have so far been silent myself about that play of his in which he brings Bertolt Brecht on the stage.

. . .

His face, I feel, has grown thinner, though no less powerful than it was in the Zürichberg villa; at that time, seen from the front, it was both softer and less aggressive. Here it is snowing; otherwise, he now seldom wears his cloth cap. But I feel his profile has become sharper.

. . .

Here I have just mentioned a name of which he disapproves: a sad affair on which he has nothing more to say. Pause. There are other things to talk about. A meeting with Herbert Wehner, the Social Democrat. He will look after the German side, and I should look after the Swiss. Sixty million people to six million, and yet we are on first-name terms. But the difference is not just numerical. He represents. What he cannot quite understand is the position of the private writer.

. . .

Here, I think, he doesn't know he is being watched: not knowing it makes no difference in him.

. . .

This is a picture of him as I do not know him, one of many. It could be a police notice: forehead, nose, moustache, chin, etc., all too definite—and particularly the expression.

. . .

Here his handwriting: graceful and ornate.

. . .

This could be anywhere—an airport or a tavern—I don't know, and it doesn't matter. He is quite conscious of being a public figure like no other German writer today, but he neither wants to be recognized, nor cares if he is, it seems.

. . .

Here he is speaking about Dürer's *Melencolia I.*

. . .

Here he is wearing a little beard, which reveals that he is in Tessin working on a book; he is showing us a cluster of snails on granite—a device for the Social Democrats—and also a scorpion preserved in spirits, which he in his capacity as house father caught and killed (August 1970).

SEPTEMBER 1970

Three airliners (Swissair, BOAC, TWA) have

been hijacked by Palestinian guerrillas and
taken to Amman and Cairo. A fourth attempt
against an El Al machine was unsuccessful: a
female hijacker (Leila) was overcome by armed
security guards, one man was shot dead, and
there was a narrow escape—a live hand gre-
nade, rolling about in the cabin, failed to
explode. The passengers in the other ma-
chines, six hundred fifty in all, are now
sitting together with the crew in the desert,
hostages in danger of being blown up along
with the airplanes unless all Palestinians
now serving sentences in foreign prisons for
earlier outrages are at once released. Time
limit: seventy-two hours.

INTERROGATION III

A. Our last interrogation began after you had been rereading
the political writings of Leo Tolstoi, with his total condemnation of any form of violence. You had not then felt able to
support that condemnation. You felt that the peasants in
czarist Russia had no other way of asserting their human
rights—

B. I still feel that.

A. What was your reaction to this hijacking by Palestinian
guerrillas, who also feel they have no other way of defending
their human rights?

B. I know some of my countrymen think the only possible way
of dealing with this violation of international law is to drop
Swiss parachutists near Zerqua, while others—the majority—
would be satisfied if Israel took over this military task. The
indignation, I should say, is general. The Swiss will not
tolerate injustice toward Swiss people. In Thalwil near
Zurich, so it has been reported, an inoffensive housewife
attacked another housewife in public with an umbrella,
thinking she was an Arab on account of her dark skin.

A. I am asking for your reaction.

B. When I heard the news I wondered at the ease with which
these kidnapings are always being carried out. Apparently

all you need is a pistol and a couple of people not afraid of losing their lives, and everything changes course. There are wrongful acts that provide a secret fascination—though one may still feel indignant . . . When I heard the news, I was glad that I wasn't in that plane. That's to say, I felt sympathy for the passengers. And then I remembered the Arabian desert near Amman. We were driving in an Opel; a woman with us who happened to put a hand on the chassis was severely burned—that's how hot it can be out there.

A. The Swiss government has yielded to the ultimatum, that is to say, it has agreed to release the three Arab terrorists sentenced in Zurich.

B. It is a matter involving Swiss lives.

A. What would you have done in the Swiss government's place?

B. It all depends how sacred you hold the law to be, the law as such. If it were as sacred as it is usually proclaimed to be, there would have been no course possible but to sacrifice the hundred forty-three passengers. I was both disappointed and relieved.

A. Why disappointed?

B. I think it is very possible that the Feddayin would not have recoiled from a massacre. The Bundesrat had to accept that they really would blow up the plane with all its passengers and crew; I was disappointed because I was brought up in the belief that a constitutional state—at any rate the Swiss state—does not capitulate.

A. And why relieved?

B. It seems it can be solved without loss of life. The plane is insured at a nominal value. The three Palestinian terrorists, sentenced in Zurich in accordance with Swiss law to twelve years' imprisonment, will be freed as soon as the hostages are freed, and they can resume their terrorist acts in the air whenever they like. . . . Though one condemns the use of force, the fact remains that the law will not be carried out; the state yields to force at the point where its own force ceases to be effective. What else could the Bundesrat do? Incidentally, it was not only the Swiss state that capitulated: the British and Germans did, too. There was no other way. Constitutional states depend on the existence of international law. But whoever wants the right to call on international law should not himself abuse it, and certainly he should not be permitted to profit when others abuse it. A country that, for example, supplies weapons to a country at war, even on a purely business basis, is in fact taking part in that war. This comes as a shock. The Bundesrat, which has no intention of putting a stop to the arms traffic, is in an embarrassing position when it comes to appealing to international law. Who, in its situation, could have acted otherwise? One cannot do business with war without having to conform to the rules of war, whatever the law may say: here it was a question of the hostages in the Zerqa desert, of saving lives—at the cost of offending against the constitution.

A. In February of this year a bomb exploded in a Swissair machine flying to Israel. Though not proved conclusively, it is probable that this was a Palestinian outrage. All forty-seven passengers died, in addition to the crew.

B. On that occasion there was nothing for the government to decide. Public mourning was enough. That is the difference: this time we had to decide. Should one hundred forty-three passengers and the crew die in the name of constitutional law? Berne's answer seems clear enough: the law is not more sacred than human life. That's what the revolutionaries think, too.

A. Meanwhile, the planes have been blown up—

B. But the hostages are alive.

A. What has that taught you?

B. That there is nothing absolute about the law, otherwise the authorities could not have reversed a sentence that had been legally passed. One would have had to sacrifice human lives— it could not have been done without tragedy, without sacrifice. . . . I have learned that our law is a humane law. And we owe our recognition of this fact to violence, however much we may condemn it.

A. How can you be relieved?

B. I understand the indignation. People are always indignant when it is not enough to be in the right. Presumably the Palestinian refugees also believe themselves to be in the right, and are indignant because this is not enough.

A. Assuming you had happened to be sitting in this DC-8, Flight Number SR 100, on the way to New York: what have the rights of Palestinian refugees to do with you?

B. Hostages are usually innocent people.

A. Do you think the disruption of peaceful air traffic by terrorist acts some of which have already caused casualties, can help to improve the living conditions of the Palestinian population?

B. The official answer is no.

A. And what do you feel?

B. I must confess that I have scarcely given any thought to the Palestinian problem before now.

A. So it needs a crime to bring a matter to your attention? Or do you feel that Dr. Habash, who is responsible for these acts of terrorism in the air, is not a criminal?

B. It all depends on whom else we call criminal. I have been reading the leading articles. In the language of our press, terrorism means only one thing: blackmail by violence—from the ranks of the oppressed.

A. And how do you define terrorism?

B. Blackmail by violence.

A. You are in favor of constitutional government.

B. I am in favor of constitutional government.

A. Yet you are reluctant to condemn violence. It frightens you, but at the same time you are relieved that our authorities have, as you say, capitulated to violence.

B. In order to remove the impression that a constitutional state can be made to yield to violence, there have already been suggestions that the condemned terrorists in Zurich should simply be pardoned; the idea is to restore faith in the contention that nothing can be achieved by violence. In fact, however—as we have seen—all that is needed is a pistol in the cockpit.

A. It is, of course, not true that the law has been set aside in order to free the hostages in the desert. The criminal law under which the terrorists in Zurich were sentenced is neither invalidated nor amended by the government's decision to exchange criminals for hostages. The Bundesrat was acting in an emergency: in emergency situations human lives are more important than laws.

B. I agree with that.

A. Do you approve of violence: yes or no?

B. There is the violence that protects lawful power, and this even constitutional states cannot do without. And there is the violence that creates lawful power. This latter form of violence is an answer to the first. But the first has always, at some time, developed out of the latter.

A. Do you approve of the pistol in the cockpit?

B. I have no right to condemn the pistol in the cockpit simply because I myself can get along without it. All I need I can have without violence, legally. Others are in a different position: my law-abidingness doesn't clothe them or house them, it does not provide them with the luxury of being able to get along without violence.

A. What are you trying to say? That violence is justified when you cannot achieve what you want without it?

B. It all depends what it is that cannot be achieved without it. . . . There is nothing I myself want which would justify the use of violence.

A. We are not talking about you.

B. Precisely.

A. You have admitted that acts of violence appall you, but you are still not prepared to condemn the use of violence in principle—

B. I have no right to.

BERZONA

An evening invasion. Asking them who they
are, I can see for myself: young people.
Five of them in windbreakers, pullovers,
etc., with a lot of hair. Best not say:
What do you want? Brought into the light, I
can see that they are not guerrillas, but
schoolboys from Basel, showing little constraint as they settle down, without much
ado. Chianti they have brought, cheese is
still on the table, but they have already
eaten. Pause. Their names? They are middle-class boys whose parents (as I suspect)
have no understanding, but houses—one in
Basel, one in Tessin. This does not seem to
bother them. The older boy, who wears
glasses and has as much hair as all the
others put together—not falling around his

shoulders, but frizzed out like an Afro—is
studying the double bass at the Conserva-
toire. But he has no intention of burying
himself for life in a symphony orchestra.
Music is provocation. I uncork sympathet-
ically. Recently, I am permitted to say, we
saw and heard the Mothers of Invention. But
that is not what he is after, either—the
provocation commercialized, Hair, etc. But
what can you do if the recording industry
grabs your music? asks his younger brother,
aged fourteen. It is easier than expected;
this is my home, but I am not required to
give opinions. The Afro will always remain
progressive. One of the others is thinking
of becoming a teacher, but is still not quite
sure, has anyway three more years of school
ahead. Since, apart from provocation, there
is no point in anything, why worry about professions? Their discussion grows more and
more lively, my presence obviously no hin-
drance. Only the fourteen-year-old is silent; he scratches around in his black pipe,
which he then grips between his teeth like a
grown-up, but it still refuses to draw. I
offer matches. When my wife says something,
they drop their dialect and speak grammati-
cally, which is quite unnecessary: it's like
being back at school. Kafka, for example
(says the second of the three brothers)—he
simply cannot read Kafka. He is seventeen,
the wittiest of the group. Even the Afro,
now stuck with his double bass, seems to
bore them; perhaps that is the reason for all
his hair, which doesn't bother me, only it
doesn't suit him. He even mentions his hair
once: the remarks he has to put up with from
his teachers or people in the street. What
they were looking for when they rang my front
doorbell I just don't know, and the question
doesn't arise. They sit there, they are the

present. What they are thinking concerns
themselves. Politics? They are not interested in Marx, the idea that all people
should earn the same. Nonsense of this sort
does creep in, but I am permitted to put the
record straight. What does interest them,
however, is Zappa and others less familiar to
me, their music, above all the private persons behind records of this sort, their way
of life a pattern to be followed: excess and
early death. The fourteen-year-old has to
leave the room, he feels sick—-the pipe, I
suspect, though he insists that it is only
the wine (two glasses). After he has vomited
I put him on a couch outside-- the face of an
elderly professor, but the skin of a child.
The longer the evening around my narrow table
continues, the less my presence seems to disturb. My contribution: cheese and listening,
and the single question—-what do they think
about marijuana? Their discussion is entirely among themselves. Marijuana is a plane of
experience on which no old grandpa can presume to teach them. Aha, so experience means
something, after all. But they don't want to
teach me: why should they? Their intellectual potential: having just learned to think,
they put all their trust in thought (without
action). Among themselves they are open to
all arguments; and these are arguments in
their own right, not just hidden excuses for
past mistakes. Their eagerness is unclouded.
The mistakes, easily identified, are the mistakes of their fathers. They suspect that an
adult, when he thinks, is basically always
defending something, that is, he is not open
to argument. Irony repels them. That is
another kind of loaded thinking, a sly conspiracy among has-beens, often completely
incomprehensible; the young person can only
suspect that the cupboard conceals a skeleton

that has nothing to do with him. So he responds to the irony with a straight face.
The fourteen-year-old, having meanwhile
washed dishes in the kitchen, now reveals
himself as an expert on drugs: he has read
practically all there is on the subject and
has statistics by heart. And why do you
smoke pot? One of them makes the excuse:
escape into a parasitical existence. The
witty one, now completely in earnest, defends it: better short and sweet, everyone
has the right to choose his own road to ruin.
He, for instance, does not want to grow old--
I beg your pardon!--not older than twenty-
five. And if everybody fixes, then your
civilization is finished--so what? The fourteen-year-old professor, who has put away his
pipe and is now smoking cigarettes, points
out the distinction between pot and hard
drugs, instructing us medically, juridically,
sociologically. Around midnight there remains something I should still like to know:
their feelings ten years, thirty years hence
--but that is exactly what doesn't interest
them in the least. . . .

CATALOGUE

Chestnuts as they burst gleaming from their green burrs /
snowflakes beneath the microscope / rock gardens Japanese
style / book printing / desert caravans with camels on the yellow horizon / rain on railroad coach windows at night / an
art nouveau vase in an antique shop / the mirage in the Anato-
lian desert, when one seems to see pools of blue water, the desert
in general / turbines / sunrise through green Venetian blinds /
manuscripts / coal heaps in the rain / the hair and skin of children / building sites / seagulls on the black mud flats at low
tide / the blue sparkling of blow lamps / Goya / things seen
through a telescope / wood shavings under a carpenter's bench /

lava at night / photographs from the beginning of this century / horses on the misty Jura mountains / maps, old and new / the legs of a mulatto girl beneath her coat / bird tracks on the snow / inns in the suburbs / granite / a face the day after death / thistles between marbles in Greece / eyes, mouths / the inside of shells / the reflection of one skyscraper in the windows of another / pearlfisher girls / kaleidoscopes / ferns, faded and bleached / the hands of beloved old people / pebbles in a mountain stream / a Mayan relief in its original site / mushrooms / a crane in motion / walls with outdated posters / snakes gliding with raised heads through the water / a theater once viewed from the gridiron / fish in the market, fishing nets drying on the pavement, fish of all kinds / summer lightning / flight of the black Alpine chough, seeing it take off over the precipice as one stands on the ridge / a pair of lovers in a quiet museum / the feel of the hide on a living cow / sunlight reflected in a glass of red wine (Merlot) / a prairie fire / the amber light inside circus tents on a sunny afternoon / X-ray pictures one cannot decipher, one's own skeleton seemingly wrapped in fog or cotton wool / breakers at sea, a freighter on the horizon / blast furnaces / a red curtain seen from the dark street outside, the shadow of an unknown person on it / a glass, glasses, glass of all kinds / spider's webs in the woods against the sun / etchings on yellow-stained paper / a lot of people with umbrellas, headlights gleaming on the asphalt / oil portrait of one's own mother as a girl, painted by her father / the robes of religious orders to which I do not belong / the olive-green leather of an English writing desk / the look of a revered man, when he takes his glasses off to clean them / the network of gleaming rails outside a large railroad station at night / cats / milky moonlight over the jungle as one lies in a hammock drinking beer from a can, sweating and unable to sleep, thinking of nothing / libraries / a yellow bulldozer, moving mountains / vines, for example in Valais / films / a man's hat rolling down the Spanish Steps in Rome / a line of fresh paint applied to the wall with a broad brush / three branches before the window, winter sky above red brick houses in Manhattan, smoke rising from strangers' chimneys / the neck of a woman combing her hair / a Russian peasant before the icons in the Kremlin / Lake Zurich in March, the black fields, the blueness of snow in shadow . . .

Etc.
Etc.
Etc.
Joy (affirmation) through the mere act of seeing.

BERLIN

On Alexanderplatz, for the first time in many
years, after passing through the lock—gates
of suspicion; the green uniforms remind me,
unfairly, of Nazi times. I feel ill at
ease. Why exactly? I belong to a state that
does not recognize this state; I recognize
it. Walk through the historical center of
Prussianism, posters of Lenin decorating the
buildings of a Communist Wirtschaftswunder.
A drive through the Brandenburg countryside
disperses my tension, a forest—clad plain
beneath a bright wide sky. Visit (22 Septem—
ber) to the poet Peter Huchel, once renowned
as a fighter against Fascism, but still de—
nied an exit visa.

FRANKFURT

Book Fair. The difference between a horse
and a writer: the horse does not understand
the language of horse dealers.

ZURICH

Nostalgic feelings in the Cooperativo, the
restaurant in the Militärstrasse; the house
is soon to be pulled down. . . . Lenin came
here often before his return to Russia.
Later Mussolini ate here, too, with Italian
workers: he was a Socialist then. A portrait
of Matteotti, whom the Fascist Mussolini put
to death, and above the brown paneling on the
smoky walls a fresh poster of the Swiss
Social Democratic party, the text a state—

ment of the obvious, though still unachieved.
A jukebox places us in the second half of the
century, and the young men are again wearing
beards. Above the jukebox a faded photograph
of their bearded ancestor: Carlo Marx. Workers are eating at the long tables covered
with white tablecloths, served by waiters in
white overalls. The cooking is Italian.
This is where anti-Fascist newspapers were
once printed, then smuggled into Italy. We
drink a beer under the smoke-stained bust of
Dante. A homely place in spite of the high
ceiling, a place of historical aspira-
tions . . .

INTERROGATION IV

A. Assume for a moment that a group of people used to handling arms takes possession of the factories in Oerlikon and threatens to blow up the Bührle plants unless a stop is put to trading in war materials—what would you say to that?

B. Leo Tolstoi condemned all use of force, including war, which he called a crime. I don't think the Bührle concern could appeal to Tolstoi.

A. Do you consider Herr Bührle a criminal?

B. I note that this question has been put neither to the court nor to the public. The right to trade in war materials, as long as it is done without false documentation, is undisputed.

A. You have read about the punishments the prosecution is demanding?

B. The offenses—falsification of documents over an extended period and arms smuggling to the value of 90 million francs —have been proved. The Federal Attorney is demanding prison sentences—provisionally deferred—together with fines that mean nothing to the gentlemen concerned. It is that which is arousing indignation among some people in the country.

A. Not in you?

B. Law is law; we are a constitutional state—I would even say a model constitutional state—even so powerful a man as

Dr. Dietrich Bührle, who has a declared income of 3,400,000 francs and a declared fortune of 125 millions, can be brought before the courts in this country.

A. Will he be sent to prison?

B. The head of the concern, Dr. Dietrich Bührle, is a colonel on the general staff of the Swiss army.

A. What are you implying by that?

B. As the Federal Attorney points out, the Bundesrat has every confidence in the Bührle concern; for this reason the Bundesrat finds these continued acts of falsification embarrassing, even if (as the defense emphasizes) they were not really dishonorable in intention, since the 90-million-franc deal was arranged not for motives of personal profit but in the interests of Swiss national defense, the Swiss economy, etc. As Dr. Dietrich Bührle himself has said, he cannot, with a turnover of 1,700 millions, attend personally to every detail. It is true he must at the time have known about it, otherwise he could not—as the defense has pointed out— have told his assistant of many years' standing "that such illegal transactions can no longer be permitted in the future." I endorse the statement: "There is not the slightest reason to question Dr. Dietrich Bührle's trustworthiness." All I was trying to say is that, if this were not so, the accused could not be a colonel on the general staff.

A. And his assistant director?

B. I do not know the gentleman personally, but must rely on the reports in the national press. Dr. Lebedinsky is not a colonel. As the defense says, this experienced assistant found himself involved in a genuine conflict of conscience, though it involved only 7 percent of the entire turnover in war materials. "He committed or approved the acts under investigation in the best interests of his employers." That is why, in spite of his dismissal, he is still drawing his salary. One must also understand Dr. Gelbert: "Like the other leading personalities in the firm, he was faced with the dilemma of deciding whether official regulations should be strictly observed, or whether, in the interests of preserving long-standing business relationships, one should try to salvage what could be salvaged"—in other words, the profits of the Bührle concern.

A. We are a constitutional state—

B. Yes.
A. There has been a public petition on the banning of arms exports. I take it that you, too, have put your signature to that. If this leads to a referendum, you can vote for Swiss trading in weapons to be banned. That is a constitutional process.
B. Of course.
A. So what is not in order?
B. The man now standing in the dock of the Federal Court in Lausanne together with a number of his assistants accused of forgery is a large employer of labor: the Bührle concern, which manufactures more than just weapons, has fourteen thousand workers. As I say, the Bührle concern is not manufacturing only double-barreled guns and the ammunition for them—one must not exaggerate. It sells guns and ammunition only in order to maintain a weapons industry of our own, as the Bundesrat well knows and appreciates. We do not incite others to fight wars; we sell them weapons because, if we did not, they would only buy them somewhere else. They could, once our weapons and our ammunition are paid for, leave them to rust, if they wish. To show that Switzerland does not intervene in the wars of other nations we supply both Israel and Egypt simultaneously. That is the way, incidentally, it has always been. During the Second World War, which concerned us closely, the Germans and the English were shooting each other in Tobruk with identical Oerlikon guns. Our arms traffic, quite apart from the fact that it is also connected with development aid, can on no account be considered an intervention in Nigerian or South African affairs: it is a simple business deal within the concept of a free market. If the Bundesrat, concerned for the credibility of Swiss neutrality, had not at that time imposed an arms embargo, this simple business deal could have been settled without false documents. The defense pointed that out before the Federal Criminal Court . . . As far as the referendum is concerned, Dr. Dietrich Bührle is not forced to comply with it: he could move his whole concern to another country any time he pleases, which means we should lose the taxes he pays, as well as his art collection. I fully understand the respect with which Dr. Dietrich Bührle is being treated; unlike other controversial cases (von Däniken for

instance), photographers are not allowed in court. Basically, we have reason to be grateful to this man. If the arms industry were to be nationalized, things would only become more difficult.

A. How so?

B. Because then the Bundesrat would have to answer for it, Parliament itself. Dr. Dietrich Bührle relieves us of this responsibility; as a free agent he delivers according to his own conscience, our country gets its share of the profit through taxes, but is not morally involved. We collect for Biafra and send nurses out to be hit by Bührle bullets. Charity is one thing, industry another—

A. The sentences have just been announced.

B. They can only be on the charge of falsification of documents. Nothing else is on trial. Aiding and abetting genocide for purposes of profit is not unconstitutional. Consequently, in our eyes the gentlemen of the Bührle concern cannot be criminals.

A. Though the Federal Attorney demanded only conditional sentences, the following are being sent to prison: Dr. Lebedinsky, Dr. Gelbert (who is incidentally a Knight of the Legion of Honor) as well as Herr Meili, and the court has also increased the recommended sentence. So one cannot call it a mild judgment. The only one to escape imprisonment is the head of the concern himself: he has been given a conditional sentence of eight months, and his fine has been reduced to 20,000 francs, since no profit motive has been proved.

B. I can understand his wide grin.

A. The question of aiding and abetting genocide for purposes of profit, to put it in your layman's words, does not arise. Consequently, the Federal Court's judgment cannot surprise you.

B. No.

A. You are also not surprised that the Federal Court (which incidentally was protected by a special police guard) was unable, while condemning the acts of falsification, to discover exactly how they were done, which middlemen made them possible, and which Federal officials, whose job it is to check the documents, for years failed to spot what was going on?

B. No.
A. That does not surprise you?
B. Our people, who believe in their constitution, are satisfied with three or four guilty persons. Apart from that, it is a matter of keeping long-standing relationships between the economy, the authorities, and the fatherland intact.
A. Do you consider the people stupid?
B. I consider myself stupid when I look at the press photograph showing the concern's boss with a wide grin on his face. He is right. The fine he has to pay to retain his freedom can be accounted for under expenses, and in any case it is a trifle compared with the bribes the concern has already paid out—expenses covering the constitutional processes that protect it from all violence.

ZURICH

```
A minor demonstration, starting outside the
art gallery (to which Bührle once donated a
million francs), marches through the Bahnhof-
strasse to the Stock Exchange; here and there
onlookers with pitying smiles, shaking their
heads. A woman says, "Bravo!" but she
doesn't join the marchers; a man keeps say-
ing, "I'm sorry for you, I'm sorry for you!"
Most, after reading the banners, immediately
walk away. A young man says, "Communists, go
to Moscow!" About a thousand marchers.
```

WORD OF HONOR

Sir, where would you prefer to live? In the first place I am no sir, and secondly; would you please remove your hand? I don't know the man at all. Sir, he says, and starts a long speech without taking his hand from my coat collar, speaking in several languages together and after a while, when he has got me in a thorough muddle, suddenly in German. A fellow countryman then. In what part of the world should I prefer to live? The question, he says, can only be put to a sir. Out of every hundred people on earth ninety-seven have no choice where they live, and from that very fact derive their reproductive strength. This is true; I think of Czech friends, Greek refugees, of millions of Indians. When I say I like being exactly where I am, he shakes me about in my raincoat and says in English, like a gangster: Come on, man, come on!—and that on the Helmhaus Bridge in Zurich. We are getting in people's way. What has it got to do with you? I ask, not taking hold of his hand again in case he starts shaking me once more. We are no longer quite alone; a few people, among them a man with a briefcase, but also ordinary people who had looked as if they were about to intervene, agree when he asks: Why don't you go and live in Moscow, why not in Havana, etc.? I was born here, I say, indicating with my head, in this district, it sounds wrong. To appear more convincing, I mention the name of the quarter, start defending myself: Have I ever said I don't like living here? At least he has now removed his hand from my collar, as if his question—Why not in Havana, why not in Peking, etc.?—were enough for the moment. We are now, in order not to disturb the traffic, standing at the side of the road, and I rearrange the collar of my raincoat without looking around for help; they all find the question a fair one, and I, of course, know the answer I owe to the majority. There are not that many present, but they have the face of the majority. What I now begin to say sounds less convincing with every sentence: Word of honor, I don't want to live anywhere else, word of honor, I was born and brought up and went to school here, and, what is more, I still live here. Do you want me to show you my passport? Should I give you the number of my pension card or the approximate number of days spent in military service with neither decorations nor punishments? Since there is to be no fight, only a few stay on. Why do I say "Word of honor" again—for the third time? It is a while before I get around to admitting that I have indeed often asked myself that very question: in what part of the world should I prefer to live? That satisfies him, it seems, I may go.

1971

BERZONA

```
Snow, a lot of snow.  The branches fluffy
white like pipe cleaners.  During the day we
shovel ourselves free, then in the night it
snows again.  Only television, Televisione
Svizzera Italiana, confirms that the world is
still going on, with visits of statesmen,
space flights, the Pope, Vietnam, music, and
sports.  So there's no need for panic.  And
mail is still arriving--pages and pages of
sociology.
```

LUCK

"I had luck, Fyodor Ivanovich, I hardly dare to think of it. Wonderful luck. As you see, I'm traveling first class. I have a passport. I have a title, I am free. Why I didn't end up in Siberia, I still can't understand, for I came close to it, God knows, very close," he said, stuffing tobacco, not into his nostrils, but into a Charatan pipe. There was also no bubbling samovar, but it was winter and he was in a railroad coach, and, when his pipe was at last drawing smoothly, the traveler said, looking through the window: "It's snowing," But it was not Russia outside. "I had no cause for jealousy," he said, as if someone were interested in hearing his story, "not the slightest cause. Natasha was already married, but I knew that from the start. Maybe I was even glad she was married. Now you are bound to be thinking that was not proper, since Natasha was married. But things are different nowadays, Fyodor Ivanovich. Her husband was a quiet, gentle man, even younger than myself, a just, but spiritless person. Perhaps Natasha failed to appreciate him. But it was for her sake I had left my wife and family. I felt then that it was wrong, but I was happy all the same. I loved her, Fyodor Ivanovich, I loved Natasha." There was nobody in the compartment who could be called Fyodor Ivanovich or Vassily Vassilovich or anything else, for in fact there was nobody there at all, but he just had to tell his story. "You see, I seldom think of it, in order not to upset myself, never in fact," he said. "I was an adult person then, a respected person, so to speak, and I believe you have guessed it, Fyodor Ivanovich, I could very well be a murderer!" The ticket collector, who happened to look into the compartment, was also obviously no Russian, but a rosy-cheeked young conductor with a red bag jogging against his knees. He was not unfriendly, but not even he had time, like people on Russian railroads in other days, to listen to reminiscences that would fill half a novel. After he had gone, the traveler said: "But do you really find it interesting?" Earlier he had been in the restaurant car; but there the people all looked at their plates or through one another. As soon as they have paid their bills, they did perhaps nod, but then it was too late to say: "I am a sick man . . . a wicked man . . . I am a repulsive person. I think there is something wrong with my liver." Who wanted to know about that? "As God is my witness, I had already raised the little ax, and Natasha was sitting in front of me, I wanted to split her in two like a log. *I* of course didn't want to, but the ax did, Fyodor Ivanovich, the little ax I held in my hand." Things like that could not been said in a restaurant car, nor in the compartment when a man entered and settled down with scarcely a greeting to read his newspaper. Perhaps his name was Hubacher or Vogelsanger, anyway he was a native of these parts, and it was not in Russia, where these frightful things had happened, that he got in, but in Grisons. "Do you know the country around Bivio?" It was all right to say that, even when it got only the surprised answer: "Why?" There was no bubbling samovar, remember, only the crackling in his Charatan pipe. "Nice pipe," he said, "isn't it?" The man sitting hidden behind his newspaper was certainly not a bad person; his coat was a good one, expensively lined. "I am a sick man, though perhaps I am not that at all, just a ridiculous man," he said out in the corridor. "And, incidentally, Fyodor Ivanovich, I told a lie just now. You probably noticed it. It wasn't for her I left my wife and family. That is nonsense. It was for myself. Later I left Natasha, too—and Vassa. . . . Now you think me an unprincipled person, Fyodor Ivanovich, but the opposite is true. She was too good for me—I mean my first wife. I never beat her, as God is my witness, but it was a blessing for her that I left her. They all admit that now. They were always too good for me, and one day I came to realize that they all suffered, you understand, sooner or later. There was always a lot of talk, every time the same talk. That's why I have traveled around so much. But today I realize the opposite is true. Why should I feel guilty? On the contrary, the minute I left them the women felt happier, or at least not more

unhappy—and there weren't so many of them, Fyodor Ivanovich, if that's what you're thinking. . . . Now we're in Biel, I
think," he said, then corrected himself: "Bienne." It was still
snowing. Trains don't stop long nowadays; no time for passengers to get out and fetch hot water, and there was no tea in
the restaurant now, only set meals. "I had no cause for jealousy," he said, resuming his story, "for it was her brothers. . . .
I don't know what came over me that night. It happened in a
ski cabin. She made some mulled wine for her brothers, because
it was cold, and during the whole evening she spoke to nobody
but her brothers, and they spoke only to her, for I was not part
of the family. I found it funny, or rather I tried to find it funny—
it *was* funny, Fyodor Ivanovich, but I am a vain man. I couldn't
bear Natasha caring for her brothers more than for me. Am I a
possessive person? I wasn't drunk, for she had made the wine
for her brothers; I didn't want any. You can imagine how lively
they were. I didn't say a word, for they were talking all the time
in French, you understand—that as well. Ridiculous. I suddenly
began to hate her, watching her from a corner, and hating her
quite soberly. At least, that's what I thought; in fact I loved her,
but hated the family feeling in her. Family feeling! I have
always thought the family tie a loathsome thing: it arouses my
worst instincts. . . . It came over me as we lay down to sleep
beside each other, Natasha and her brothers and I—or, to be
more precise, Natasha between her brothers and me. It was cold.
I had kept the log fire going the whole evening, but she had made
the wine for her brothers. They were already snoring when rage
seized me, I could feel it suddenly whipping away my blanket,
this rage, seizing me and setting me upright in the darkness. . . .
Did I tell you that her brother, the elder one, was an officer?
He was the stupider of the two, but Natasha never rebuked him.
The younger was a dancer, a choreographer or something—
anyway, an artist. It was this one Natasha particularly admired.
I realized for the first time who I was: her lover. . . . It is possible that in the darkness Natasha may now have asked me if
I was unwell, whispering so that her brothers could keep on
snoring, but I didn't hear her. I have been to the best schools,
but I am and always will be a primitive person. Natasha didn't
believe I had it in me. And her brothers, knowing no more than
that I was in love with Natasha, didn't believe it either. . . .
It was winter, as I already told you, and it was night—I didn't

know where to go. Out into the deep snow. I wanted to be frozen to death, you understand, while they snored in the cabin." He stopped to let someone go by in the narrow corridor. "Do you believe in God, Fyodor Ivanovich?" he asked, then, without waiting for an answer: "Now I could have been fifteen years in Siberia for a stupid murder. Perhaps I should have learned to believe. It needs very little, that's all I know for sure. Perhaps, Fyodor Ivanovich, I should have learned to believe in God's mercy. Now all I believe in is luck." He scratched out his Charatan pipe as the man whose name might be Vogelsanger or Bärlocher or anything else took up his leather briefcase and vacated the compartment, not without a nod. "To put it in a few words," he said, settling down again in the upholstered compartment, "I wanted to freeze to death. I loathed myself, Fyodor Ivanovich, I was ashamed of myself. It was not cold enough to freeze, it was just unbearable. A starry night. My stiff corpse in the snow on the following morning—that was not only a mean and ridiculous plan, it was also impossible to carry out, for, when the light began to dawn over the mountains in the east, I was only shivering. Natasha was still asleep. She knew nothing of my plan, no one under the whole wide sky knew how ridiculous I was—except myself! . . . Now we are in Brugg, I think"—with a glance through the window—"Brugg or Braden." These are no epic distances. "Perhaps I am boring you, Fyodor Ivanovich, but you are the first person to whom I have told my story. . . . When I at last went back to the cabin, I thought I was in full possession of my senses, coldly resolved to put on my skis and in the first light of dawn to run down to the valley, where I would write Natasha a letter. She also was much too good for me. An angel! . . . I don't know if you have experienced it, Fyodor Ivanovich, this feeling of being mean and ridiculous: it is more terrible than a starry night in the snow, or so I felt as I heard her brothers snoring above my head. What had they done to me, after all—that officer and that dancer? Their sister had given them mulled wine, and I can understand French well enough. . . . So I took up the little ax to chop wood, because I was freezing after my ridiculous two hours in the snow. Even my bones felt frozen. I had made a fire for her, now I would make one for myself. It makes a noise, of course, a log like that when the ax sticks in it and one thumps both log and ax against the chopping block. The family snoring stopped. I was glad now

that I was shivering, for that gave me the right to chop logs and
slit them up into firewood the way we do, you know, even at
the risk of hurting ourselves. It must have looked funny, but it
was not all that funny. Fyodor Ivanovich. When Natasha came
down and asked me what in God's name I was doing, I said;
'Making mulled wine.' She was sleepy and not her usual lovely
self, as she had been the whole of the previous evening, and,
because she was sleepy, I put it even more clearly: 'Mulled wine
for myself!' Yet I felt ashamed. Her air of sweet reason, Fyodor
Ivanovich, her sweet feminine reason! You don't know Natasha,
of course. We had been in love three years, and I thought her
the very soul of unreason, a real human being. But her reason-
ableness now, at five o'clock in the morning, was infuriating.
'Mulled wine,' I shouted, 'go away!' Natasha thought she knew
me, otherwise she would not have sat down on the block as if
that were what it was there for—Natasha in a blue overall,
her hair uncombed, still warm from sleep. The brothers, whom
my chopping had awakened, were of course listening. She
said, '*Qu'est-ce-que tu fais?*' I said again, 'Mulled wine!'—you
know, in a meaning sort of way—I don't know whether she took
it for a joke or just a pigheaded way of annoying the rest of them
—and not only her two brothers. I forget to tell you that there
were other people in the cabin, sons and daughters and so on,
a whole tribe, when I said to her; 'Go away!' and raised the ax
to chop firewood . . ." He began again to scratch out his pipe,
in order to stop himself speaking, yet he could not. "now we're
in Schlieren," he said, with a glance through the window.
"Fyodor Ivanovich, have you ever thrown a chair out into the
street—and then another and another? I've never got any better,
you see. This was later—with Vassa. That time I did have cause
for jealousy, and I was drunk, a drunken pig. Iron chairs they
were, my rage seized them and flung them off the terrace onto
the road, and I didn't become a murderer, Fyodor Ivanovich. How
do you explain that?" He was silent until his pipe was again
drawing smoothly. "You believe in God, Fyodor Ivanovich,
otherwise you wouldn't smile at my folly. Tell me frankly that
you're sorry for me, Fyodor Ivanovich, for being such a stupid
and shallow person. I'm not sorry for myself . . . I wasn't mad,
I knew exactly that at this instant my ridiculous behavior had
nothing to do with Natasha, who was looking at me, nor with
her brothers, it was only that I couldn't hold the ax back any

longer, though Natasha was sitting in front of me and looking at me. I believe I couldn't even speak her name, her so beloved name, all I heard was: *'Qu'est-ce-que tu fais?'* Then the little ax was embedded in the block, she standing beside it, I still holding the log I had wanted to split—and that was all, Fyodor Ivanovich: Luck!" He was still looking out of the window. The yellow lights of a station flashed past. "Altstetten already," he said indifferently, and it was now time to take down his coat and gradually collect his other possessions—not much, a little parcel, perfume for his wife. Since the loop was almost invariably missing from his coat, he was in the habit of just throwing it on the rack and, when he looked around for it, he seemed surprised to find Fyodor Ivanovich sitting opposite, almost directly beneath the coat, smiling a little: "Little father, that is your whole story?" In the corridor people were already pushing and shoving. "No," the traveler said, now leaving his coat where it was, in an equally mocking tone: "Fyodor Ivanovich." The other man was rather short, not old, but his curly hair had gone prematurely gray, and he had unusually glittering eyes. He wore an old overcoat, evidently from a first-rate tailor, with an astrakhan collar, and a tall astrakhan cap. When he unbuttoned his overcoat a sleeveless Russian coat and embroidered shirt showed beneath it. "I am Pózdnyshev," he said, as if one ought to know the name, and then: "Won't you have some tea? Only it's very strong." The tea, which he had brewed at the station before the last, was really like beer. "Pózdnyshev," he repeated bitterly, speaking in a voice that sounded as if his throat needed clearing: "Little father, why do you not tell your whole story, your real story, when you see someone is listening?" One could tell by one's feet that the train was now beginning to brake. "Well then," the traveler said, "I'll tell you," as if he had not heard the guard, who was putting his head into every compartment, calling out: "Zurich main station. All change!" He paused, rubbed his face with his hands, and began: "If I am to tell it, I must tell everything from the beginning. I must tell where I was born, and who raised me, who my friends were, what I studied, and all the things that led up to my miserable story. . . ."

```
NEW YORK, February

We have rented an apartment, belonging to a
```

child psychiatrist whom I do not know. Her
diploma on the wall. A psychiatrist's couch:
one doesn't sit and one doesn't lie, but re-
laxes with results—these, then, are things
that I have repressed:
a. My father
   (Died 1932.)
b. The general strike of 1918
   (Students in college caps driving street-
   cars, behind them soldiers with steel helmets and fixed bayonets to protect the
   strikebreakers.)
c. My first effort at reading newspapers
   (I wanted to find out whether a motor-
   cyclist, who collided with our hand cart
   when we were fooling around and fell off
   his machine, had died.)
d. Poverty
   (Stealing orchard windfalls.)
e. War children from Vienna
   (I preferred playing with them, they knew
   different games, but it could only be done
   in secret, and when I was caught there was
   trouble: I was a traitor.)
f. The fear of God
   (Swimming trunks in the bathtub.)
g. The fear of other people
   (To become a member of the gang you had to
   clamber through a sewage pipe, barefoot in
   the stinking water, in the distance a pinpoint of daylight.)
h. Lenin
   (The thin little man going in and out of
   the house next door; my father said he
   wanted to destroy everything in the
   world.)
and several other things.

INCIDENT

No cause for panic. Nothing can happen. The elevator has

stopped between the thirty-seventh and thirty-eighth floors. It has happened before. The current is bound to come on again any moment. Humorous comments in the first minute, then grumbles about the house management generally. Somebody flashes a cigarette lighter, perhaps to see who is standing in the dark cabin. A woman with shopping bags on both arms has difficulty in understanding that there is no point in pushing the alarm button. She ignores all advice to put her bags down on the cabin floor, where there is room enough. No cause for hysterics: nobody will suffocate in the cabin, and the idea that it might suddenly hurtle down the shaft remains unspoken— it is technically impossible, surely. One man never speaks a word. Perhaps the whole neighborhood has been cut off: that would be a comfort—then a lot of people would be working on it, not just the caretaker down in the lobby, who perhaps hasn't yet noticed anything wrong. Outside is daylight, maybe the sun is even shining. After a quarter of an hour it is more than annoying, it is downright boring. Two yards up or two yards down and we should be at a door, though that wouldn't of course work either without electricity—an insane piece of machinery, really. Shouting is no help; on the contrary, you feel even more abandoned afterward. Somebody will certainly be doing all he can somewhere to mend the breakdown: it's the duty of the caretaker, the house management, the authorities, civilization. The crack that at least the woman's shopping bags will save us from starvation comes too late: nobody laughs. After half an hour a young couple tries, as far as that is possible among listening strangers, to talk to each other quietly about everyday things. Then more silence; now and again someone sighs, the exaggerated sort of a sigh that signifies reproach and annoyance, nothing more. The current is, of course, bound to come on any moment now. What can be said about the incident has already been said several times. Somebody says there have been power cuts lasting two hours. Luckily the boy with the dog got out before it happened; a whining dog in the dark cabin would have been the last straw. The man who doesn't speak is perhaps a foreigner who doesn't understand much English. The woman has meanwhile put her shopping bags on the floor. Her anxiety that the frozen foods will thaw arouses little sympathy. Somebody else perhaps wants to go to the toilet. Two hours later there is no more indignation and no talk either, for the current must come on at any moment; one knows the world won't end like this. After three hours and eleven minutes (according to subsequent reports in the press and on television) the current is restored: lights go on over the whole district, where it has meanwhile turned to evening, light in the cabin, and a touch on the button is enough to send the elevator rising as usual, and as usual, too, the doors slowly open. Thank God for that! And it isn't as if we all immediately pile out at the very first stop: everyone selects as usual the floor he wants. . . .

EMERGENCY DIAL 911. OBSERVE THE FOLLOWING RULES OF SAFETY WHILE WALKING THE STREETS:

1. Try not to walk alone at night—have someone accompany you through the streets.
2. Have a friend or relative meet you at the subway or bus station.
3. When you arrive at home, ring your bell to alert a relative or neighbor and have a key ready in your hand to open the door.
4. DO NOT enter an elevator with a stranger of any age.
5. Walk in an area that is well lighted; don't take shortcuts.
6. Know location of police call boxes and public phone booths in your area.
7. If there are doormen in your neighborhood, know when they are on duty; they may be helpful.
8. Remain *alert* while walking; *look around you.*
9. If you observe any person or group that appears suspicious, do any of the following:
   a. Use a police call box and call for assistance.
   b. Go to a public phone booth and dial 911.
   c. If no phone is available, enter any store or residence and call police. Your neighbors are willing to help.
10. DO NOT carry large sums of money, conspicuous jewelry, or other valuables; when you cannot avoid this, secrete the cash and other valuables on your person, NOT in your wallet or handbag.
11. DO NOT place your house key together with other keys. Keep them separate. If you lose identification papers together with your house keys, someone may have access to your home.
12. Carry a whistle or a cheap battery-operated alarm when possible.

13. Carry your purse close to your chest. Don't dangle it loosely at arm's length.
14. If you hear screams, day or night, try to pinpoint location and help your neighbor by calling 911 immediately.
15. DO NOT answer your downstairs bell unless a caller is expected and known to you.

Ptl. Charles E. Delaney
Community Relations Office
26th Precinct

NEW YORK, February

It appears to be true: a fellow Swiss describes how on 10th Street (where we live) he suddenly, at eight o'clock in the evening, felt three knives pressing on his body, two at the back, one in front. His assailants (all blacks) asked only one question: "Where is it?" When they discovered only ten dollars in his change purse, their knives became more threatening. Luckily he kept still, until they found another twenty dollars in his wallet. They then threw his wallet and passport into the road, so that he had to retrieve them while they disappeared. A passerby to whom the distraught man appealed merely shrugged his shoulders. . . .

Seminar at Columbia University in German: Problems of Style and Expression. Who are the students? Their college fees amount to $2,500 annually; a student costs his parents $5,000 to $6,000 per year. Who are their parents?

Demonstration in Times Square: with the same banners against the same war as last spring, but with fewer marchers. They go around and around an enclosure erected by the police, neatly separated from the ordinary citizens in the street. As in an exercise cage: "Peace now!" The police, though numerous and

equipped with helmets, truncheons, and ra-
dios, coolly instruct the majority outside:
"Keep moving, please keep moving." One reads
that the majority (70 percent) is now against
the war. Demonstrations are no longer an
effective method.

An elderly taxi driver explains why he is
going home after this trip, why he no longer
drives at night: "Too many characters, you
know." But he can understand them, he says:
they return from Vietnam, don't know what to
do for a living, then start taking drugs.
Heroin is expensive, so they attack him and
take his entire day's earnings. That's why
he prefers to go home around this time. But
there are nice people, too, he says: they
tell him at the end of the journey that they
have no money, he then gives them his address; some really do send along the three
or four dollars they owe.

Alcoholics Anonymous. They meet three times
a week. An attractive, youngish woman talks
of her experiences with alcohol: she is now
cured. Very frank, direct, not at all sanc-
timonious. Sole condition of entry: a genuine desire to give up drinking. There are
about a hundred fifty men and women of vary-
ing ages, poor and better off, black and
white together. A person who wants to join
in the discussion first introduces himself:
"Joe. I am an alcoholic." This man then
asks the speaker how she dealt with relapses.
They understand one another. One man is very
drunk, says something, then after a while
leaves. Nobody is annoyed: all here know how
difficult it is. I see him even managing to
cadge a dollar before he goes. Only a few
look as if they are drinkers. In the next
room children are playing a noisy ball game.

There are free cups of tea. Somebody who has
mercifully fought free of the temptation ac-
companies an addict to parties and tries to
restrain him, without condescension, for he
himself has known alcohol, and the demon who
promises this glass will be the last, and the
excuse that today there is something to
celebrate. An old Negro, when I asked him
for leaflets, first gives me his hand and
says, "Bobby." I say, "Max."

WOMEN'S LIBERATION

—and every time he finishes up by saying he is in favor, entirely
in favor, but we women must win it for ourselves. Then he
pulls the blanket over his bare shoulder, this nineteenth-cen-
tury creature. I could kill him, just because he knows I can't.
Why not, though? A creature that snores isn't a human being.
We'd been living in harmony for months. The myth of vaginal
orgasm—he allows that for the sake of peace and quiet. If I
mean to kill him, he says, I had better learn first how the car
engine works, and other such nonsense. I didn't know what I
was marrying. A woman's body just happens to be different, he
says, which is what I say, too, though I mean it differently. He
wants to know if I've read Norman Mailer. He doesn't even
fight when one answers back, just says again he's entirely in
favor. Women on the level of blacks, he admits all that, but what
does he do about it? And now there's this June, who is making
eyes at him, this June with her cart-horse legs who can't even
realize that he doesn't take her seriously—that's the last straw.
Why do I take *him* so seriously? That's what he asks before he
goes off to sleep. I ask myself too. And I don't read Norman
Mailer. They never learn. Even *Lysistrata* is a man's invention,
that hoary old man's joke about a sex strike by women being
bound to fail because there are always scabs like this June with
her underdeveloped consciousness. The nearest to a progressive
thought he has ever got: that women's emancipation so far has
turned out to be a boomerang, because it hasn't freed women;
on the contrary, it has just slotted them into categories of male
thinking. That's exactly what we're saying. If he can condescend

to be serious even for a moment, he admits it can't go on like this. And he has at least dropped certain habits. He used to say: *your* children. Then he casually quotes Margaret Mead, about the paternal function of the human race being a socially orientated invention (yes, you heard—invention), not a natural phenomenon like menstruation (that's right)—socially orientated and therefore repressive. I don't think all that long hair suits him particularly—perhaps because I know him. Joe isn't a lion. They just pretend to be progressive, these artists, and then he gives himself away: women aren't creative, he says. Helen sorted him out, better than I can: she doesn't get upset when he argues. He doesn't argue with me any longer, but is always nice—and not only when he has the urge or feels I have the urge, either. Still, he does admit he wouldn't like to be a woman. But I *am* one. Or, if a woman, then a Lesbian, he says. And that I'm not. When he tries to imagine being me, it turns out that I'm lazy (compared to him), because he thinks messing about with his Plexiglass is work, and I'm emotional, because he thinks *he* is always reasonable about things he doesn't agree with. It's always the same. He says I'm maternal and side with the children when he throws them out of the studio. He says I'm not stupid (still compared to him, of course), so he thinks it all the more stupid of me not to see when he is in the right. I could kill him. There's only one woman he'll listen to: *la mamma* in Bologna. The fact that young women—and not only June, whom he himself doesn't take seriously—fall for him doesn't make me jealous: it just stops him ever learning. He calls me possessive, but I don't *ask* him to put himself in my place. Then he says I have qualities (compared to him): it's a quality, for instance, according to him, that I'm sensual, etc., and Irish. That's the sort of thing he says. Women, he says for all to hear, are conservative by nature. He really still does believe such things. Free Our Sisters—all right, he'll go along with that if they're in prison—but I *am* free, he says. And if I threaten to leave him? Then he suddenly brings up Strindberg, which I consider a load of trash, apart from the letters, of course. Helen says we mustn't argue, we must build up facts. And now he's snoring, this thirty-one-year-old patriarch who thinks the same as Norman Mailer, whom I am not going to read. Everyone knows and has known for three thousand years what they think. They've learned nothing since. Anyway, not Joe. He

thinks Gertrude Stein is great, but I tell him he wouldn't be
able to live with her: he can hardly even live with me. Now
he's snoring, because the minute he falls asleep he can't shut
his mouth—just like a baby.

NEW YORK, March

One wakes up, goes out into the street, and
survives. That makes one feel cheerful, almost reckless. Nothing special needs to happen: it's enough just to survive from one
ordinary day to the next. Somewhere a murder
is going on, and here we are standing in an
art gallery, enthusiastic or not as the case
may be--but present. It is no lie when I
answer back, "Thank you, I am fine."

Awakened at 3:30 in the morning by a detona-
tion. Two bangs owing to the echo. A few
minutes later police in the next street. Too
tired to stand at the window for long, and
there's nothing to see anyway--just the reflection of the rotating blue light on the
house fronts. Half asleep, I think: Somebody has shot somebody. Voices. Then a
noise, which continues almost an hour long:
splintering glass, and splintered glass being
swept up. Unable to get back to sleep: when
I open my eyes, still the rotating light from
the police car on the ceiling; but eventually
I do fall asleep. . . . It was in the New
School on 11th Street, a smallish bomb, damage to the vestibule: in the lobby the usual
collection of students (adults) at the library counter. When I ask the doorman the
possible reason for the bomb, he shrugs his
shoulders. Nothing new. Such things happen.

At the Fillmore East, a year ago, a psyche-
delic light show was suddenly interrupted. A
rock player came to the front and asked us to

look under our seats to see if a bomb was
there. They had had a phone call. The
theater has 2,884 seats. Most of us bent
down briefly to look under our seats, rather
as if a woman had lost her purse; others
remained lying in their seats, obviously in a
trance. Three minutes later the band started
up again. I asked my young neighbor with
Jesus hair and gentle eyes why there should
be a bomb here. Reply: "For no rational
reason," and then, since I still didn't
understand: "You know, in these days. . ."

Seminar on the narrator's function:
a. Homer
b. The Apostles
c. <u>Don Quixote</u>
d. <u>Anna Karenina</u>
e. Today

Where political action is hopeless: sects of
all kinds, Krishna children, etc., the eclec-
ticism of salvation doctrines. One can't put
one's head through a brick wall, but one can
decorate it with bright Indian ribbons. They
look picturesque. What started out as a
revolutionary impulse dissolves in introspec-
tion, atrophy of the will, atrophy of the
critical sense. Without the growing criminality due to drugs, the rulers would have no
need to worry: their revolutionary children
are destroying themselves.

Yesterday in the neighboring street (9th
Street) a young man was murdered. Today
with sociologists again. There is little
that they do not at once translate into their
own language. Man can take his choice of
doctrines.

Stroll after work through the asphalt cities,

of which one day nothing will remain "but the wind that blew through them" (Brecht)—it sweeps and swirls the rubbish through the rows of streets, which look like the aftermath of a battle. Rust and decay, houses as garbage. Elsewhere, not far away, new high-rise buildings are springing up. Deserted as the streets are, one feels no fear in them: an occasional limousine. Fear is where the white-gloved doormen stand on wall-to-wall carpets. No stop lights here, one can really stroll. A blue evening: airplanes drawing their brown veils of jet poison over Manhattan. This is not even a slum: ruins on the borderlines of capital, they are not worth pulling down; the capital is at present earning interest elsewhere. Just land, privately owned, that Nature is claiming back with weeds. Former warehouses, they started to collapse long ago, or were burned. Not a single hope left—not even for dogs. An overpass: showing that we are in a metropolis and not at the end of time. I don't know why, but it all makes me feel cheerful when I stroll here. We come on shining water, but from close to it is a blackish cesspool, barges with dredgers clearing the slime. Names recall the Dutchmen who once landed here; the pier is rotten, the sun goes down behind brown smoke.

The doorbell rings and I simply open the door. I still haven't learned. A man with work kit: I ask him what he wants, and, when I don't understand, he just walks in. Window cleaner! He wipes for ten minutes, demands nine dollars. Presumably the house management has sent him. Afterward I am told I was lucky; but he really did just clean the windows.

One learns about the war crimes from witnesses who, interviewed on television (Chan-
nel 13), describe what they did in Vietnam
when ordered to take no prisoners. Free fire
zone: everyone can be killed, including children. Reward for killing three Vietnamese: a
week's leave on the coast. As proof of killing one brings along ears or genitals. None
of the witnesses, who give their names and
present addresses, can recall anyone ever
being punished or even warned for violating
prisoners. The public meeting is run by a
Columbia professor of law. If no killing,
then for one reason only: to allow for interrogation, where all kinds of torture are
practiced—and, incidentally, sexual urges
satisfied on both women and men—before the
victims are shot. The incidents, described
by the young witnesses as quite usual, date
from 1967, 1968, 1969, 1970. Although they
now talk from a different perspective (all
very factual), they still, when talking of
the Vietnamese, use the expression "gook."
Asked by press reporters whether they had not
been conscious of the criminal nature of such
conduct, they all admitted, "You soon get
used to it." What happens if somebody refuses to join in? The young man, now a commercial employee, shrugs his shoulders: disciplinary transfer, a further six months in
Vietnam. One just becomes an animal. None
of it shows in their faces, however. Usually
the prisoners are shot from the front, but
for a change they can be tied to a helicopter
and dropped from a certain height. An old
man rises in protest against the witnesses:
his son, his only son, died in Vietnam; he
had persuaded him that he would be fighting
for his country and for freedom, and that is
what he had done, his only son. Then he

starts to weep. The chairman calls for
further questions. . . .

WALL STREET

Lunch on the sixtieth floor . . . Even in the elevator (doors
of chromium or brass?) only gentlemen, dressed for work as
if they were going to a concert: dark gray to black, hardly any
blue. In spite of the crush in the elevator (the lunch break
has just started) an air of inviolable correctness. Their skin
is fresh and smooth and usually taut, their gaze alert, their
voices not quiet, but confident and manly; an occasional laugh
sounds almost shocking, boyish in contrast to their very sedate gestures. Even with their hands in their pockets they
remain unmistakably gentlemen.

RECEPTION IN THE LOBBY:
I am a successful writer, hence this invitation; the other guests
are from the diplomatic service. We look down on the lower
skyscrapers of Wall Street between the two rivers, immediately
agreeing: a wonderful view. Our host, though used to this view,
leaves us time to admire it. Unfortunately a misty day: otherwise we could see Brooklyn, etc. Whoever comes here for lunch
must have a good head for heights: the people down on the
street, when one looks down, move about like maggots or lice.
Really, one shouldn't look down. Wall-to-wall carpets, glass,
leafy plants. It is quiet here, Manhattan a panorama under
glass. Here there are only gentlemen meeting gentlemen, an
intact world with, incidentally, no old men to be seen and no
stout ones besides myself; they obviously have little time, yet
betray no haste. They are used to knowing that their time is
precious. I am more tense: here one does not dare to doubt. The
imputation of being somehow in accord with it all is as silent
as one's steps on the carpet. Only my baggy corduroy trousers
don't really fit in, but that makes my invitation all the more
of an honor. We go to lunch in groups. A separate room, with a
round table, art on the walls, a new view of Manhattan. Unfortunately, it is misty, but we have already said that; all the
same, we can see the Statue of Liberty. We drink iced water,
no alcohol: high finance is puritanical here, but cheerful. The

day's news (among other things): the Russian royal family was not murdered, but is said to be alive still, somewhere in America. If that should turn out to be true, it raises questions of property, now lying in London, millions of old rubles. I no longer remember what we ate. Four of the guests are Germans. Question: who will be Chancellor, Barzel or Schröder? But never a word out of place against the present Federal Chancellor, Willy Brandt; it is considered possible that the Social Democratic government might last until the elections. In spite of its policies towards the East. Unless, of course, it comes a cropper on the economy. Franz Josef Strauss is not mentioned, although he was here recently and was robbed by two prostitutes. Schröder is considered a more likely candidate than Barzel, I hear, and can assure my American host that the subject does not bore me in the least; the gentlemen know a lot that one does not necessarily learn from the newspapers. I have already noted the art that the Chase Manhattan Bank collects: Lichtenstein, Lindner, Dine, Fontana, Glarner, Bonnard, Dali, de Kooning, Sam Francis, Hartung, Segal, Albers, Calder, Goya, Vasarely, Steinberg, Pomodoro, Beckmann, Nevelson, etc.—these I know from the galleries. What surprises me more: that there is no hint of American imperialism. Did I say something? After the experiences in Indochina, it is rather to be feared that the American people might revert to isolationism, in other words, there could be a reduction in American aid for Latin America. And later? About the theater I have little to say. If any country is imperialistic, it is Soviet Russia (I don't deny it), which is losing vast sums of money in the Arab countries—as our host says: Luckily for us. But this is not our main lunchtime topic. We have none. There is not much to be said either about the World Trade Center, 1350 feet high, now under construction, although we can see it through the window; it will bring a further eighty-five thousand commuters into the city, to dissipate their energies in the daily traffic. Who can do anything to stop that? Then my eternal question to the experts: why use gold as a cover? What has it got compared with oil or manpower, etc.? The answers vary. A Swiss banker once said gold was a pure myth. Today's answer: Nothing in our world is secure except gold, which has kept its value from time immemorial and will continue to do so. Why? Without gold the only feasible economic system would be state owned, in other words, dictatorship; but a free economy needs a hoard, stability—not to forget that gold has its uses for jewelry, etc. My incomprehension does not help the conversation. What am I writing at the moment? That there are some idealists among the hippies I agree without argument; also that there is no unrest in Switzerland. We eat with pauses. It would be foolhardy to mention Vietnam. They know more about it. No one at this table represents power, they are simply at one with it, and to this extent wise. Asked about my experiences with "my" students, I can assure them these are well behaved, no great conflicts. I take coffee. On the other side of the table they are discussing Japan: gaining markets through low prices, but in Japan, too, wages will rise. They have the figures. China? They have the figures. They are confident that throughout history the sole motive has always been profit. Unfortunately, there are no cigars, and the gentlemen must get back to their work. I thank them sincerely: for a writer it was more interesting than they think. Our host insists on accompanying us down to the subway personally; marble all the way to the barrier, then one goes through the turnstile—outside.

AUSTIN, TEXAS, end of March

A skunk running around the park at night: first time I have seen one in its natural state; but you shouldn't get too near, says my friendly host, a German scholar, a dean on the edge of the prairie. The flight from New York was as long as from Zurich to Moscow, but at both ends the beer is the same. So the capital of Texas is Austin—not Dallas, as I previously thought. The Capitol with its classical dome, floodlit at night, proves it. When was it built? Here it is already summer, the oleander now fading. It is not really a city, but one huge park: nothing urban in its generous use of space, simply an oasis of comfort.

Recently, a year ago, a young man climbed up

to the observation tower at the university, a
madman with an arsenal of ammunition, to
shoot down blindly into the crowd on the wide
square below and kill some fellow students. . . .

Embarrassment in the excellent motel. Everything there that a person in his wildest
imaginings could possibly need. And everyone
so friendly—the furnishings, too. Living
couldn't be made easier. Outside (so I picture it to myself) the prairie, while here I
have everything—and clean. It is a park
here, too, summer night with rows of gleaming
cars and illuminated signs. Everything quite
recognizable—not familiar, but completely
recognizable. I do not know where I am.
There is no Here. I have no wishes (they
have been asking me again)—but a contained
sense of panic.

Lieutenant Calley found guilty of having
murdered at least twenty-two Vietnamese civilians at My Lai, under nonemergency conditions. All that now remains is the sentence
(death or imprisonment?). The findings
alone have caused nationwide protest. Someone has written on his limousine: I Killed in
Vietnam, Hang Me Too. The young and (according to the photographs) soft-looking lieutenant did not reckon on being found guilty,
and can only repeat that he served his country. Today the court is being accused of
besmirching the army's honor, sixty thousand
telegrams to this effect, even after it became known that the death sentence had not
been imposed. First Agnew and then Nixon
admonish the legal authorities.

Lecture on Bertolt Brecht.

QUESTIONNAIRE

1.
When you are in a foreign country and meet compatriots, does this make you feel homesick, or precisely the opposite?

2.
Is home to you something with a flag?

3.
Which could you most easily do without:
a. a home?
b. a fatherland?
c. foreign countries?

4.
What do you call home:
a. a village?
b. a town or a district within it?
c. places where the same language is spoken?
d. a continent?
e. a house or apartment?

5.
Assume you are an object of hatred at home: can you deny that it is nevertheless your home?

6.
What do you particularly like about your home?
a. the scenery?
b. the fact that the people have similar habits to yours, that is, that you fit in with them and can therefore rely on their understanding?
c. its customs?
d. the fact that you do not have to speak a foreign language?
e. memories of your childhood?

7.
Have you ever had thoughts of emigrating?

8.
Which foods do you eat for nostalgic reasons (for example, German vacationers in the Canary Islands have their sauerkraut flown in daily), and do these make you feel more secure?

9.
Let us assume that home for you means tree-covered mountains
and waterfalls. Do you feel moved when you see similar mountains and waterfalls in another part of the world, or are you
disappointed?

10.
Why are there no displaced right-wing intellectuals?

11.
When you pass the customs barrier and know you are home
again, does it ever happen that, in the very moment your home-
sickness vanishes, you feel even more alone? Or are your feelings of possessing a home country strengthened, for example,
by the sight of familiar uniforms (railroadmen, police, soldiers,
etc.)?

12.
How much home country do you need?

13.
When you and your wife do not share the same home country,
do you feel excluded from the other's home country, or do you
both liberate each other?

14.
To the extent that home is, both in a social and a scenic sense,
the place where you were born and brought up, it is not inter-
changeable. Are you grateful for this?

15.
Grateful to whom?

16.
Can you think of any regions, towns, customs, etc., which make
you feel in your heart that you would have been better suited
to a different home country?

17.
What makes you a homeless person:
a. unemployment?
b. banishment for political reasons?
c. a career in a foreign country?
d. the fact that you tend increasingly to think differently from

people who call the same place home and rule over it?
e. an oath of allegiance misapplied?

18.
Have you a second home country? If so:

19.
Can you imagine having a third or a fourth home country, or do you then find yourself reverting once more to the first?

20.
Can you turn an ideology into a home?

21.
Is there any place that fills you with horror at the idea that it might have been your home—Harlem, for example? And do you then try to imagine what this might have meant, or do you just simply thank God?

22.
Do you feel the world as a whole to be a place where you feel at home?

23.
Even on foreign territory soldiers are said to have died for their homeland. Who in your case decides what you owe to your homeland?

24.
Can you imagine yourself without a home at all?

25.
For what reasons do you conclude that animals such as gazelles, hippopotamuses, bears, penguins, tigers, chimpanzees, etc., which grow up behind bars or in enclosures, do not feel the zoo to be home?

Washington Square, the first shimmer of green
on the trees, one had ceased to expect it
from their gray skeletons. "Spring, the
sweet spring . . ." Yesterday I saw nothing
but decay, leprosy, faces with diseased skin,
the faces of young people, the whole city a

single gigantic ulcer—it's never correct,
what I think, never for more than an hour or
so, or a day at most. Today, for example:
morning in this bare park, beside these elegant houses where Patricia lives, and this
light, these buoyant skyscrapers in the blue
haze, earlier the atmosphere of goodwill at
the drugstore breakfast. Today I am taking a
day off, glad to be here. Sitting reading on
a public bench: an old man out for a walk
stops and speaks to me, interested in compar-
ing his pipe with mine, and then we swop tobacco. A few young blacks are lounging in
the sun. Or are they lounging? I am not
sure what, if anything, is going on. One of
them sits down beside me, as close as in a
bus, though the long bench is empty. Unfortunately, I have no cigarettes. But he
stays, digging a crumpled cigarette out of
his pocket, silent. I can give him a light.
Inside his checked jacket I see a first-rate
camera with telelens. What does he want? A
girl approaches leading a dog, pedigreed, and
she herself is fashionably elegant, with fair
hair and mauve sunglasses. Now the black boy
beside me gets up, wanders to the right
around the fountain, so that the girl will
have to pass him. What does he want? But he
has guessed wrong: the dog chooses another
direction, and the encircling tactic inconspicuously fails. No police. The girl,
incidentally, does not quicken her pace, in
fact she even stops once to allow the dog to
sniff, and now the others in the park are
also wrongly positioned; they would have run
to get in the young lady's way before she
disappears through the gateway. I go, too:
perhaps my bookshop will now be open. Here,
on 8th Street, another youngster with a skin
disease: she is begging—not out of hunger.
Marijuana can cause it, too. She looks at me

vaguely: You know, don't you? In a shop window (among other things), plastic vaginal
vibrators, worked by batteries.

Evening with a student couple. He, a poet,
works in Brooklyn during the day, combating
illiteracy. Does that still exist? It's
getting worse, he says, now 7 percent. Mainly Puerto Ricans, citizens of the U.S.A.,
mother tongue Spanish; but the teachers speak
only English. When their school education
ends, they can neither read nor write. Some
signs they of course know from experience—No
Exit, Walk, Stop, Bus, No Entrance, Closed,
etc.—but in fact they can't really read a
thing, people of twenty and thirty. What
jobs are open to them? They can just about
copy their own names. To test their intelligence he gives them (for instance) a camera,
and the results are often astounding: what
they see, how they see it. All the same, the
number of illiterates in Greater New York increases year by year.

6 April. Dinner with Jorge Luis Borges, the
poet. He is seventy-two and blind, speaks in
monologues. When others at the table talk to
him, he can't see who it is, and so he is
happier when he does the talking. Now and
again he politely asks who somebody is, one
open eye staring into space. Tremendous
knowledge. A grand seigneur. He wears his
fame like an inherited right, easily and
naturally. The lady seated at his side shows
him which glass contains water and which
wine, then he carries on from memory. When
it emerges that I am Swiss he can even address me in dialect: "Das isch truurig"
("That is sad"). Altogether an obsessive
linguist. He has read Gottfried Keller in
the original. He is fond of my country (he

says, looking in what he takes to be my direction): Gstaad, Wengen, Grindelwald, all
places I don't know. But in general he
speaks exclusively about literature, in very
good English.

SCHOOL OF THE ARTS

The black students feel themselves misunderstood in class and
accuse the white teachers and students of treating them unfairly. Meeting in an overheated hall. Even before the discussion the blacks demonstratively segregate themselves from
the whites. The head of the school, Frank MacShane, has to
ask all present to pull in their chairs and form a circle. Only
six black students are there; they excuse the absentees by saying reproachfully that the meeting was fixed for an impossible
time. An alternative date convenient to all the aggrieved blacks
cannot be arranged. What has happened? The black students
giggle and exchange looks among themselves, as if to show that
the very question is ridiculous. Their teacher, a Jewess born in
Vienna, cannot judge their literary work, they say, because
she isn't black herself. I had attended an earlier class: the work
they handed in was conventional, not unskillful, the literary
criticism extremely cautious. The main speaker on behalf of
the blacks is a black teacher, an unsuccessful writer. He takes
the line that all art is propaganda, all propaganda art. Something the whites cannot understand. A clever and (so the teacher
tells me) very talented black girl student gives examples:
her work (she says) has been praised—(she laughs: praised!)—
while the work of her black comrades is often criticized. What
is literary quality? A white idea. The argument that there are
such things as objective literary criteria produces—like all
other arguments—only a thin snigger, combined with a cold
look directed past the other participants. Even when they speak,
they do not look at the white people. Shakespeare is a racist,
a white man, no use to them. The remark of a white student
that the important thing is the language, not the content, raises
a storm. When the teacher asks them to believe that her intentions at least are good, there is open laughter. The discussion becomes outspoken, but only on the side of the black stu-

dents. The whites may say what they like: every one of them is in fact the descendant of a slave owner. Again and again we are told: A white man cannot criticize a black man, for they come from a part of the world in which the white man has never lived. So what is she to do in class? the teacher asks. Reply: "We don't have to solve your problems"—with a laugh that sounds almost contented. Invited by the head to say a word, I try to describe Brecht's ideas on the role of literature in class warfare. All they know of Brecht is that he was a white man. Even the admission that *l'art pour l'art* is always the art of the ruling classes fails to bring their eyes around to the speaker. They are not left wing; even a black millionaire is one of us, they say. Some of them incidentally, say nothing at all: the supernumeraries of arrogance. How proceed? They admit, after a great deal of talk, that the teacher has never said that there is no such thing as black literature; all the same, the fact remains that they feel humiliated. The criticisms of their work may look simply literary, but basically they are racist. Demand for black teachers. Only there are none available at present. Then more scorn about their white colleages, whose only concern is literature itself: "your short stories about nothing." A young white student's attempt to justify himself (insofar as his black colleagues will allow him to speak) by saying that he, too, has been trying to describe a conflict, but it just doesn't happen to be the racial conflict, produces a collective sigh of unspoken mockery: That's what we mean! Now we are just running around in circles. The harried teacher defends herself ineffectively: firstly, she is not conscious of ever having made derogatory remarks; secondly, she had drawn the attention of a white student to the same artistic error with the self-same words; thirdly, she had praised the clever girl very highly. The girl: "It is for the whites to say what hurts us and what doesn't?" Even the praise she had been given was racist in character: the black people's experience had not been taken into account, her piece was praised on purely literary grounds. And then she mimics the teacher's gesture—a white person's gesture. Her racial colleagues laugh like children. Why they go on attending this school I cannot find out. Incidentally, they themselves talk of paranoia; somebody, a black man, was working on his first novel when something happened in the street (you know): for days he was unable to continue with his novel. . . . The meeting finally disintegrates, the white people reduced to helplessness; that seems to satisfy the black students for the time being.

P.S.

Weeks later, a party at Frank MacShane's place: the new black teacher also there, a large African badge on his chest. What did he think about that meeting? He seemed maliciously pleased that I had been of so little help to the whites. . . .

23 April 1971

Young men with and without beards, Vietnam war veterans, throwing their war decorations down on the steps of the Capitol in Washington. Each one gives his name and the length of time he served in Vietnam, then tears the decoration from his throat—in silence or with an oath.

24 April 1971

Antiwar march in Washington: numbers estimated at 300,000, mainly people between twenty and thirty years of age. Between the speeches a song by Pete Seeger: "The Last Train to Nuremberg." A mass meeting free of violence or acts of destruction. The speeches a single-minded protest against a dirty war, against the impoverishment of the poor, against injustice. Attacks on Nixon and Agnew and FBI-Hoover, but faith in American democracy, "All power to the people," hope unmixed with political doctrine: the tone moralistic throughout, and the crowd stands firm—no shouts, only hands raised repeatedly in the peace sign and an occasional clenched fist, with friendly applause for demands, "Peace now!" Speeches by Martin Luther King's widow, his successor, Angela Davis's mother, a white senator, students. The faces in a crowd, picked out on tele—

vision, are good natured, naïve. Not a revolutionary crowd, by any means, but more
like a sect meeting, brothers and sisters,
solemn in the face of war crimes and air pollution——all rather touching. No real criticism of the system. President Nixon is at
his country house miles away; no representative of the administration is there to receive a deputation of war cripples from all
parts of this huge nation.

STATICS

One morning, shortly after eight, he reports to some desk or
other. A policeman at the entrance down below had been unable
to direct him precisely. When, after a long wait, with hat in
hand, he at last reaches the desk and bends down to repeat
that he has come to make a charge against himself, the official
does not even look at him, but gathers his papers together. He
must wait outside with all the others who have parked their
cars in the wrong places and have now come along with the
usual excuses. But he doesn't sit down on the yellow bench,
for he has received no summons and has no hope of ever being
called. In order not to show his face, he stands looking out of
the window, hat in hand. He does not cry out.

. . .

It comes in spurts. Sometimes it lasts only an hour and afterward he cannot understand his own horror: the official would
have laughed, or perhaps not; the significance of his having a
married sister in Scotland would not be understood, nor the
fact that he has a son to whom he regularly sends money.

. . .

He never touches alcohol.

. . .

At that time his students notice nothing at all. They are amused
by the careful way in which he writes in chalk on the black-

board, always with a sponge in the other hand to wipe out
without delay any mistake he might happen to make. He has
little hair—just a bald pate with a few perspiring locks at the
back. When he eventually turns again to face the class, he
always wipes his hands in an embarrassed manner, his eyes on
the floor.

. . .

Eventually he sits down on the yellow bench like the others
before him. Presumably this department is only partly concerned with his case. Down below in the entrance there are
the usual police notices hanging up in cages, with photographs
of particular instruments of murder (knives), a 5,000-franc
reward rising to 10,000 francs; the longer it takes to find you,
the more expensive you become. He looks at his watch: it is
Saturday. He wonders whether, in view of the fact that the department is obviously overworked, he should have chosen today
to make a charge against himself. . . .

. . .

His wife still thinks it is forgetfulness, absentmindedness.
Since it has been raining all day long, he must have noticed
when and where he went out into the rain without his hat. But
he hasn't the least idea—a wet head, but no idea.

. . .

His subject: statics for architects. In practice, the calculations
are always left to the engineering department, and all that
architects need is a general appreciation of statics. He always
shows them slides: cracks in concrete.

. . .

He is nicknamed "The Crack."

. . .

His visit to the police station is not repeated; but some weeks later he tells his wife that he must give up his job. He is fifty-three.

. . .

He has never killed anybody, not even in a street accident. Once as an assistant on a building site he witnessed an accident that had cost a worker's life, but he had not been in charge, and the engineer who was had been exonerated anyway. He had only happened to be there because he was bringing some measuring instruments; all the same, he is now frightened that he might suddenly get the idea that he *has* killed somebody.

. . .

Not that he believes in the law . . .

. . .

Architecture is all very well, but stress is stress. One must never forget that every load we omit in our calculations must be paid for, witness the slides: cracks above the support: shearing, torsion in the pillar, collapse. Then he always says, "You see?" During the intermission he stays in the auditorium, preparing his notes. When, to help his students, he sits down on the bench beside them, he always smells of stale sweat.

. . .

The first sign those nearest to him notice is a nervous habit: he says at every opportunity, "That I don't know"—even when he has not been asked whether he knows or what he feels about it. Nobody takes it seriously, just treats it like any other habit of speech, such as "Oh, I see," or "Precisely." But it isn't a habit of speech, he is fully aware of what he means when he says "That I don't know." As a rule, what it is he doesn't know is unimportant. Why should he know where the sea is deepest? Of course, it is hardly possible to make his ignorance known immediately on every occasion; the others go on talking in the assumption that one does know, and it is only after a while, when the subject is finished with, that he can sum it up: "That I didn't know." To understand how carefully he listens and how far his remark is from being a mere habit of speech, one would have to notice that he never says "That I don't know" twice over to the same point. Once is enough; then his lack of knowledge on a certain matter has been recorded, and he never forgets the things of which he knows nothing.

. . .

He is not interested in being appointed dean.

. . .

His memory is not failing; on the contrary, it works actively against him. He suddenly remembers that he still owes his sister in Scotland her part of the inheritance. A complicated affair, but what comes into his mind is 80,000 francs. Plus interest. Or some foreign word occurs to him, a word he doesn't need at the moment; it just occurs to him that he still doesn't know what it means.

. . .

Usually the lost hat is hanging in his anteroom. On one occasion a student is surprised when, after helping the professor into his coat and then indicating his hat, the professor maintains that it is not his. He goes off without it.

. . .

His students like him.

. . .

It is not only sharpened yellow pencils that lie side by side on his desk: everything is like that. He fears untidiness. He is one of those people who always have dirty fingernails and can't do anything about it.

. . .

At the police station, when a youngish policeman asks him after
an hour what he wants, he remains seated on the yellow bench—
like somebody not knowing how he came to wake up in this
place . . .

. . .

Only his face has collapsed.

. . .

His wife, who still adores him after nineteen years, suffers less
from his lack of knowledge than from his nervous habit of
feeling bound to draw attention to it every time. Sometimes
she even puts a hand on his arm in advance to stop him saying
"That I don't know"—at least in front of other people. She is
never successful; her friendly hand tends rather to startle
him, as if she were trying to warn him: Here comes something
you don't know—and so he confirms it: That I don't know.

. . .

There are little things that come into his mind, particularly
in the early mornings when it is still dark outside. Then he goes
barefoot down into the kitchen to get something to eat: cheese,
stewed fruit, even cold spaghetti if there is nothing else. It
doesn't help much even if the incidents his memory throws up
are funny ones: he is still alarmed. And it often leads to feelings
of alarm assailing him in a whole series. . . . That time the
cemetery informed him that his mother's grave was to be annulled and he failed to answer—that was a piece of remissness
which keeps coming back into his mind. But instead of sitting
down at once and writing back that he would of course pay for
an urn, he found himself recalling that at the time of her death,
in 1940, he had been right indeed even courageous in the way
he dealt with that major. His memory (as he stands barefoot
in the kitchen) reproduces the entire argument, and what he
had said to the major: it was feeble stuff. At times it is only a
feeling he recalls—of a kind one no longer has at his age—or
a smell.

. . .

One day he hands in his notice of resignation. . . .

. . .

He remembers: a stolen football; playing doctors in the cellar, homosexual games, the fear afterward, and then the detective coming down to the cellar after he had told his mother, his betrayal of the young gardener. He remembers that he had been given pocket money by the young gardener. He remembers: that he failed his exams at high school.

. . .

Later his nervous habit disappears again: he just lowers his head the moment he hears something he does not know, and listens. Birds sometimes slant their heads like this, and then you don't know where they are looking. He hardly ever says "That I don't know"—just stays silent with his head in this slanting position. . . .

. . .

But he cannot speak of all this, or, if he does, it sounds incomprehensible; one can remind him at once that he is a respectable professor, not a crook, a father who at least means well, no anti-Semite, a colleague respected for his modesty. Nor (for God's sake!) is he a murderer, etc. At such times he doesn't argue or even nod, but simply looks into the distance. They are thinking in moral terms. All the same he is dismayed. . . .

. . .

His resignation is not accepted, since he is unable to give any reason for it; he is in good health; the university grants him the use of a secretary.

. . .

All he understands is that there is no way of stopping it.

. . .

At the airport he fails to recognize his married sister from Scotland, and he returns to find her sitting in his apartment, looking as if she had always been there, though of course a bit older. But after that everything runs smoothly, the harmony unbroken.

. . .

Statistics for Architects, a manual containing a summary of his teaching over many years, is translated shortly after publication into three languages, including Japanese.

. . .

In fact, everything is running smoothly. . . .

. . .

His wife thinks him crazy when he tells her he deserved to lose that court case. . . . It happened a long time ago, and had been the cause of much head-shaking ever since. A scandal. He had sued a firm that had commissioned an expert statical opinion from him in the days before he became a professor; the firm, though paying him part of his fee, had disregarded his opinion in erecting the building (a factory with large halls) on the grounds of economy. It was his sense of responsibility that led him to sue. But the firm, as it turned out, was registered in the principality of Liechtenstein, and the case had to be heard in Vaduz. He had to engage a second lawyer, one from Liechtenstein, and this man, as he only subsequently found out, was the firm's tax adviser. These were things he had not known. By the time the halls were completed and a settlement proposed (payment of the remainder of his fee on condition that the case was withdrawn), he had not only spent all his fee on legal costs, but he had also placed his career in jeopardy. In order to force a settlement, the firm had commissioned opinions from other experts. The Swiss Engineers' and Architects' Society, which has powers of arbitration in such cases, warned him of the dangers of challenging the expertise of colleagues; he should not forget that these colleagues, though not directly involved in the choice of a new professor, had a certain amount of influence. Though it was cowardly of him (according to his ideas at the time) to protect certain colleagues in order not to jeopardize his professorship, he was all the more determined not to accept a settlement from the firm, cost what it might (namely, that part of the inheritance which he still owed his sister). . . . Now at breakfast he suddenly comes out with the admission that he deserved to lose the case. Certainly the buildings in question are still standing, but that is not the reason for his admission. He has none.

. . .

Then a few more weeks without stress . . .

. . .

He himself always puts the slides for his lectures into the cassette with his own hands, holding each one up to the window beforehand, as if he feared one might creep in unawares to make a fool of him. There had been laughter once; the auditorium was in darkness, so he could not see what had caused it. The slide, showing a collapsed hangar with three-hinged arch (an example of what an unforeseen wind can do), he removed permanently from the cassette.

. . .

His sister has made a wealthy marriage: when he mentions the matter of the inheritance, all she cares about is that her husband (a banker) doesn't ever hear of it. Apart from that he steers clear of family reminiscences. Fortunately their mother's grave has not yet been annulled. The sister from Scotland, incidentally, stays only two days (in a hotel), and in this short time she does not discover exactly what it is that makes her feel sorry for her brother, who after all has a professorship, a very nice wife, a son who has just been promoted to lieutenant, a state pension, etc.

. . .

Then comes this congress in Brussels, which he knows from a previous visit. After the room in the hotel (which he also knows) has been booked, the tickets bought, etc., he suddenly confesses that he has never been to Brussels before. His wife has letters from him written in Brussels, even photographs she can show him, but he still cannot believe it.

. . .

The question is now simply when they will notice that he knows nothing about statistics—a question of time. It is still nine years to his pension. His son appears to know already.

. . .

Sitting on the yellow bench in the police station, hat in hand, he does not know what his memory released during the night; he assumes that they know, in fact he almost hopes they do.

. . .

Then all of a sudden he might put this very same hat on his head. Without a moment's hesitation. When he arrives home, he simply has his hat back. The hackneyed joke about absent-minded professors annoys him: in fact, he forgets less and less.

. . .

Once, in the middle of the street, he takes off his hat, stops and looks around to see if anyone is watching, then hangs it on the iron railing of a garden fence and walks on.

. . .

At times now he is surprised to find how high his head is above his own feet, walking down there on the pavement.

. . .

When he gets sick, he is glad.

. . .

One sees him since his recovery hanging on his wife's arm. He nods shyly when one greets him, but he still remembers his former pupils who have got on well, even their names. He is better now, he says politely, his head held sideways. He still wears the same sort of felt hat with a sweaty headband. He has not gone back to work. His wife, guiding him across the street, also acts as if nothing has happened. The visible fact that his pupil's buildings (housing developments, congress halls, hospitals, office towers of steel and glass) have none of them collapsed so far does nothing to alter his inner feeling: that he understands nothing of statistics, had never understood the things he taught. . . .

> A trip into the country, upstate New York,
> and, as always on such trips, the question:
> Where are we exactly? Indian country, though
> there's said to be nothing here now but
> snakes. Paradise without people. A notice
> on trees: Crimes on This Property Will Be
> Prosecuted by the Police. House built of
> wood, white on a green lawn in park lands
> merging into the wilderness, a large pond,
> presumably with fish, and again the notice:
> Crimes on This Property, etc. After a few
> moments of peace we do indeed see a fish, in
> fact, two. The owner is away in Europe. Or
> in Egypt? The notice doesn't mean us: we
> have the key to the house, permission to turn
> all this nature to our own use. A few things
> in bloom. Our companion, a youngish pro—
> fessor of sociology, has frequently been on
> visits here before, and he manages to find a
> can opener. Sitting in front of the house,
> we see: one hare, some very lovely birds, a
> white horse grazing alone on the meadow. All
> property, as far as the eye can see. Two
> hours away from Manhattan. At night the

whistle of railroad trains, but no footsteps:
no robbers. Next morning the hills are all
still there, the pond, too, and the birds,
etc.

QUESTIONNAIRE

1.
Can you remember from what age it has seemed natural to you
to possess something, alternatively not to possess it?

2.
To whom, in your opinion, does (for instance) the air belong?

3.
What do you regard as your property:
a. something you have bought?
b. something you have inherited?
c. something you have made yourself?

4.
Even when you can replace a stolen object (pen, umbrella,
watch, etc.) without difficulty, does the theft of it as such annoy
you?

5.
Why?

6.
Can you feel money by itself to be property, or must you buy
something with it before you feel like a property owner? And
how do you explain the fact that the more you feel envied for
a certain thing, the more you are conscious of being its owner?

7.
Do you know what you need?

8.
Assume you have bought a plot of land: how long does it take for
you to feel that the trees on this plot belong to you, that is, to
feel happy or at least confident that you possess the right to
have them cut down?

9.
Do you regard a dog as property?

10.
Do you like fenced enclosures?

11.
When you stop on the street to give something to a beggar, why do you always do it as hurriedly and inconspicuously as possible?

12.
How do you imagine it feels to be poor?

13.
Who taught you the difference between property that loses in value and property that increases in value, or has nobody ever taught you that?

14.
Do you also collect art?

15.
Can you name a free country in which the rich are not in the minority, and can you explain why in such countries the majority always imagines itself to possess the power?

16.
Why do you enjoy giving gifts?

17.
How much landed property do you feel you would need in order to have no more fears for the future? (Reply in square yards.) Or do you find your fears mounting in proportion to the size of the property?

18.
What risks are you not insured against?

19.
If property were confined only to things that you use and not to things that give you power over others, would you want to go on living under such conditions?

20.
How many employees do you own?

21.
How so?

22.

Do you sometimes feel burdened by your responsibilities, which you cannot delegate to others for fear of endangering your property, or is your happiness due to these very responsibilities?

23.

What do you like about the New Testament?

24.

Since the right to possess undoubtedly exists, though effective only when property is available, would you be able to understand your fellow countrymen if a majority of them—in order to assert their own rights—were one day to dispossess you?

25.

And why not?

YALE UNIVERSITY, 5 May

Without the television set in the hotel one would imagine oneself in an idyllic world of Gothic architecture. A stroll through the bookshops--they have got everything: Georg Lukács, for instance, Germaine Greer (The Female Eunuch), Beckett, Solzhenitsyn, Borges, James Baldwin, Freud, Hermann Hesse, Fanon, etc. It is a land where thought is free. . . . On television: another antiwar demonstration in Washington. No acts of violence: they, the people who think differently, simply block the entrance to Congress and to the Law Courts, leaving the forces of law and order (police, Federal troops, paratroopers) to arrest people "without making specific individual charges of wrongdoing." Among those who end up in the detention camp is a whole wedding party, which carries on with its festivities inside. A total of 12,700 arrests in four days.

"This morning, immediately after the Swiss National Bank gave up its attempt to maintain the standard exchange of 4.2950 francs to the dollar, Swissair announced that it would no longer sell tickets for dollars. . . . The central banks of Switzerland, the Netherlands, Belgium and Austria followed suit. They had been deluged with so many dollars that they could no longer absorb them under present conditions. In accepting the surplus dollars up to today, the Europeans, in effect, had been helping the United States finance the war in Vietnam and helping American companies buy European industries."

—*The New York Times,* 5 May 1971

BROWNSVILLE

Here people are living behind cardboard, a substitute for house walls that have collapsed, amid rubble, debris, puddles, etc. Black children swarm over the rubble or at windows covered with mesh screening. One knows it all from picture books. A slum? No, these are middle-class (brownstone) dwellings, as in an ordinary city, and there is even an avenue, here and there schools, sports grounds equipped for basketball, etc.; on the horizon one can see Manhattan. It was formerly a Jewish middle-class quarter; now the orthodox Jews from the East have moved out, but the houses still belong to them, as also the shops and the land, though its value has depreciated through the poverty of the blacks. Depreciation is followed by decay. There are ruins that have no owners, so valueless have they become. The synagogues are being rented for other purposes. Only blacks with an income can keep their houses maintained, and there are few of those. There still remains the Jewish Hospital and Medical Center of Brooklyn (to look after ninety thousand deprived inhabitants) with its Comprehensive Approach to Child Health. A brave enterprise: I don't know where I have ever seen anything quite like it, and I can only nod as I am led around by a succession of white doctors, male and female, whom I follow respectfully. Here four thousand children are being cared for; I see one of them in the playroom, a boy with crinkly hair and large eyes fixed trustfully, as I observe, on the blond woman doctor. In the corridor I am given lessons in social pathology: people without identity, alcoholism, misery due to neglect rather than to starvation, unemployment owing to a lack of training facilities, disintegrating families, illiteracy, etc., and the trouble they are trying to treat here—the mental effects of poverty. I hear of a program, started with federal funds, that has now been handed over to the separate states to carry on by themselves, but New York has no money for it: there is uncertainty whether the whole venture can be continued next year. . . . No lack of churches in the district—All Are Welcome—but no church buildings: one identifies most of them only by a crucifix outside. There is also talk of a housing scheme, ostensibly to improve the lot of the hopeless. The streets are wide, but full of holes, and when it rains there are puddles; the asphalt is disappearing, but we are not in the country—there are stop lights. A city of weeds. When, as happened recently, the people lose their tempers, they set fire, not to the houses of the distant bosses, but to the houses here: charred ruins are dotted all about. That may be tactically sound, but now and again children set fire to an occupied house. Who cares if you are homeless? Whole families in a single room: what that looks like we have also seen in the picture books. Our guide quotes figures: the authorities are familiar with them. A hot summer's day, but we get out of the Volkswagen only where our guide, who has worked here for years, is known. Winstons Chicken Bar: the food is all right. A beer costs more in the ghetto than elsewhere: the customers have no other choice. Impossible to see what people do all day: there is no production, no factories, no offices. Things of no more use are dumped on the roadside or in yards: cars with raised hoods, gutted and rusty, wrecks without tires, glass, seats, etc. (the metalwork unfortunately does not disintegrate). But we are not in Africa, not outside the industrial world; it does not surprise us to see polished jumbo jets flying overhead. An avenue of shops shows we are not in another country: the brand names in their windows are the usual ones. There are even banks, smaller than over there, but built with the same marble—savings banks, they are called. Some children have managed to open a water hydrant and are enjoying the deluge; on the horizon we again see the silhouette of Manhattan. . . . Previously they came, blacks from the South, to look for work; now they come to rot in one hideout or another, free, unskilled, and workless. Brownsville is not Harlem; the people here do not know their neighbors. They are all refugees—and for a lifetime. Here there is no way out—not even in their dreams. Racial segregation through misery. Those who do not die in infancy live on and multiply without knowing how or why, and millions live on welfare, which just about keeps them fed. The state pays their rents in crumbling welfare hotels, privately owned; there is nothing one can do about that—without profit the world cannot go on. . . .

One knows all that.

Once we see two white policemen. There is nothing for them to do: they just walk along, looking straight ahead—incidentally the only whites to be seen here, apart from the white doctors in the hospital, whom I admire. I ask them for figures: how many suicides (very few), how many alcoholics, how many mentally disturbed children. Something is being done—it is just not true to say that nothing is being done: it's just that there's a lack of money, a lack of qualified teachers, a lack of enlightenment; incidentally, since the advent of drugs there have been fewer serious riots, but more crimes. And then, there are marked differences: between Puerto Rican children and black children— the latter cannot work off their aggressions in speech, only physically.

Any other questions?

Visit to a Puerto Rican family in a tower house: this is now Manhattan, not Brownsville. Three rooms with kitchen and bath, view across a yard. A mother with six children; four daughters in two beds. One son has brain damage, wants to be able to read, but will never learn. The other son goes to school and is also working. Doing what? He doesn't say exactly. But he wants to know what I write novels about. We are given beer to drink. On the refrigerator a Portuguese Saint Martin, above the sofa with its stuffing hanging out a blond Jesus. The children's father has run off to Puerto Rico, and the family lives on welfare. One of the daughters, fifteen years old, is brushed and combed as if for a ball; but, pretty as she looks, she is going nowhere—her childish make-up is only for a dream. The son says he wants to learn a trade of some kind. Among themselves they speak Spanish. They are Americans; but at home, in Puerto Rico, there is no hope, they say.

> We shall win, for the United States have
> never lost a war. Woe to the seekers after
> peace, who no longer believe in God and the
> mission that God has entrusted to the Ameri—

can people! Thus a clergyman with double
chin and a Bible in his hand. Why, Jesus
himself has said . . . As soon as the young
man, a veteran of the war in Vietnam, tries
to argue objectively, the clergyman reads
from the Bible, equating (for example) the
parable of the Good Samaritan with the U.S.
army in Vietnam, in Cambodia, in Laos, or
anywhere else: the army is helping the de-
fenseless, who have been set upon by robbers.
What can one say of those long-haired young
people who loiter in front of the Capitol?
And now Mao's Little Red Book comes out of
his pocket; here you can read what communism really is: they want to win in order to
destroy the world with materialism. Mao
("this guy") says quite openly: They want to
soften up the United States. The young man
now brings up certain historical facts concerning Indochina that are available to all.
In vain. What does Jesus say? He says, for
example, that all they that take the sword
shall perish by the sword. This is well
known, of course, but it needs some explanation: it is communism that has taken the
sword, and it is God's professed will that
the U.S.A., as the strongest nation in the
world, should impose his sentence. And this
is no fiery preacher speaking, but a placid
clergyman on television, used to his congre-
gation's approval. Regarding Lieutenant
Calley: even women and children and aged people are our enemies (a fact the young Vietnam
war veteran concedes, even if he bases it on
what the Vietnamese people have learned from
the whites), and enemies must be killed, says
the clergyman. So Calley acted rightly, in
an upright and God-fearing way, and the cow-
ards in this country who call for peace are
only helping the Antichrist, since peace can
be achieved only by weapons, through the

victory of the U.S. Army, for freedom is
God's gift to us, and one day Cuba will also
be free again, if we believe in God like our
fathers, who in consequence never lost a war.
The clergyman is not to be put off his stroke
by a bearded intellectual who mentions the
extermination of the Indian population: those
were also victories, it was God's will. A
third man at the table, a former ambassador
in Asia, tries to make a joke of it: Does
God's grace extend to only one nation? He
asks: Should Cuba and Chile be invaded? The
clergyman is modest: he does not presume to
tell the President what to do; as a Christian, he can only hope that God will choose a
determined President. As regards the question of God's grace, joking aside, it is at
any rate certain that God can have no love
for the Soviet Union. For God is on the side
of freedom and decency and morality. What
does it say in the Bible? There is only one
thing that can stop the preacher in his flow,
and that is the next piece of TV advertising:
The Beer That Made Milwaukee Famous. So the
Bible has spoken, and the duty of every American citizen is plain: Communists must be
killed, Americans prisoners freed, bombing
attacks on North Vietnam continued and in-
tensified. A reminder that prisoners of war
are only released on an exchange basis or
after a peace treaty has been signed causes
the clergyman no difficulties: there can be
no peace treaty with the Communists as long
as they refuse to release prisoners ("American lives"). The debate, incidentally, is
never bitter: the diplomat and the clergyman, though of differing opinions, are constantly proclaiming their sense of mutual
identity through jovially loyal laughter.
Only the bearded young intellectual remains
humorless, with his figures and his Geneva

Convention. Even the chairman of the discussion is alive to the need for some harm-
less light relief: after all, the millions of
televiewers, who have to put up with advertisements every seven minutes anyway, have a
right to be entertained. The fact that there
are zones in Vietnam where the Americans
themselves are known to take no prisoners,
but to kill all in sight, that the clergyman
considers militarily justified: when the
American people goes to war, it is out to
win, otherwise in the world "that God has
given us" there would be neither peace nor
freedom nor decency nor morality. . . . After
an hour of this I switch off.

THE NEW YORK TIMES

Mrs. George C. Barclay is a silver-haired, 67-year-old Manhattan
housewife who wants to die with dignity. So she recently signed
the Euthanasia Educational Fund's "living will," in which she
requested that, if she becomes ill and there is no reasonable
expectation for her recovery, she be allowed to die and not be kept
alive by "artificial means" or "heroic measures."

Her husband, a retired banker, and their three children know of
the will, and have told Mrs. Barclay they agree with her decision
and will try to see that it is carried out.

Mrs. Sydney Appel, 54, is a Brooklyn housewife who also signed
the document. But her four children are vehemently opposed to
the will, because they don't believe such a death could be handled
in "a responsible manner."

"What about the woman whose children felt she was an inconvenience?" asked Mrs. Apple's son, Douglas, 17. "If she had already signed the will, it would be no great difficulty for the children
to do away with her."

To the people who are active in this country's two major euthanasia groups (the Euthanasia Educational Fund and the Euthanasia Society of America), euthanasia generally means one thing:
the right to die with dignity. Indignity, to them, means deterioration, dependence, and hopeless pain. But to many other people,
euthanasia (derived from the Greek for "good death") means
"mercy killing."

Proponents of euthanasia predict that family discussions such as those that occurred in the Barclay and Appel families are going to become quite common in the next few years as the subject of death, and whether the patient has the right to decide how and when he wants to die, is brought out into the open.

There are indications that this is on the verge of happening now. A "right to die with dignity" bill was recently introduced in the Florida Legislature, stating that a patient suffering from an incurable, fatal and severely painful illness should have the right to ask that his life be painlessly terminated. The bill is now in committee.

Courses on death have been filled to capacity this year at both New York University and Union Theological Seminary. The technical advances in the medical arts (new life-sustaining drugs, organ transplants, artificial kidneys, auxiliary hearts, defibrillators, pacemakers, and respirators) have resulted in dialogues among young medical students, who do not always agree with these artificial means of keeping dying patients alive.

Making own decisions

And the recent liberalization of abortion laws in several states has added fuel to the arguments of those who believe that people should have the right to make their own decisions regarding life and death.

"All of my friends like to talk about death nowadays," said Mrs. Henry J. Mali, 67, of Manhattan, president of the Euthanasia Educational Fund. "It's even a subject of conversation at cocktail parties. People seem charmed to find somebody else who wants to talk about it."

Almost 20,000 persons have requested the "living wills" in the 18 months that they have been available, according to Mrs. Elizabeth T. Halsey, executive secretary of the Euthanasia Educational Fund, at 250 West 57th Street. She said that she received 50 requests a day for the wills, which are not legally binding, and recently ordered 10,000 more.

How does one die with dignity? One of the lines in the "living will" says: "I ask that drugs be mercifully administered to me for terminal suffering even if they hasten the moment of death."

At present, doctors who carried out this wish could legally be charged with murder. This is perhaps the major reason why people consider euthanasia abhorrent—or because it is often used interchangeably with the term "mercy killing", which in turn is usually associated with the killing of babies who are born with mental or physical defects. (To many others, euthanasia is equated with Hitler's program of killing mentally and physically handicapped persons.)

"It is a common misunderstanding that we advocate mercy killing," said Jerome Nathanson, chairman of the board of leaders of the New York Society for Ethical Culture, and a strong proponent of euthanasia. "But actually, mercy killing is the complete antithesis of what we seek.

"The question is not one of killing people," he added. "It is the question of letting one die."

Mr. Nathanson, whose wife died of cancer in 1968, said he believed that the new honesty and openness among American youth might help change public attitudes about euthanasia.

"Sexual relations are one's private affair," he said, "and one's attitudes on death should be a private affair."

Mr. Nathanson said he knew of a doctor who, if a patient is suffering from a terminal illness, leaves three pills on the bedside table and tells the patient, "Take one every four hours. If you take them all at once, they will kill you."

"I don't know why all doctors can't be that way," he said, "and leave the decision up to the patient." Many doctors make a distinction between "active euthanasia," where a drug or other treatment is administered to hasten death, and "passive euthanasia," in which therapy is withheld and death is hastened by omission of treatment.

Most religious groups condemn active euthanasia, especially the Roman Catholic Church. Last October, Pope Paul VI said in a statement to Roman Catholic physicians that euthanasia, without the patient's consent, was murder; and with his consent, suicide. "What is morally a crime cannot, under any pretext, become legal," he added.

But the Pope also seemed to espouse the religious community's more lenient attitude toward passive euthanasia when he said that while doctors have the duty to fight against death with all the resources of science, they are not obliged to use all the survival techniques developed by science. Prolonging life in the terminal stage of incurable disease could be "useless torture," he said.

A statement by Pope Pius XII is included in the literature distributed by the Euthanasia Educational Fund. It says: "The removal of pain and consciousness by means of drugs when medical reasons suggest it, is permitted by religion and morality to both doctor and patient; even if the use of drugs will shorten life."

The Euthanasia Education Fund is a nonprofit, educational organization that finances studies and seminars on euthanasia for physicians, clergymen, social workers, nurses and lawyers. Contributions to the fund are tax deductible, while contributions to the Euthanasia Society of America, an action organization seeking political change, are not. Both groups have offices in the same room at the West 57th Street address, and claim 1,200 joint members. Last year the membership was 600.

The Rev. Donald W. McKinney, pastor of the First Unitarian Church of Brooklyn and vice-president of the Euthanasia Educational Fund, said he believed that the fact that the "living will" was not legally binding was "rather irrelevant."

"Its great value," he said, "is that a tremendous burden of guilt is lifted from the family and children when a person signs the will. And it is also a great deal of help to doctors."

He said that more and more clergymen had to wrestle with the moral question posed by euthanasia: Whether it can be reconciled with the commandment, "Thou shalt not kill."

"The primary commandment is reverence for life," he said. "It is not a question of killing, but a question of honoring life, a question of dignity.

"The process of dying is changing today," he went on. "With all the new medical advances we have, we have to determine if life is really being served by prolonging the act of dying."

The fact that there is no clear definition of death that is acceptable to everyone is one reason why many doctors are opposed to euthanasia. Some doctors consider death to occur when the brain dies; others, when the heart stops functioning. Sidney D. Rosoff, legal adviser for both euthanasia groups, said: "A patient is dead when a doctor says he is." But even this definition has not always held up in court cases.

"I tend to be basically moved towards it (euthanasia)," said Dr. Barry Wood, a Manhattan internist who is also an ordained Episcopal priest, "but I become more conservative as I see the possibilities. One possibility is to declare certain people unfit—and this has happened in the past."

Dr. Fred Rosner, director of hematology at the Queen's Hospital Center and a leading critic of euthanasia, said: "If euthanasia were legalized, the next logical step would be the legalization of genocide and the killing of social misfits. And who can make the fine distinction between prolonging life and prolonging the act of dying?" he added.

Another argument

Other opponents of euthanasia frequently argue that a dying patient should be kept alive as long as possible because a cure for his illness could be just around the corner.

"There is a paucity of overnight miracles," Mr. Nathanson rebutted. "Physicians generally know what's going on in the field.

"And what if a person can't stand the pain for five years? If I say, 'I can't stand it,' and the doctor says, 'Look, your suffering may help other people,' that's the worst ethical indignity that can be done to a person."

The Hippocratic oath that all physicians take when they graduate from medical school is used as an argument by both proponents and opponents of euthanasia. The oath states that it is a physician's duty to relieve suffering, but it also says he must preserve and protect life.

In Great Britain, which has an active Euthanasia Society, there have been two recent controversial proposals by doctors that an age limit should be set at which doctors should stop "resuscitating the dying." Dr. Kenneth A. O. Vickery suggested the age of 80; another said that anyone over 65 should not be resuscitated if his heart stopped.

Dr. Vickery, who said he thought geriatric patients were overloading hospital and welfare services in Britain, recalled the frequently quoted lines of Arthur Hugh Clough, the 19th-century English poet, who wrote:

> Thou shalt not kill; but need'st not strive
> officiously to keep alive.

This country's two euthanasia groups are opposed to age limits. "The people in Britain are thinking of society," the Rev. McKinney said, "we're thinking of the individual. We believe that even people in their twenties and thirties should have euthanasia, if they need it." Mrs. Appel, whose children are opposed to her desire for euthanasia, said she came to her decision after watching her senile, 87-year-old mother die a painful death after suffering a broken hip.

"I made up my mind I didn't want my children to see me that way," the dark-haired woman said. "I don't want to leave them with the mental image of deterioration."

Mrs. Appel's son's argument that families might let a patient die for ulterior motives is another frequently used argument against euthanasia. Some family members, the opponents reason, may wish to relieve their own suffering rather than the patient's; or else the heirs may have their eyes on the patient's estate.

Most people who have signed the "living will" have chosen doctors who are sympathetic to their wishes. Mrs. Barclay said she picked her doctor because she knew he was a contributor to the Euthanasia Society of America. Mrs. Mali, who is the wife of a retired textile executive, said her physician was a man who had promised he would let her die "peaceably, rather than having my arms stuck full of tubes.

"Now that I'm old, the next celebration is death," Mrs. Mali said in her East Side town house. "And what I'm most interested

in is how my death can be made an honorable estate, like matri-
mony."
By Judy Klemesrud (Copyright by NEW YORK TIMES 1971)

NOTE FOR THE HANDBOOK

*One advantage of being old is that there is no longer any point
in being considerate, and an aged person does not require
anger—the recklessness of anger—to make him speak the
truth. Often things are as he sees them, and of course others
know it, too, but keep silent out of consideration for themselves. An old man is not a prophet, he is just calm and without
fear. What the prophets of old, mostly blind men, had to say
was usually only what was clear to all, but the others could
not afford—out of consideration for themselves—to admit it:
to their own detriment.*

So this is how they look, the small criminals, today's collection of thieves,
burglars, drug pushers, muggers, elevator
pickpockets, etc.—the routine haul of the
policeman's round. They sit waiting on the
long bench in the right-hand corner of the
room. The night court is public. Behind the
justice of the peace the Stars and Stripes;
above him, cut in marble: In God We Trust.
. . . Almost all of them are blacks or Puerto
Ricans, some in colored shirts, others gray
and torn, female delinquents among them.
Quite a number seem to know the place already. Routine on both sides. Four prose-
cutors and lawyers, all young and Jewish,
proceed without fuss. Unfortunately, it remains more or less a dumb show: one hardly
hears who is speaking—the low murmur of
routine. Only the justice's decision, after
a hearing of five or seven minutes, is audi-
ble to the public: $1,000, $500 (bail presumably); occasionally a sentence—five days'
imprisonment, three days' imprisonment. A

331

beefy man in shirt sleeves holds the reports
in his hand. Now and again he says, "Silence!" Everything is orderly, matter of
fact, unceremonial. The secretary is an
African with sideburns, white shirt and tie,
large round spectacles; he looks somehow historical as he sits there, motionless as a
statue; his brow gleams like bronz, but now
and again he yawns. Only the justice wears a
robe. It looks like a stage rehearsal, movements not yet exact. particularly the entrance of the sinners, interjections, to-ing
and fro-ing; but the sentences are real.
Then a look around the audience: is some
relative there who will pay? There may be.
Someone waves a handful of notes. Sometimes,
however, just a shrug, if it's not enough, or
there is nobody there: then off through the
doors, followed by a lot of policemen in blue
shirts, and one catches a glimpse of bars
opening and closing. Like coops for hens.
Only one white man struggles as the shirt-
sleeved official with the rosette grips his
arm to show him the way, which he knows.
When the long bench is empty, the next batch
is admitted. Many young people. It looks
more like an employment agency. No excitement. The night justice thumbs through the
reports in front of him, not looking at the
delinquent. Meanwhile the attorney questions
the delinquent, his manner not unfriendly,
and then addresses the justice, who seldom
asks a question: he knows all the answers.
Only one black schoolboy maintains distinctly
and obstinately, though quietly, that he is
not guilty. But it seems to be untrue. Unfortunately: for, as we know, the prisons are
overcrowded; at the moment four people in a
single cell. It is midnight. Most of the
cases have to do with drugs, just now the
easiest way for unskilled people to earn a

living. An old man, black as the first
generation of slaves, appears not to understand what the lawyer is saying; hat in hand,
as if he feels honored to take part in this
act of state, he looks now at the lawyer, now
at the prosecutor, now at the justice, as
trusting as if he were in a medical clinic.
The sentence: three days' imprisonment, and
he nods like a patient. It is not a farce;
the legal niceties are observed. Beside me
sleeps the child of a black mother who is
still waiting for her son. There are ac-
quittals, too: a girl, slightly crippled,
slovenly, but she can go. However, it seems
she has no money for the subway, and begging
is not allowed in court. How is she to get
home—to Brownsville, maybe? We leave at
about one in the morning, but the court is
still sitting and there is still a large
pile of blue reports waiting. . . .
P.S.
Something I didn't know, but that Uwe
Johnson, ever reliable, told me in Berzona:
outside that building (courtroom and jail-
house in one!) there are places where bail
can be borrowed short term at exorbitant
rates of interest. Five hundred dollars on
the table and you needn't go to jail now,
but you must find six hundred by Saturday.
How? The nation of Stars and Stripes (In
God We Trust) does nothing to stop it: this
is Free Enterprise, a matter of course—the
basis of Western freedom.

"You have the right to defend yourself. You are not accused of
anything, but despite that you may still want to defend yourself.
For example, you live in a society you consider infamous, you
have demanded changes, etc.: that is evident from your many
words, if not from your deeds. Or do you feel that you have acted
in accordance with your expressed beliefs? According to your

dossier there is nothing against you—no complaint against your beliefs as such, nor against your way of life as such. As the civilization you accuse understands it, you have committed no crimes worth mentioning; according to your dossier your life differs hardly at all from the lives of others who are content with the social order from which they benefit."

. . .

"Do you wish to plead resignation?"

. . .

"The jury you see here is the one you have been allowed to choose for yourself. They might have been different people. But you have chosen: an old school friend to whom you consider yourself much indebted, Tolstoi and Kafka and Brecht and other writers, your own children, and, besides these, neighbors who know a lot about your daily life, some friends, colleagues, women, a Jew, a worker, a Negro—people, in short, from all walks of life, including some philosophers (to the extent you imagine yourself to have understood them), a teacher now dead, and finally a hippie, who has not turned up."

. . .

"Although you pronounce society vile, you have never wielded power or even sought it. Perhaps, in a modest way, you might have been able to achieve something. Why did you never seek power?"

. . .

"As I have said, there is no charge against you, unless you raise one yourself. So you have been content to remain comparatively guiltless?"

. . .

"You are silent."

NEW YORK, May

Donald Barthelme says: "You (Europeans) are
happier than we are." In what way? Marianne
prepares her popular barbecues of veal, ham,
onions, and rosemary; I build the fire, if
with unfamiliar sorts of wood. What is different in Tessin? The nearby stream ripples
in the same way; and in Tessin, too, one must
watch out for snakes. . . . Recently Jürg
Federspiel turned up, later Jörg Steiner
dropped in for a visit, two writers from
Switzerland; news from home is soon told; in
a foreign country people have more to say to
each other. . . . Now and again I feel surprised how easy it is to start calling people
by their first names within an hour of meeting them for the first time: Donald, Mark,
Elisa, Joe, Frank, Lynn, Harrison, Ted, Patricia, Stanley, Steven, etc. I cannot say
which of these people I should be addressing
in German in the intimate Du form, and which
not. American friendliness is not necessarily more superficial, as is often claimed, it
is simply expressed more ambivalently than in
our language, in which the intimate Du form
can be cheapened by overhasty use. . . . A
meeting in the street, surrounded by millions
of other people, can at times seem like an
encounter in a village; but we are not in a
village; we know the others can get on very
well without us, and do not feel offended.
This makes for naturally warm feelings on
both sides. People are more forthcoming
than in small towns, and one becomes like
that oneself—in a spirit of mutual gratitude. When one comes on an acquaintance in
the crush of a party after not seeing him for
weeks, it is like two people boring a tunnel
from either end and meeting in the middle.

One says, "How wonderful to see you!"—and it is true.

The seminar ends.

Afternoon in a bar on the Hudson River. Dock workers playing billiards, drinking beer out of cans. One is greeted even if one has been there only once or twice before, perhaps without having spoken a single word. . . .

QUESTIONNAIRE

1.
Do you fear death and, if so, at what age did you begin to fear it?

2.
What do you do about it?

3.
If you do not fear death (because you think materialistically, because you do not think materialistically), are you frightened of dying?

4.
Would you like to be immortal?

5.
Have you ever believed yourself to be dying? If so, to what did your thoughts then turn:
a. to what you would leave behind?
b. to the world situation?
c. to a landscape?
d. to a feeling that it had all been in vain?
e. to the things that would never get done without you?
f. to the untidiness of your drawers?

6.
Which do you fear more: that on your deathbed you might abuse

someone who doesn't deserve it, or that you might pardon all those who don't deserve it?

7.
When yet another acquaintance dies, are you surprised by the ease with which you accept the fact that others die? And if not, do you feel the dead person is one up on you, or do you feel one up on him?

8.
Would you like to know how it feels to die?

9.
If there was an occasion when you wished yourself dead, but did not die, do you afterwards conclude you had been wrong— that is to say, do you then take a different view of the circumstances that made you feel that way?

10.
Do you ever think: Serve you right if I died?

11.
If there are times when you do not fear death, is this because you are finding life difficult at the moment, or because you are enjoying life at the moment?

12.
What is it about funerals that upsets you?

13.
If you have pitied or hated somebody and then hear that he has died, what do you now do with your pity or hatred for him?

14.
Have you friends among the dead?

15.
When you see a dead person, do you feel you ever knew him?

16.
Have you ever kissed a dead person?

17.
If you think of death, not in a general way but personally in

relation to your own death, are you always dismayed, and do you feel sorry for yourself or for the persons who will survive you?

18.
Would you rather die in full awareness, or be cut off suddenly by a falling brick, a heart attack, an explosion, etc.?

19.
Do you know where you would like to be buried?

20.
When breathing stops and the doctor confirms death, are you confident that at this moment the person has no more dreams?

21.
What agonies would you prefer to death?

22.
If you believe in a place to which departed spirits go (Hades), do you find comfort in the thought that we shall all be reunited in eternity, or is this the reason why you fear death?

23.
Can you imagine an easy death?

24.
If you love someone, why do you not wish to be the one left behind, but prefer leaving the sorrow to your partner?

25.
Why do dying people never shed tears?

NEW YORK, May

Trees putting on their green in courtyards, trees like real trees. One looks down on their budding leaves with some emotion: the courage of chlorophyll!

Phone call from a fellow Swiss who lives here. Since his English is confused, I reply to him in Swiss dialect. Whereupon, even

more confused, he asks (in English): "But who
are you?" He is speaking on behalf of a
friend from Gockhausen in Switzerland, and he
does not believe that it is myself on the
phone; he wants to speak to my wife, who is
out. He repeats; "Who are you?" In spite of
hearing his native language, he still won't
believe me; he prefers confirmation from my
wife that the news of my death, cabled
through by United Press, is false. He is not
familiar with Mark Twain's reply in similar
circumstances ("The reports of my death are
greatly exaggerated"). After we have talked
together for quite a while he again asks:
"But who are you?" Incidentally, Mark Twain
used to live in the same street opposite.

Friends have a black daily help who is now
learning to read and write; she is having
four lessons a week and asks for a book
which I have written—her first book. She is
sixty-five. Our help, also black, has
stopped coming; I heard her laughing loudly
and talking, she was standing in the room, a
cigarette in her almost toothless mouth,
gazing through the wall—she hears voices.
The new help, a black from the West Indies,
cleans thoroughly but doesn't enjoy her work,
as she amicably tells us; she composes songs
that she sings herself, and is looking for an
agent to get her on records; she wants to
play us her songs sometime on tape. Music is
the only thing in the world that makes sense,
she says. She is about fifty and lives in
Brooklyn.

A dead man in the street (Bowery) in the
afternoon: the police already there, a
couple of them; that's all right, then—we
drive on like everybody else.

RIP VAN WINKLE

He always feels the same when he returns home after some time. He is surprised to see everything stand in its usual place.

. . .

The ravine in which the drinking and ninepins-playing company of gentlemen kept Rip van Winkle busy for years as pot and pin boy could have been in what is today Morningside Park or still further out, where the Rockefeller Cloisters are.

. . .

Awakening on the black cliffs of Manhattan, his gun beside him, he rubs his eyes, startled but clear-headed, though his breath smells of brandy. It was presumably a distant clap of thunder he heard in his sleep. Not the noise of the balls. However, he did not dream the brandy. The thunderstorm has passed. Evening over the Hudson River. Years could not have gone by; his dog, for instance, is still young.

. . .

He has a wife and in his dreams has not forgotten her, has been telling the gentlemen in their antique Dutch dress about her for years. But in his dream he could never get away.

. . .

The path (now Broadway) is long; on the way night falls, and he is assailed by fears that there might be no one left who still recognizes him. How would he feel then?

. . .

That company of gentlemen with their ninepins!

. . .

When he gets back to the village (New Amsterdam) and looks

around in the dawning light, nothing is changed. Even the hens are still there. None missing. They are just asleep, his contemporaries. Ships in the harbor: one has sailed off in the meantime, another now lies at anchor. What else? Time has stood still. His wife doesn't believe a word he says, tells him it is Wednesday. Of course she has been worried; something might really have happened to him out there.

. . .

Nobody believes his tale. . . .

. . .

His house with its small windows, steep steps, familiar crockery, etc.—he doesn't look about him, knowing that everything is in its proper place. Edam cheese, herrings from the barrel, sausage —he gobbles down whatever is to hand, looking through the window. Everything is as it should be: so this is his home.

. . .

Not even a death in the village.

. . .

It's not as if they no longer recognize the old Rip. His assistant says a customer has been in twice, raising hell. Nothing new. It is known that he drinks; they have often had to point out to Rip van Winkle where his house is. But now he is sober.

. . .

Why does he tell such tales?

. . .

True, he goes on as before: making barrels as he has been taught. After work he plays cards, speaks Dutch, and drinks; on Sundays he goes off to Coney Island to shoot hares, or to the black cliffs of Manhattan. This is his life. He is surprised when they greet him as if nothing had happened. All the others—his good wife and the neighbors, his customers and his mates, who laugh at his famous story—believe that this is his life. . . .

S.S. FRANCE, 8 June

Europe in sight, the ship now in the hands of a pilot, we stand on deck, the luggage packed, but we are still moving, no one is in any sort of hurry, we are pleased to see that we are still moving. . . .

BERZONA: THE COLUMN

The big Brockhaus Encyclopedia doesn't mention it, though now and again a guest does, touching it to find out what it is made of. Granite? Yes, granite. A rough and rather pathetic column. Some ask at the first sight of it, "Was that always there?" Our village has no chronicles, only inscriptions on the deserted chapel and on a few houses: 1682, 1664, etc. Probably a stonemason, working away from his home valley, which had no job for him, carved the column for his own pleasure. He invented nothing and was no Carlo Maderna, who also came from this district. Really, there is nothing more to say once one has laid a hand on the column and said knowledgeably: "Tuscan!" The base, incidentally, is somewhat chipped, but not too badly. It will outlast us. A gray and rough local stone. Brockhaus reliably describes Doric columns, Ionic columns, Corinthian columns, all as learned in school and since seen in Sunium, Corinth, Olympia, Athens, Delphi, Paestum, Selinus, Baalbek, etc.; but the column supporting our little loggia never reminds me of journeys. As we sit drinking coffee it divides the valley in two for us. Its lower half is somewhat bulbous: it is altogether not very happy in its proportions. We sit in basket chairs, watching the summer lightning in the night sky, before us the column of which all we know is that someone carved it, for there it stands, supporting. During the summers, so I imagine, he carved for rich foreigners or in churches down south, where he worked for a master; in the winter he had to go home and had time, a lot of time, for granite. Why he had to return home I don't know:

probably he had a family here. Granite is not marble; the form he had in mind is frailer than the rough granular stone. And then, above all: it stands alone. Everything else about the house is as to be expected: the rustic beams, the window ledges of this same granite, the huge fireplace, etc., are not related to it. The column is a guest. It is not quite a man's height, but it stands on a balustrade; one can, when standing talking to some-one, rest a hand on its capital, and now and again one does so, for it is not forbidding. At times I even knock out my pipe against it. We know its large family, of course, including those smooth bastards outside banks all over the world. But it doesn't know its own origin. Some people don't even notice it, so it seems, and then I don't introduce it. But later, when conversation dries up, the usual question comes: Was that funny column always there? No, not always; someone once carved it. I could imagine that he was proud of it. Only the cornice beneath the capital looks classical, but it, too, has turned out plump, like a sausage. When one has read the day's newspapers and put them aside, idle for a while in the knowledge of one's own helplessness, there it stands, unshaken, not proud, but good and true. When one touches it, it is rough and full of the heat of the departing day. Against the pale evening sky it offers its excuse: the weath-ering of centuries, its smudgy profile black against the sharp light of dusk, just letting in the first star.